STILL ALIVE!

OLU AKINOLA

Copyright © Olu Akinola, 2022

First Published in Ireland, in 2022, in co-operation with
Choice Publishing, Drogheda, County Louth, Republic of Ireland.
www.choicepublishing.ie

Paperback ISBN: 978-1-913275-56-3
eBook ISBN: 978-1-913275-57-0

A CIP catalogue record for this book is available from the National Library.

This is a work of fiction. Names, characters, places and incidents either are the
product of the author's imagination or are used fictitiously. Any resemblance to
actual persons, living or dead, events or locales is entirely coincidental.

Still Alive!!!

No Matter What
I Won't Give Up
I Will Appreciate My Life
I Will Love Myself
I Will Continue To Fight
Because I Know That
There Is Light
At The End Of The Tunnel
And I Will Get There.

This book is dedicated to Thomas Potter who is now Home in Heaven, and his wife Linda Potter, the most kind-hearted mother that I have ever known.

PREFACE

Matthew, a security guard was wrongly convicted and got ten years sentence for drug possession, he's a family man that loves his wife and children wholeheartedly. He intends to fight for his conviction to be overturned, but he would have to be incarcerated for about three years pending his appeal.

In prison he comes across some of the most dangerous criminals in Ireland. His wife stopped taking most of his calls and stopped replying to his letters after spending one year in prison.

A notorious criminal, John the daddy devil who was about to be released from prison has divulge his mission to Matthew to kidnap and kill his ex-wife Cathy, Matthew's mission is to stop him from committing further murders because he has already revealed that he killed his father in-law and kidnapped his ex-wife's best friend Lucy whom John associates has locked up in a cage on a farmyard.

Can the police stop John from killing Cathy and rescue Lucy from the farmyard?

Will Matthew's conviction be overturned? Will he be reunited with his wife and children?

Will John's vengeance to kill Matthew in prison come to manifestation after his informant in the police told him Matthew ratted him to the police?

Chapter One

Judgement Day

Matthew Williams sat in one of the cubicles of the prison truck, he was dressed in black suit, blue checkers shirt with a blue tie and a black shoe, he's about five feet, ten inches tall, an averagely built man in his late thirties. It was summer time, in the middle of April, the sunny weather beamed through the small window in one of the cubicles of the prison truck, it was around 5pm, the journey from the court house in Wexford to Cork prison was about one-hour drive. Clinging to his holy bible and uncontrollable showers of tears trickling down from his eyes, he has just been given the mandatory ten years sentence for the drug offence he was convicted for by the jury of six women and six men three months earlier at the circuit criminal court in Waterford City, notwithstanding that his barrister Eamon Duggan, his solicitor Luke Hoare and his senior counsel Darren O'Kelly had all advised him that the next step is to take his case to the Court of Criminal Appeal, based on the ground that he didn't get a fair trial at the Circuit Criminal court, they believe they have a chance that his conviction can be overturn, but he has been told that his Appeal won't come up until in about another nine months. He couldn't stop thinking about his wife Delilah, whom he calls sweetheart, and his two lovely innocent children, Samuel his son, whom is three years old, and Debbie his daughter whom is one year old, and all his other dependants, how on earth are they all going to cope with his incarceration, he blamed himself for all the problems he has unintentionally brought upon himself and his loved ones. In fact, there is no day that passed by since he was arrested by the police about twenty one months earlier with a package containing drugs that he doesn't blame himself for been naive and selfish not to have thought about what would happen to all his loved ones, most especially his wife and innocent children if he's taken away from their lives. He blamed himself again and again for his naivety for getting himself involved with the guy that put him in this predicament, notwithstanding that his innocence was abused and used by this criminal to commit this heinous crime, Matthew said to himself in his thoughts as tears stream from his eyes down unto his shirt *"you are very stupid, your life is now messed up, locked up, and the real criminal is out there, and he will continue to use naive idiots like you to collect his drugs."* He became angry again thinking in retrospection of when he was first arrested after signing for the package with the drugs and pleading to the police to follow him to where he was told by the real culprit to deliver the package, so that the police could apprehend the guy at where he was waiting for him to deliver the package, but the police refused to immediately go to the location, instead, the police took him straight to the police station and locked him up in a cell for about two hours, and later took him out to the interrogation room to ask him to tell them if there were other people involved in the drug importation and supply, when it was too late to arrest the real culprit, the number the guy that sent him to collect the package which he immediately gave to the police when they arrested him was now giving a message that the number is not in service when the police rang the number two hours later, and that was the only contact number that the guy gets in touch with him from. He described the guy and the black jeep that he drives but that didn't helped the police when they went to the location he told them the guy was waiting for him to deliver the package an hour later after his arrest *"you know what, you have to start telling us the truth Matthew, you knew about these drugs that came from India"* one of the three police officer said to him in the interrogation room after showing him the white powder that was conceal in the carton that was used to bring in the mobile phones that he was asked to go and collect by the real culprit. *"Please I never knew or was told that drugs would be coming with the package, please help me,"* cried Matthew as he begged the police officers.

He thought about the ten years sentence as he sat in the prison truck, he has been told by one of the prison guard that put him in the cubicle that with good behaviour, he can be released and get out of prison in seven years' time and become a free man again, because he already spent three months in prison before the sentence, and another three months in prison when he was initially arrested with the drugs twenty one months earlier when he had to fight for bail before been released on bail with a surety that had to deposit seven thousand Euros to the court. His wife had to start pleading to people that she knew could afford the money and could come forward to stand as surety for Matthew, it took over two months to get a good Samaritan, a man name Jim introduced to his wife by the father in-law of one of the prisoners he met in prison. Matthew now remembers in retrospection how he came out on bail that night after spending three months away from his wife and children, then, his son was two years old and his daughter was three months old, he had really missed them, his wife and his kids only came to visit him once within the three months in prison, he wasn't allowed to touch them because of a transparent glass that was used as a barrier to block any physical contact between prisoners and visitors, prisoners and visitors can only talk through the glass and the visit only lasted for about one hour, it was very emotional and harrowing for Matthew and his wife and children that they couldn't have a physical contact visit, it was him crying first, then his wife and then the innocent children started crying. So; getting out on bail from Cork prison that night, it was about 8pm, a little bit dark in the month of September, he was given his money that he had saved up in his prison account that was kept by the prison authority within that three months of his first incarceration which was about ninety-five Euros, and also a bus ticket to pay for his bus ride home. Matthew breath in the air of freedom as he walked for about fifteen minutes through the front of the two company building walls on the right hand side of the outside walls of the prison, and further through the housing estate of about forty houses to the bus station, all his thoughts in the bus was about his wife and children. He didn't have any phone to call his wife, because his mobile phone had been seized by the police to be used as evidence for the communication between him and his partners in crime to use as an exhibit to convict him in the law court, but he spoke to his wife earlier that day in the afternoon when he called her from the prison phone, and his wife told him that he would be released because his bail had been granted and approved by the judge, and that he would be coming home. In retrospect, Matthew remembered how he got home that night at around 10pm, they lived in a two bedroom apartment in a building that has twenty other apartments in Waterford city, the apartments are in blocks of three storey building, Matthew, his wife and children lives on the third floor, Apartment 30, he remembered knocking on the door, and his wife asked who it was, and he replied *"sweetheart it's me"* and she immediately opened the door, and they both just hugged themselves passionately, overwhelmed with joy and started crying, Matthew immediately went into one of the two bedroom apartment to his daughter's baby court in the main bedroom that he shared with his wife, and discovered that she was sleeping, but Matthew picked her up, and went to the single room, his son's room, he was sleeping as well, but Matthew kissed him on the forehead, holding his daughter, hugging his wife, crying and apologized to his wife *"I am really sorry sweetheart to have put you and the children into this trauma and ordeal, I am really sorry"* he said apologetically as he held unto her still carrying his daughter, but his wife just replied smiling "I am just very happy that you are back home, come on, I made your special meal" she held his hand and asked him to follow her to the kitchen, but he said he had to take a shower first, and immediately after taking the shower, he changed into his pyjamas, and it was a very beautiful night to be back home to his loved ones after three months separation.

The blaring song of *"I will survive!!!"* by Gloria Gaynor from the radio in the prison truck brought him back to reality from his retrospection, he still felt very uncomfortable in the small cubicle because of his Claustrophobic nature, notwithstanding that he wasn't handcuffed by the prison guard that put him in the cubicle, because the guard knew him from the prison that he's a good and well behaved prisoner, the guard also gave him a newspaper to read, and asked him if he wanted him to buy him mineral water before they left the court house, but Matthew said no, because he was fasting, he fasted every day without food and drink till 6pm, he has denied himself breakfast and lunch since his incarceration praying for God's divine help to intervene in his ordeal and safe him from this nightmare, and reunite him with his wife and children, so; every were he goes, he goes with his holy bible, and even now, that he's more overwhelmed because of the ten years sentence, that he felt that he was going to die in prison because of the duration of the long years of separation from his wife and children, he still believed that the only thing that can get him quickly back home to his wife and children is the fasting and prayer that would help him to get divine intervention at his appeal. He managed to stand up and looked out of the small window at the top of his cubicle and could see that they are in a traffic in Cork city and just about five minutes' drive away from Cork prison, the car parked to the side of the prison truck was a white Mazda saloon car with a couple, a man and his wife that looked in their middle thirties with their two lovely kids, a boy and a girl about the same age with Matthew's children, they looked like they were coming from the beach from the way they were dressed up, the man was at the wheel and the woman sitting very close to him and putting her hand on his shoulder, that reminded Matthew of his wife and children, he pictured his children, he really felt like hugging them, and his heart started palpitating, he started crying as he pictured his wife crying at the court house when the sentence was passed by the judge earlier on that day, he pictured his pastor Joseph Potter that he's in his late sixty's and his wife Ruth Potter in her early sixty's consoling his wife, he pictured them in retrospection trying to reassure his wife *"God is going to make a way sister Delilah, and everything will be alright"* says Joseph Potter, he pictured one of the three prison guards that knew him from the prison nodded his head at him as a signal for him to say goodbye to his wife, and he remembered how she hugged him and both of them crying, and his pastor came to him and prayed for him, and hugged him, and also a lady Lorraine Donavan the manager of the charity shop that Matthew used to do charity work for, also hugged him in tears, and also a lady called Elizabeth from the church that is in her early fifty's also hugged him, everyone crying, it was very emotional, to Matthew, the ten years sentence sounded like a death sentence. Earlier in the court that day, Ruth and Joseph Porter, Elizabeth and Lorraine had all spoken as a character witness on behalf of Matthew for the judge, Paula Doyle, to be lenient in sentencing Matthew, but the judge still gave him the mandatory ten years sentence, because he pleaded not guilty, she even said on sentencing that Matthew should have gotten more because the prosecutors were asking that he should be given twelve years for wasting the time of the court by not pleading guilty, but the judge put Matthew's cooperation from the start of his arrest to help the police apprehend the person that told him to pick up the package which the police refused, and the reason the police gave for not wanting to go with Matthew to the place he was begging them to come with him to arrest the real culprit was that they believe Matthew wanted to escape. The prison truck finally stopped at the prison gate, and Matthew could hear the other prisoners in the six other cubicles singing *"home sweet home, it's good to be back home"* after about ten minutes the prison truck door opened, and the door to Matthew's cubicle was the first to be opened, he was taken to the prison reception by the same prison guard that put him in the cubicle in the prison truck, for him to be signed back in to the prison by the two prison officers at the reception, they took him to the holding cell by the prison reception, and after about another fifteen minutes he was joined by the other five prisoners from the prison truck, three of them he knew from the prison, and the other two were just newly transferred from another prison to Cork prison because they were misbehaving from the better prison that they were previously housed, one of them was brought from Weathfield prison, a better prison than Cork prison, with a bigger library, built within the last twenty years, more modern and far cleaner as well, the prison has in built toilet in the cells, Cork prison doesn't have in built toilet in the cells, the prisoners have to pee or defecate in a potty whenever they feel like going when they are locked up inside their cell, then, they have to throw their excretes into one of the four toilets at the end of the corridors on the landings that is meant for about fifty other prisoners whenever the cell doors are opened, most of the time in the morning at 8:15am.

Back on his way to the landings on the first floor, Matthew's cell is one of the last four cells on left hand side used to house prisoners that works in the prison kitchen, because the prison kitchen is right at the back of those cells, and the four cells is after the governor's office, after the entrance to the prison kitchen. *"Hi Matthew,"* Patrick, one of the prisoners that Matthew works with, in the prison kitchen, walked up to him at the front of the governor's office, he's in his late fifty's, he's about six feet tall, a bit taller than Matthew, and doing fifteen years for drugs, he has already done two years of his current sentence, but this was not his first sentence, he did ten years sentence before for drug sale and supply as well, and was released after serving seven years of the ten years sentence, but got arrested after five months after his released from prison for dealing in drugs again, Patrick is a very nice guy and very polite as well, but he's just a guy that can't do the normal legitimate job to earn a salary or weekly wages, because of his avarice for wealth, he believes he's wasting his time, he wants and loves fast quick money, and that is the reason why he's planning another drug deal in prison even though he still has to spend about another eight years in prison before been considered for early release on good behaviour. *"You are lucky that you didn't get more Matthew, that judge was fair to you, he gave you the mandatory ten years, it's all over the news, I can tell you that I am not surprised, I was even thinking you'll get more for not pleading guilty, you are one lucky man Matthew, I told you to plead guilty, even though you said you were just used by whoever sent you to collect the drugs, that you were not aware that you were collecting a package containing drugs, you're still guilty in the eye of the law, and if you had pleaded guilty maybe the judge would have been lenient with you and given you six years or even five,"* says Patrick *"but I can't plead guilty to an offence that I didn't commit, I am appealing the judgement"* Matthew hysterically replied *"I bet you that if you appeal your sentence, you'll definitely be getting more years"* Patrick said this convincingly, *"I am telling you categorically that all the prisoners that I know that appealed there sentence even though they pleaded guilty got more years, not to talk of you that pleaded not guilty"* he said again, *"but I am innocent, and needs to fight my case and get true justice,"* Matthew replied immediately before walking to his cell in frustration, then closed the cell door, notwithstanding that it was around 7pm, and the prison guards locks the cell doors around 7:45pm, he was just not in the mood to be discussing his sentence with anyone apart from focussing on his appeal.

He shared a cell with another inmate that got five years for drug offence as well, his name is Widodo, an Indonesian guy, he's about five feet, five inches tall, in his late thirty's as well, but he's small in stature and very nice guy, he also works with Matthew in the prison kitchen, before his incarceration, Widodo used to work as a cook on a ship, cooking meals for all the sailors on the ship, and travels from country to country in the ship, he was arrested for trying to smuggle drugs through the Waterford port into Waterford city when the ship he came with from Indonesia arrived at the port, he was sentenced a week earlier, and has been very depressed and asked his lawyer to appeal his sentence because he pleaded guilty and he was thinking he would be getting lesser years, because it was his first offence committed in the country, he has a two year old daughter and wife waiting for him in Indonesia, but the lawyer has advised him that if he appeals his sentence, he might get more years because of the quantity of drugs found on him that carries a ten years mandatory sentence, but the judge gave him five years because of his guilty plea, so he decided not to appeal his sentence, just previous week, two days after he was sentenced, he got a terrible news that his mother died in Indonesia of heart attack at the age of fifty eight years old, Widodo was total devastated when he came back into the cell after hearing the news because he's the only child of his mother, and he believed that it was the news of his five year sentence that killed his mother, Matthew had to console him, notwithstanding that he had his own problems that he was overwhelmed with, because he was going to court the day after to get his sentence. The more he tried to console Widodo, the more he cried, and Matthew started crying as well, he was there for Widodo, he encouraged him to be strong, to have faith, and to be positive that things would be okay and also advised him to look after himself for his wife and daughter, that really helped Widodo to calm down, and he thanked Matthew the next morning.

For the past three months that Matthew has been back to Cork prison after his conviction by the jury, before today's sentence, Matthew has been working in the prison kitchen during the day time, and still manages to go to the prison school in the morning, afternoon and evening, because prisoners are let out of their cell at 8:15am for twenty minutes to get breakfast and also to empty the excretes in their potty, and then let out again from between 9am to 11am to go to see the governor of the prison for any queries they have, and also to go to the prison school or the prison gym, or to go outside in the small yard that is hundred metres long and fifty metres wide, which is always crowded because sixty percent of the prisoners in Cork prison comes out to the yard to either take a walk, play football, smoke weed or take drugs or mostly fight one another. Also in the yard, there are about six telephones boxes mounted on the wall immediately after the entrance gate by the right hand side for prisoners to make three minutes phone call once a day to their family or friend, and also to call their solicitor, but a prisoner is only allowed to make call to one of the three different contact numbers that must have been approved and processed by the prison authority, and then a unique pin number is issued to the prisoner for the prisoner to first dial, and the prisoner can then choose one of the three numbers approved for the call to be able to go through, but all calls to family or friends is been listened to by the prison authority, but calls to solicitors are not been listened to, there are many prisoners that are institutionalize to the extent that they don't want to communicate with their family or friends through the telephone in the prison, they believe that they should concentrate on doing their time, they believe that any member of their family or friends that wants to communicate with them would write them a letter or come to visit them, so; they only have to call their solicitor once in a while when they have appealed their sentence in other to know when they would be going to court, so what they do is sell the slot meant for putting numbers for families or friends to another prisoner, because Matthew works in the prison kitchen, three other prisoners approached him to tell him to give them a phone number that he would like them to put on their list to be processed, and after getting the prison authority to process the number that Matthew gave to them, they gave Matthew their Pin number for him to enter into the prison telephone for him to be able to dial the processed number that Matthew gave them, so Matthew agreed to bring them some extra food and fruits from the prison kitchen after the day's work, and because of that, Matthew is able to make four calls with four different pin numbers he has, so; what Matthew does is, he calls his wife in the morning, afternoon and in the evening, and also calls his mum in the afternoon, and most of the time when he's seriously depressed, he goes to the office of the reverend father on the second floor of B block to call his mum or wife, for him to call from the priest phone. Matthew doesn't need any Pin, all he has to do is to give the reverend father the number he wants to call, and he calls the number for him, and hands the receiver to him immediately his number begins to ring, and he's able to talk on the phone for about ten minutes, the reverend father is always ready to help him because he goes to his Mass every Sunday morning, and most of the time when the reverend father is passing by on the first landing on B block on the first floor, he and Matthew discuss about the Bible, so anytime Matthew comes to his office, mostly about three to four times in a week, the reverend father is always happy to give him a chance to make his phone call.

Prisoners are also let out of their cell at 12pm for about twenty minutes to get their lunch, and also let out at 2pm till 4pm to go to prison school or to the gym, or to also to go to the prison yard, on the way back, prisoners queue up to get their dinner and get locked up again till 5:30pm and finally let out of their cell again till 7:30pm to go to the prison school or gym or to go outside in the prison yard for a walk and to make phone calls. What Matthew does is that, he works in the prison kitchen in the morning from 7:30am to 9am to help get the breakfast ready and clean up, and then go to the prison school at 9am to 11am to study a course that he applied for which was Introduction to Information Technology, that was the first course he applied for at the prison school, it was a certificate course that takes one month to be completed if the prisoner attends all the morning classes four days a week, so Matthew completed that within a month, and applied for a degree course that would take him four years to complete, he actually applied to study Information Technology, he did this while he was awaiting for his sentence, but he was told by the prison school principal that he couldn't be allowed to start a degree course unless they know that he's been sentenced over 7 years in other for him to be able to complete the course, so Matthew had to change his plans and started going to the Art and wooding technology class in the school to pass time before his sentence. In the Art class Matthew's teacher was a lady by the name Maria Mclean, she was a very nice lady, and she always offered her students, about four of them including Matthew, nice cakes and foods that can't be gotten from the prison shop, but Matthew always says no when she offers him the cake, he tells her he can't eat it at that time of the day, and tells her that he's always fasting in the morning and afternoon because he was awaiting his sentence and needs divine intervention, and he also told Maria that his wife and children needs financial help, so; Maria promised Matthew that she would help him with some money to give his wife and children, and told Matthew not to tell or mention it to anyone that she wants to help him, because she would get into trouble because it's not allowed for her and any prison staff to support or give financial help to any prisoner, that it's against prison rules, so, Matthew promised and thanked Maria that he would never tell anyone about it.

The cell door opened, Matthew was standing by the bunk bed that he shares with Widodo, one of the prison officers, Mr O'Sullivan who is the supervisor at the prison kitchen was at the door, *"I heard you got ten years, don't worry you'll be alright Matthew, just keep your head down like you are doing, and before you know it, time flies, if you need any help that I can help you with, let me know,"* he said. Mr O'Sullivan is one of the nicest prison guard that Matthew has ever come across in the prison, he put Matthew in charge of the prison kitchen store to take stock records of stuffs in and out of the store after three weeks Matthew started working in the kitchen because the prison was short of staffs, and the prison officer that normally does the job had to help in another department in the prison, so Mr O'Sullivan spoke and vouch to the governor that Matthew is reliable to do the job successfully, so the governor approved Matthew to do the job for an extra income of fifteen Euro weekly, because each prisoner gets fifteen Euro weekly from the government as a gratuity to buy things in the prison shop, and for working in the prison kitchen Matthew gets another fifteen Euro, and with the extra fifteen Euro for working as a store keeper, Matthew earned a total of forty five Euro weekly in the prison, but Matthew doesn't spend his money at the prison shop, he saves all his money up and gives it to his wife whenever she comes to visit him, notwithstanding that Matthew loves to see his wife and children every minute and seconds, it's always very emotional and traumatizing when they come to visit him because they are just looking through the transparent glass and can't touch each other, most especially Matthew's daughter that is about twenty one months old, she always wants Matthew to carry her, she's always trying to get through the transparent glass to Matthew, crying and screaming, so; Matthew managed to convinced his wife to come once in two month, and whenever she comes, Matthew makes arrangement with the prison for all his saved up money to be given to his wife, whenever he needs anything from the prison shop, he waits for the time any of the prison officers that works in the kitchen ask him if he wants anything in the prison shop. They always ask him at least once in a week, most especially Mr O'Sullivan, because they like him because he's very hard working, most of the prisoners that works in the kitchen will always give excuses to say they are sick and won't come to work for at least three days in a week, but Matthew has never missed a day's work since he started working in the prison kitchen, he works seven days a week because he has more freedom working in the kitchen than just getting locked up in the cell most time of the day, and also because of his claustrophobic nature, he always wants to be outside his cell, that is the reason why he's the only prisoner that has been allowed to work full time in the kitchen and also allowed to go to the prison school anytime the school is open, because he always get his job done, sometimes he does the job that is meant for two other prisoners like washing the plates and also go on to sweep and mob the floor, the prison officers just like him, even other prison officers at other departments like in the school and in the gym, and also officers on duty on the landings likes him, sometimes when he wants to take a break for some few minutes from working in the kitchen, he can tell one of the officers on the landing to leave his cell door open when other prisoners are locked up in their cell during the day because he works in the kitchen, so Matthew always have freedom to walk through the landings and go to the toilet or bathroom or to the reverend's office to make extra phone calls to his wife or mother, and most of the time, the officers in the kitchen offers to give Matthew extra phone calls to his family, most especially Mr O'Sullivan, so; that evening as he was advising Matthew to keep his head down, Matthew said, *"thank you sir, I am still alive."* *"That's the main thing Matthew,"* Mr O'Sullivan replied smiling and left for the kitchen, Widodo came straight to Matthew to pat him on the back to encourage him *"I brought you some food from the kitchen"* he said as he started opening the white nylon bag on one of the two tables in the cell and brought out the sets of covered paper plates with food inside, because he knows Matthew fast during the day every day, one good thing about Widodo is that he always pamper Matthew with food, he always tells Matthew that he'll take care of him, and Matthew always encourages him as well when Widodo is under the weather. Matthew thanked him and told him he has to quickly take a shower before the final lockdown at 7:45pm because it was getting to half seven. That night has he laid on the bed, Matthew cried in silence and prayed thinking about the ten years sentence, he didn't have the appetite to eat any food as he was utterly overwhelmed by the sentence, but thinking about his appeal gave him some hope that he won't be doing the ten years sentence, he closed his eyes, tried to picture himself with his wife and children, tried to remove himself from his current predicament, his imagination was back and forth with flashbacks of been incarcerated and free from his ordeal, it took him over one hour after closing his eyes before he finally drifted to sleep.

Chapter Two

Cork Prison

The noise from the door to his cell that just opened woke him up, Matthew knew immediately that it was half past 7am in the morning, that is the time the prison guards opens the cell doors for prisoners that works in the prison kitchen to get ready to prepare breakfast for all the prisoners in the prison, Matthew knelt down and bent down his head on the pillow on his bed in a crouching position to quickly say a five minute prayer, that's the first thing he does every morning immediately the cell door opens when he gets up from sleep, after then, he changes into a white prison kitchen uniform and white shoe that he wore back from the kitchen the previous day at the end of the day's work, he then picks up his own potty on the floor on the left hand side by the cell door, that he used in the night to pass excretes, and then go and empty it in one of the four toilets basins in the only toilet room meant for forty prisoners on the first landing on A block. The architectural way Cork prison is built is that, there are four houses on the prison precinct, and all the four buildings are linked to each other through a secured gate that needs to be unlocked with a PIN code entered by a prison guard or any prison employee authorised with a personal code to unlock the gates, and after unlocking the main gate from one building to get into another building, you might then need to unlock several other gates in the same building depending on the direction you are going to in the building. The first building after the prison entrance gate houses the cork prison reception, and two holding cells for prisoners that has just been brought into the prison awaiting to be processed into the prison, and also in the same building, you have about 350 lockers in a room for prisoners to put in their personal belongings like clothes, shoes, jewelleries and other stuffs that is not allowed or permitted in the prison, and you also have the governor's office, and the chiefs of the prison office, and all other offices in the prison is in the first building. The second building is a three story building that has got three wings for prisoners cells, Block A, Block B that has three floors each and it's for prisoners that are doing time for drug offences, thefts, and other crimes apart from murder, but there is another section of the building called Block C which is for prisoners doing life time for murder and Block C sometimes houses prisoners that are doing a very long time for drug offences, and also in this second building immediately at the back of Block A on the first landing at the back of the cells meant for the prisoners that works in the prison kitchen is the prison kitchen, and on the second landing in Block A, you have the priest office which is directly beside the prison clinic which is just two rooms used to treat minor injuries or used to apply first aid treatment to severe injuries before the ambulance arrives to take the prisoner to the hospital, Cork prison is in the middle of cork city, any serious injury or sickness, the prison calls for an ambulance to come and take the prisoner to the main hospital in the town which is just about fifteen minutes' drive from the prison, but the prison guards always escort the prisoner to the hospital and wait there with the prisoner to bring the prisoner back immediately after treatment. The third building has two floors, the first floor is where the prison gym is, and the second floor is where the prison school is, the fourth building you have the kitchen and restaurant for the prison guards and prison employees.

After Matthew emptied his potty that morning he went to one of the three officers on the landing on A Block to put down his name to see the governor at 9am, he needed to speak to the governor about been transferred to another better prison in Portlaoise called the Midlands prison, where he'll be able to have physical contact to his wife and children when they come to visit him, he's being told by other prisoners that were transferred from there to Cork prison because of misconduct that Midlands prison is far better than Cork prison because you have toilets in the cells, you get a contact visit, and you can even have a single cell to yourself if you work in the prison as a cleaner or work in the prison kitchen, the best you can get in cork prison is a two man cell, there is just one prisoner that has got a single cell to himself in Cork prison, his name is Kevin, and it's because he's doing double life for killing his wife and best friend. Kevin has been in Cork prison now for about six years, he's over six feet tall, an averagely built guy in his early forty's, and a very lovely guy, that's the reason why most people that come across him in the prison wonders why he killed two people, when you hear the story behind his crime, you'll be shocked how human brain can just go haywire to do something utterly barbaric.

Kevin used to be an architecture and had his own company and doing very well financially and had been married for three years, but Kevin's wife Ann had been cheating on Kevin for several months with Kevin's best friend David, whom they both work together as partnership in business, Kevin only found out through one of his neighbours, the extra marital affairs normally happened when Kevin goes away, sometimes he goes away for about four days on a business trip, David comes over and sleeps with Kevin's wife, most of the time he slept overnight and the neighbour, an elderly lady in her seventy's that leaves directly opposite Kevin's house, most of the time sees David leaves the house the next morning, and because the elderly lady goes to the same church that Kevin and his wife goes to, one day, she asked Kevin in private when she saw that Ann was talking to two other ladies about thirty metres away from them, that were also members of the church after the service, *"do you have a brother Kevin?"* the old lady asked. *"No,"* Kevin replied, *"you see, I have been wondering if I should tell you this or not, but there is this man that comes to your house whenever you're not around, I think he drives an Audi, a black colour, I believe he always pass the night because the car is parked in your driveway overnight and gone in the morning, do you know this man?"* the lady asked, notwithstanding that Kevin was gobsmacked and somehow terrified to hear what she just said, but he immediately put on a poker face and smiled, *"ooh his name is David, he's my friend,"* he replied. *"Okay, he's your friend, well, I just believe I should let you know,"* the lady said. "Thank you so much," Kevin said, *"I'll see you next week then,"* the elderly lady quickly said as she saw Ann coming, and quickly walked away to her car. Kevin still stood where he was overwhelmed by the information that he had just been given by the elderly lady, wondering what can be going on between David and his wife, but he decided not to discuss it with any other person including his wife and David because he had a plan to investigate what was actually going on, so; the next day which was on a Monday, when Kevin came back from work he told his wife that he had to travel for business trip for four days from the next day which was Tuesday, he already managed to convinced David earlier that day in the office that he had to travel out of the country to attend a business meeting that would be beneficial to getting a contract for their company, David was very excited when he heard the news. Ann had just received seven million euro life insurance will from her father's death, and since there was no prenuptial agreement before their wedding, Kevin was entitled to half of the money, Kevin's thought and plans was that he would gather evidence of any infidelity of Ann to use as proof to file for divorce, so; on his way back home, Kevin bought some video recorders that he later planted in the house, one in the sitting room, and another in the bedroom when his wife was sleeping in the night. Tuesday morning Kevin packed his travelling suitcase and kissed his wife *"I have to quickly get to the airport, my flight is at 9:45am,"* Kevin said to Ann as he kissed her on the forehead. *"I am going to miss you"* Ann said as she wrapped her arms around Kevin's back kissing him on the lips, Kevin smiled back, *"I have to go, I'll miss you too, but I should be back on Saturday morning,"* Kevin replied and left the house, but instead of going to the airport, he drove to an hotel which was about fifteen minutes' drive from his house, and packed his car at the back of the hotel hidden it away from the road, he checked into the room he booked the previous day. Kevin sat on a single couch and kept checking the two video cameras he installed in his house from his laptop that was placed on a coffee table, when it was around 10pm he saw David came into the sitting room, he saw Ann and David kissed, saw them go into the kitchen, and then saw them came back into the sitting room with a bottle of brandy and wine glasses, he saw them drank from the bottle of brandy, he saw Ann moved closer to David, he saw them kissed and then they started undressing themselves hurriedly, they both became naked kissing passionately, then Ann held David's hand, and gently led David to the bedroom, so Kevin tried to switch to the video camera in the bedroom on his laptop, but he couldn't bring it up, he tried several times, but still couldn't, so after twenty minutes trying and battling to bring up the video camera to no avail, he decided to go to his house, he drove and parked his car three houses away from his house, and walked stealthily to his house, parked at the front of his house right at the back of his wife's car, that was packed on the driveway was David's car, the black Audi, the house is a semi dethatched two bedroom bungalow with no gate, so Kevin walked furtively to the house and stealthily opened the entrance door with his own key and got into the living room that was dark, but he could see on the table two glasses of wine cups and one empty bottle of brandy, he tip toed to the main bedroom that was meant for himself and his wife, the door was slightly opened, he peeped through the opened door and saw David and his wife cuddled up together on the king size bed sleeping, the bedroom light was turned off but the light from the street light pole reflected into the room, so; Kevin could see both of them clearly naked, they were both in very deep sleep, which must have been as a result from the brandy they drank earlier on, standing there at the door gobsmacked, his heart palpitating and extremely infuriated, Kevin subconsciously went into the kitchen, he saw a set of knives on one of the shelves, he picked up the biggest knife, and went straight back to the bedroom were his wife and David were still in deep sleep, he jumped on the bed, he stabbed David five times in the neck and then stabbed Ann four times in the neck and went back to David stabbed him again several times in the chest and went back and stabbed Ann several times again, they couldn't defend themselves, he stabbed them to death, he quickly changed his clothes that was covered with blood, then drove back to his hotel room crying holding his head, then around 7am the next morning, he rang the police to tell them what he had done and told the police were he was for them to come and get him. Kevin got double life, not withstanding that he cooperated with the police and pleaded guilty.

Matthew was standing in the queue with seven other prisoners waiting to see the governor of the prison, it was getting to 9am, and in another fifteen minutes, it'll be time to go to the prison school, but he knows he won't be late because he is the next prisoner on the line to see the governor, and if he's late, because of the kitchen uniform that he was wearing, the prison guard at each gate on his way to the prison school are always happy to unlock the gate to get him to the prison school, but the problem is that he would need to go through about five locked gates from the kitchen to the school, and sometimes he might get to some gates where there is no prison guard to unlock the gate, so; what Matthew normally does is to get one of the prison officers that works with him in the kitchen to get him to school, and not withstanding that it takes about eight minutes to go through all the gates to get him to school, the officer only need one master key that opens all the gates, and the officers are always happy to bring him to school because they like him. *"Good morning sir,"* says Matthew to the governor, he was lucky that it was governor Kavanagh that was in charge that morning, because he's the most liberal and compassionate governor of the three governors in Cork prison, he's always ready to help most well behaved prisoner that works in the prison and hasn't been causing any troubles, and from the way he smiled immediately he saw Matthew, it showed that he was curious to know why Matthew has come to see him, *"please sir I want to put in a transfer to the Midlands prison because it's been very difficult for me, my wife and most especially my two innocent children whenever they come to visit me here sir, my children always want to touch me, most especially my one year old daughter, it's been very harrowing experience sir."* Matthew paused to control himself from crying has he tried to explain the reason why he really needed the transfer urgently, but because his eyes was already welled up with tears as he vividly remembered the last visit by his wife and children in flashback seeing her daughter desperately trying to go through the transparent glass at the visiting room to touch him, and when she couldn't she started crying, his son started crying, then his wife, and then he started crying, has he remembered that, stream of tears dribble from his eyes, *"okay, I understand what you are trying to tell me, We'll see what we can do to try and arrange that transfer for you Matthew."* The governor immediately interrupted and turned his head to the right side to speak to the prison chief officer that sat beside him, *"can you please get him to complete the transfer sheet form and we will process that for him"* the governor said to the chief. *"Okay, you get him the form today and bring it to me,"* the chief said to one of the two prison officers standing by the door behind Matthew *"okay sir"* the prison officer replied, *"you see Matthew, there are loads of other prisoners that has already put in an application for transfer, even some applied over a year now and hasn't gotten it and still waiting because the way it's done is that, if any prisoner misbehaves in Midlands prison, then they transfer the prisoner to us here, then another prisoner can then be taken from Cork prison to Midlands, so, unless there is a space in the Midlands, that is when we are able to try and get someone from here to take that space, it's like a prisoner exchange, if you get what I mean, but having said that Matthew, I still advise you to put in the application for transfer, like I said, I'll see what I can do,"* says the governor.

Immediately he got to the prison school, Matthew went straight to one of the three phones that was hung on the wall in the corridor for prisoners to make calls, it was half past nine in the morning and he has been apprehensive since he woke up from sleep, thinking about his wife and children every minute and seconds, and that's the way it has been since he came to prison, he's always overwhelmed with their thoughts, sometimes he gets overwhelmed that he runs to the toilet to cry or tried to hide his feelings from fellow inmates because it's a sign of weakness when you're found or discovered in that plight, but after speaking to his wife on the phone always gives him some relief, notwithstanding that after twenty minutes he's back in the same plight overwhelmed with the feelings of not been around them and missing them badly, and always looking forward to make the next phone call to hear his wife and children voice again, and most of the time on the phone, their conversation is always, *"am missing you badly, we need to be strong, I love you, we'll get through this."* The call is a three minutes call, and it goes very fast, but Matthew always wants to tell his wife goodbye before the call get disconnected, there is a beeping tone that sounds like about five times for the last twenty seconds of the call before the call finally gets disconnected, so; Matthew will just quickly use the last ten seconds to tell her, *"I love you with all my heart"* and would quickly tell her when next he would call her. Sitting down in the office of Anne Marie, the head of the prison school, his eyes welled up in tears as he was speaking to her about his ten years sentence, *"Please I really need to start a degree course, I can't be wasting my time doing nothing in here, I miss my wife and children every seconds every minute, I have been here for three months locked up, and I don't think I can survive the ten years sentence if I don't do a course that would at least make me feel that I am not wasting my life in here"* says Matthew. *"You need to be positive Matthew, I will try my possible best to process the application for the degree course for you, and I think with your record in the prison and also with the length of your sentence, you'll be getting the approval by the deciding committee, and I also belief that you'll focus on doing the course successfully after getting it because it would be a big achievement to get that degree, it would help you to get a good job when you've finished your sentence and out of prison"* says Anne Marie. *"Thank you, thanks a million,"* says Matthew as he stood up and left her office, sitting on the chair outside her office waiting to see Ann Marie was Jude, he stood up immediately he saw Matthew came out of the office, and called him aside signalling with his head for him to come with him to the far end of the corridor that has more opened space for them to talk, Matthew followed him, it was just about ten meters from Ann Marie's office. Jude is about six feet tall, but athletically built, he is in his late twenties, he was wearing a brown chino's short, with a white tea shirt and a white runners, he looked very clean, and that's how he is when coming to the prison school, always clean because he's always trying to get the attention of Miss Walsh, a female prison officer that teaches the basic computer course in the prison school, Jude used to be Matthew's cell mate on the third landing on B block before Matthew started working in the kitchen, he had told Matthew to help him to discuss with Mr O'Sullivan, the head of the prison kitchen that he wants to work in the kitchen, and Matthew was very happy and willing to help Jude because Matthew believes he owes Jude a lot for helping him through his father in-law to get someone that stood for him as a surety when he got out on bail after he first got arrested and charged for the drug offence, but when Matthew told Mr O'Sullivan, he said he would get back to him, so, after two days, Mr O'Sullivan said he can't let Jude work in the kitchen because the officer on Jude's landing said he's been in a fight twice with other prisoners in the past three months that he arrived at Cork prison, so Matthew told Jude that he has to stay out of trouble for some time for him to be able to persuade Mr O'Sullivan to give him the job, and that's the way it is, Mr O'Sullivan always doesn't want to take any prisoner that has gotten into a fight with other prisoners to work in the kitchen, just because of safety purpose, because in the kitchen you have knives and other sharp objects like scissors that can be used has weapon, that is the major reason why any prisoner that is in for murder, manslaughter or any other offence that has got to do with fighting or violence is an automatic no, and not allowed to work in the kitchen, and apart from that Mr O'Sullivan said Miss Walsh reported Jude to one other female officer for trying to seduce her in the computer class, and it's the truth because Matthew was right there that morning, when Jude said to Miss Walsh *"Hi Beautiful"* and Miss Walsh, yes Miss Walsh, that's what I call her, and that's the way most prisoners address female officers by calling them Miss and then with their last name, that's the reason why when Jude said *"Hi beautiful"* to Miss Walsh, she was infuriated and warned him not to ever call her beautiful, and sent him out of her class and immediately brought him back to his cell and locked him up. Miss Walsh is a beautiful lady in her mid-twenties, about six feet tall, athletic figure and has a blond hair with ponytail. She actually likes Matthew because of his personality, because when it comes to courtesy and respect for both male and female officers, Matthew is very good at it. One day when Matthew was struggling with a page on the computer and using the mouse on the desktop computer, Miss Walsh came out of no were and just placed her hand on Matthew's right hand on the mouse, *"I'll quickly fix this for you,"* she said smiling as she corrected the mistake on his work that was on the computer screen, Matthew couldn't remove her hand from his, he allowed her to move his hand with the mouse has she corrected the mistake, when she was done, she looked at him smiling and giggling because she sensed the tension and surprise on his face, Matthew just said *"thank you Miss."*

Jude was doing four years for drug offence, he was arrested at his home in Waterford City after collecting a package of Cannabis drug at the post office in Waterford City that was sent from west Africa, he was caught with about twenty kilos of Cannabis and he only got four years because he's married to the daughter of a top Politician in Waterford City, and his father in-law used all his political connection to get him a lighter sentence, most of the prisoners that was caught with lesser amount of drugs got twice his sentence, Jude was very lucky because his father in-law likes him a lot, he comes with his wife and daughter every week to visit him, and whenever they come, they leave him money on his prison account to buy stuffs in the prison shop, he was with Matthew in a two man cell before for two weeks before Matthew started working in the prison kitchen, Matthew had the top bed on the bunk bed and Jude had the bottom bed, in Jude's corner on a table in the small cell that is just about six metres long and four metres wide, you'll see loads of different types of cereal, biscuit and loads of other food that can only afforded by few prisoners, but on Matthew's table it's always empty because he never buys stuffs from the prison shop, he saved all his money to give to his wife whenever she comes. When Jude first got arrested and brought to prison, that was the first time he first met Matthew in the prison yard, it was two months after Matthew was first arrested and brought to Cork prison and trying to get out on bail, Jude also was trying to get bail too, it took Jude one week before he got bail, and for that one week before he left Cork prison on bail, any prisoner he comes across he always boasted and bragged to them that he's getting out and won't be coming back, he bragged about his father in-law been a top politician and would use his power and connection to get him a suspended sentence, and he would brag and brag, that's the reason why he has been in a fight with other prisoners about three times, Matthew witnessed two of the fights, one happened in the prison gym, and it all started when all the prisoners, about twenty four of them were taken to the gym that afternoon, and the way the gym is used by prisoners is that, when the prison officer opens the final door to the gym, all the prisoners just runs to the few excising machines that is in the gym, and there were just about twelve excising machines in the gym, there were two treadmill equipment for walking, running and climbing and four exercise bikes used for exercise, to increase general fitness, for weight loss, and for training for cycle events, and two rotocycle used to improve cardio to workout lower and upper part of the body, and also there were three rower excising equipment used for the mimicking of a rowing a boat in the water that helps with full body work that really helps with weight loss, toning and building muscles, and one iron man for building muscles, and also loads of other gym equipment's accessories like band rollers, band elastic, and the use of this equipment is based on whoever gets to the equipment first, uses the equipment, so, on the that day, Jude was looking forward to use one of the three bikes, but other prisoners got to it first, so Jude asked the prisoners when they'll be finished so that he can use the bike, normally the time spent in the gym is one hour thirty minutes and that includes the time for taking a shower, because there is a shower room that had two toilet cubicles and three opened shower cubicles, so what most prisoners do is to use the first hour to excise and the last thirty minutes to try and get into one of the three showers, and that's what Jude normally does, but that day when he asked the prisoners on the bike when they'll be finished for him to be able to use the bike after one of them, one of the guys said after thirty minutes that he'll be finished, but when Jude went back to him after thirty minutes, the guy said he has decided to continue to use the bike for another thirty minutes, so Jude got mad telling the prisoner to get off the bike because the prisoner was a small guy in stature, about five feet tall and weighs about 120 pounds, while Jude weighs about 200 pounds, so Jude thought he can bully the guy off the bike, but what Jude didn't know was that, the guy had four other guys that were members of his gang, so when Jude was trying to push him off the bike, three of the guys jumped on him, punched and kicked him, this lasted for about one minute before the two prison guards in the gym could jump in to get them off Jude, and by this time some damages had already been done to him, one of his eyes was badly punched that he had to be taken to the hospital for treatment, and with all his bravado that he won't be getting a custodial sentence when he goes for his sentence, he got four years but the final two years was suspended by the judge, so he only had to do eighteen months for the two years on good behaviour, but when Jude came back to Cork prison after his sentencing, after been out on bail for fifteen months before his sentencing, just after six weeks into his sentence in Cork prison, he was transferred to Loughan House Open Centre, an open prison for prisoners regarded as requiring lower levels of security risk because of his father's in-law political connection, but after a week at Loughan House, Jude was brought back to Cork prison because he got into a fight with one of the prison guards over there. So, Jude now standing with Matthew in the corridor asking him if he has been given the degree course that he went to discuss with Anne Marie *"I am still on it, Anne Marie said she would put in my request, and try and get it processed for me,"* replied Matthew, *"lucky you, I have been trying to get the same degree course since I came back to prison after my sentence, and I have been told that I can't get a degree course because I didn't completed the computer course with Miss Walsh, how can I complete the course when she kicked me out of her class,"* says Jude, but what he didn't say is that he didn't completed two other certificate courses in two other different classes that was not taught by Miss Walsh. As they were there, talking on the corridor, Patrick, the prisoner that has got Tattoo all over his head came to them, *"Matthew my Nigger!!!"* he said as he extended his hand in handshake *"what sup Patrick"* says Matthew as he took the handshake, Patrick ignored Jude and continued to walk towards the Art Class, *"what is that Matthew?"* Jude said with angry face *"what?"* Matthew curiously asked *"why would you be happy with that idiot calling you a Nigger?"* asked Jude frantically. *"What do you mean?"* Matthew asked, *"what is wrong in him calling me a Nigger?"* Matthew asked again *"what!!!"* says Jude *"you call me Nigger all the time, is it because Patrick is white? I don't see anything wrong in him calling me a Nigger, if you can call me a Nigger, then any other person either white or black can call me a Nigger"* says Matthew. *"I have to get to class"* says Matthew as he started going into the Art class to try and finish up with the sketchy drawing of the family picture of himself, wife and his two children, he started doing the drawing about two weeks earlier before going to the court for his sentence. There were four other prisoners in the art class, one of the prisoners was Marcello, he is in his late thirties like Matthew, he's five feet seven inches tall, he's doing twelve years sentence for ten kilos of cannabis he got caught with while trying to sell the drugs to an undercover police, that was his first offence, so other prisoners wonder why he got twelve years for half of the quantity of cannabis that Jude was caught with, and for the mere fact that he pleaded guilty, his sentence was supposed to be lower than the ten years mandatory for drugs, but some prisoners that knows the judge that sentenced Marcello said the daughter of the judge died of drug overdose a week earlier before Marcello was brought for sentencing in front of the judge, they said that was the reason why the judge was very hash in giving him an unfair sentence, after his sentence, Marcello thought he got twelve months, so; after spending nine months he applied for early release, it was then that Marcello was told again by the prison authority that he got twelve years, by then it was too late for him to appeal his sentence, because after any sentence is passed by a judge, the prisoner has twenty one days to legally appeal his sentence, what other prisoners says is that he got a bad solicitor that was recommended to him by the police. Marcello has been in Cork prison for over seven years, so; he still has another two years to go before he can get out on parole on good behaviour, and if anyone deserves early release, it is Marcello, because he hasn't been in trouble with the prison authority since his incarceration, notwithstanding that he has been in fight with some prisoners, it has always been because he defended himself from bullies, but another problem with Marcello is that he has never completed any course or training that he has attempted in the prison school, most of the time after doing the course or training half way, he just doesn't show up to complete it, he just stays in block B where his cell is for several months and only comes out to collect his food and take a shower may be once in a week, notwithstanding that in Cork prison prisoners are allowed to shower twice a week, on Tuesdays and on Saturdays, some prisoners said he's very depressed most of the time because after he was arrested, Marcello's wife that people call princess because of her beauty, left him after she learnt that he's doing twelve years and not twelve months, for the first nine months that Marcello was locked up, princess visited him every week thinking that he was doing twelve months and would soon be released, but she stopped visiting him after learning that he was doing twelve years, and two weeks after learning that, he wrote Marcello a letter that she's moving on with her life, and after a month after receiving the letter, one of Marcello's friend wrote him a letter that his wife has moved with Marcello's three year old daughter to another county to live with another man, that totally shattered him, because when he got the letter, he didn't come out of his cell for a week, the prison officers had to get the prison priest to go and talk to him after trying to speak to him to get him out of the cell, and he didn't, but after the priest spoke to him, that same day, he came out and took a shower and started coming out of his cell, God knows what the priest said to him to get him out of his cell, but sometimes he still hibernate in his cell, that is the reason why the prison teachers don't take him really serious when he starts a course or training because they know he won't complete it, and sometimes he would only go to the prison yard for several months most especially during summer to play in the football league that is organised by some prisoners during summer, he plays as a goal keeper in a six man a side team, and he's always very serious, his actions of trying to keep any ball fired towards his goal post away from going into the post proofs how serious he is with the game, most of the time Marcello is always soliloquizing, talking to himself laughing at the goal post, even when he's walking the hundred metres length of the prison yard on his own, it's like there's someone beside him walking with him and talking or having a conversation with him, it was like he was going insane, but it is only when you go and have a conversation with him that you know that he still got his sanity, Marcello is very hairy too, with loads of beard, which was always very untidy, because he seldom cut or trim his beard, but he is a very lovely guy if he's in the right mood, he gives Matthew good advice about staying out of trouble and always asking Matthew about his wife, about how his wife is handling the ten years sentence given to him, he does that almost every day, sometimes he comes over to Matthew's cell to ask him if his wife is still picking his phone calls when he calls her, and when Matthew tells him yes, that his wife still picks his call and talk to him and still encourages him not to forget about her and their children, Matthew always noticed the astonishment on Marcello's face that his wife is still talking to him, even after the ten years sentence, just now when Matthew came into the art class, Marcello came over to him and asked him, *"have you spoken to your wife today Matthew?"* and immediately Matthew said *"yes, she's alright"* the disappointment was very obvious on Marcello's face, it's like Marcello was always expecting him to say *"no she hasn't been taking my calls"* and Marcello waiting to tell him *"she's left you for another man"*, the picture Matthew was trying to finish sketching was taken at a father Christmas ghetto two days before the last Christmas in a shopping complex that was minded by Matthew when it was originally been built, the site has now been completed into a beautiful shopping mall with about one hundred shops with various types of businesses, notwithstanding that it's built in a remote place away from the closest village which is about fifteen minutes' drive, people still come there to do shopping and business, the place is always bubbling with people because of the variety of businesses like good eateries, restaurants, clothes and shoe shops just to name a few that the shopping complex houses, and the car park is always filled up with cars. As he looked at the picture in reminiscence, he got lost in his thought to when he finally got his bail out of Cork prison after spending three months for the first time away from his beautiful wife and children after he was first arrested with the drugs.

Chapter Three

Out On Bail

Two years earlier, Matthew was in the prison yard walking the hundred metres length from wall to wall with Peter his first cell mate, it was a sunny day, it was the second time that the prisoners had been let out of their cell for recreation for the day which would last for one hour thirty minutes, they had been let out since half past 2pm, and it was gone twenty past 3pm, they already done fourteen laps back and forth, there were about sixty other prisoners in the yard, about twenty five of them walking and doing the same laps as Matthew and Peter, they walked in rows, some walked together in rows of two, some rows of three and some doing the walk on their own Soliloquizing, talking to them self, people like Marcella. Peter was doing eight years sentence for drugs, he was caught at the Cork airport with four kilos of cocaine in his baggage two years earlier, he travelled from Nigeria enroute Ireland to UK, so, he was only on transit for three hours in Ireland to connect to his next flight to his final destination when he got stopped by the Irish customs, since he got sentenced, he has been trying to go back to UK to finish his sentence, because he leaves in UK with his wife and three children, but he has been told by the prison authority that he has to do half of his sentence in Ireland before he can be allowed to be transferred to UK prison to complete the remainder of his sentence, so that means he has to do four years in Ireland, which means he had another two years to go for him to be qualified to be moved to UK, Peter is about Matthew's height, and the same stature, but the difference in their physical appearance is that, Peter's hair cut style is pompadour because he has loads of hair, and Matthew has clean shaved head, they held there school folder in their hand as they did the laps, there plans was to go to the prison school that afternoon, but they were told by the officer that was supposed to take them to prison school, that the school had been closed for staff meeting that afternoon, so it was either they go back to their cell or stay in the yard, so they decided to stay in the yard. At the other far end of the yard, away from the entrance to the yard is a small building block where the three toilet rooms is housed, that is where some prisoners go to jostle to smoke drugs that had been smuggled into the prison by another prisoner, sometimes they can be up to about eight prisoners jostling to smoke one gram of cocaine, sometimes the drug is thrown over the prison's fence into the yard for the prisoner that it was meant for to pick it up, and most of the time, the drug is thrown in during the time prisoners are out in the yard, so there is always a problem because when the drug is thrown in over the fence, it gets picked up by another prisoner that it is not meant for, but first found the drugs, and if the prisoner refuses to release it or give it to the rightful owner, there is always a serious fight that would last for about five minutes before the prison officers comes in to separate the fight, sometimes it can be four prisoners fighting one prisoner that picked up the drug and doesn't want to release it to the rightful owner, there was a time that one new inmate that had just been in Cork prison for two days got into a fight with five other prisoners, and he beat them all to the ground, this guy was about six feet tall, had athletic stature, a bald headed guy and walked and tip toed like a ninja, he was dressed in a black track suit with white runners, the way he fights was crazy, he ran after each of the five guys that surrounded him one at a time back and forth from knocking down one guy then another guy, he took them down one after the other using his legs and fist, he did it in a very calculative way as if it was in a movie were every steps and action has been rehearsed before the fight, before the prison guards arrived at the scene of the fight after about four minutes after the fight started to rescue the five prisoners that he was fighting with by taken him away, he had already passed the drugs to another prisoner.

Back in the cell later that day, Peter received some documents from his wife sent by registered post from London, he was brought to the officers office on the landing to sign for the post, he then came back to the cell and opened the letter, he discovered that it was a divorce papers asking him to sign to accept the divorce, Peter smiled as he looked from the letter to Matthew that was sitting on top of the bunk bed, *"she's asking me to sign this divorce papers"* he said as he handed the papers to Matthew, it was getting to about 8pm after the final lockdown for the day, and it was a little bit dark on the side of the top bunk bed, so; Matthew couldn't see properly, so; he climbed down from the top of the bed to stand under the florescent light in the cell to read the documents, fidgeting from shock and his heart palpitating from the news of the divorce given to him by Peter, as he read the document *"what are you going to do Peter, you are definitely not going to sign it, or are you?"* Matthew asked. *"No, I am not going to sign it, she has been ignoring my calls for the past six months, I have only been able to speak to my children when I call the house phone, and whenever I ask my children were their mum is, they always tell me that she's in the neighbour's house, the house next to my house, and you know what Matthew?"* says Peter. *"What?"* asked Matthew curiously. *"My neighbour that she goes to meet is a single guy that has been interested in my wife before I came to prison, it was my wife that reported this same guy to me when I was in Nigeria before getting into this ordeal, she said the guy is always giving her a seductive looks, and always wave to her to get her attention whenever he comes across her, but said she ignores him, but now that I am in imprison, this same guy has been the person my children tells me that my wife spend most of her time with at his house, and my children said, the guy also comes down to my house to see my wife,"* says Peter. *"That is crazy, I believe she's definitely having an affair with this guy, that might be the reason for her asking you for a divorce, my God!!!"* Matthew replied.

Peter's first son is twelve years old, and his two younger daughters are ages nine and seven. Peter and Matthew has now been a cell mate for three weeks, Peter is in his early forties, he's four years older than Matthew, and he's well respected by most of the prisoners because he's like a legal consultant to most of the prisoners going for their appeal, he helps most of them to write letters to the judge, most of the time some prisoners that are awaiting their sentence comes to him to ask him to help them write a letter to the judge in charge of their case, a letter that will explain mitigating reasons for why they should get a lighter sentence, in most cases the reason for mitigating factors would be that they cooperated with the police, and that they pleaded guilty at the earlier stage of their arrest, and after helping them, most of the prisoners would buy him stuffs from the prison shop, and some offer him protection, Peter is like an unofficial solicitor in the prison, and sometimes he goes into the prison library to read or study some cases to know the legal law guiding the crime committed by the prisoner that he wants to write a letter for, most especially the prisoner fighting a conviction and going for appeal, and after finding all the legal facts, he'll then write a letter for the prisoner and the prisoner would then send the letter to their solicitor, telling the solicitor the section of the law to concentrate on to use to proof the reason for wrongful conviction, and also give the reason why the conviction should be overturned, and apart from all this, Peter is a very lovely guy just like Matthew, but another difference in their personality is that peter is coping better been locked up and doesn't have claustrophobic nature like Matthew, also, Peter has been locked up for almost two years before Matthew's arrival at the prison, and also Peter is asking to be sent back to London in another two years, because he knows when he gets to London, he would be immediately sent to an open prison, then released on probation and allowed to go home because he would have served half of his sentence which is the law for early release on good behaviour in UK after serving half of the sentence, so he just believed he's gone on top of the mountain in his sentence and he's on his way down the mountain and almost out to freedom, and also the more reason why Peter stopped worrying about his incarceration lately is because his wife is asking him for divorce and he believes it's karma that has caught up with him because when he was outside before getting into the drug business that brought him the prison ordeal, he used to be very promiscuous sleeping around with different women which his wife and son knew about his infidelity, and he didn't have a good relationship with his wife and son, notwithstanding that Peter worked at Heathrow airport as a manager in one of the duty free shops and earned a decent salary, but because of his adulterous lifestyle, he needed money to fund that type of lifestyle, because he loves to travel to Africa almost every three months for a week because he lives like a king whenever he goes over there, when he changes the pound sterling currency into naira, the Nigerian currency, he's able to woo as many as three women on each travel, and it was one of this women that introduced him to the drug baron that gave him the drugs to bring back to UK that got him into this ordeal. For the past three weeks, what Peter and Matthew does every night at 12am, they sing some Christian songs and say some prayers till 1am, and whenever they are saying the prayers, other prisoners could hear them, and some prisoners would scream *"Fuck You!!!"* and screams other fowl languages at them, but some prisoners would commend them the next morning or even tell them to say some prayers for them when next they are praying.

Seven weeks after Matthew arrived at Cork prison, after his first arrest, it was the first lock out in the morning, Matthew was in the prison yard on the phone talking to Delilah, Matthew asked Delilah to go to his solicitor to ask him to ring Ronald Kent, his last boss that he worked with, to tell him about standing as surety in the court, in other to get him out on bail. After the call, Delilah immediately carried Debbie on her back, and put Samuel in the stroller to quickly go to the solicitor's office, the solicitors office is about twenty five minutes' walk from where she lives, when she gave Ethan Ahern, Matthew's solicitor Ronald Kent's number to ring, the solicitor told Delilah that he would ring Ronald Kent later, but Delilah immediately rang Ronald Kent on her mobile phone, when Ronald came on the line *"hello sir, my name is Delilah, I am Matthew's wife, Matthew said I should give your number to his solicitor to ring you to ask you to help him to stand as a surety for him to be able to come out on bail, because that is the reason why he's still in prison"* says Delilah. *"Okay, I am sorry to hear that"* replied Ronald Kent, *"Matthew is a good employee, not withstanding that he was working for our company through Watchcat security company, you can give my number to his solicitor to call me, I'll see if I can help"* replied again Ronald Kent. *"Well, Matthew's solicitor is right beside me here sir, if you want to talk to him now"* says Delilah. *"Yeah, give him the phone"* says Ronald Kent, Delilah quickly handed the phone to Matthew's solicitor, when the solicitor took the phone from Delilah, he got up from his chair and then went into an inner office talking to Ronald very quietly, but Delilah could still hear him talking *"Hi Ronald, my name is Ethan Ahern, I am the solicitor representing Matthew, I know your family, most especially your father"* says Ethan Ahern. *"Okay"* replied Ronald Kent *"before you get involved with this case Ronald, I mean before you want to consider standing as a surety for Matthew, I'll want you to consult with your solicitor, because this is a drug case,"* says Luke. *"Okay"* replied Ronald. *"Thank you Ethan,"* says Ronald, then the call ended, Ethan came back into his office and handed the phone to Delilah, *"he said he has to go and speak to his solicitor before he can decide if he can stand as a surety for your husband or not,"* says Ethan to Delilah. The next day, Matthew was on the phone to his solicitor again. *"The Gardai says if you agree to plead guilty, you'll get six years sentence, instead of ten or even more if you go to trial and found guilty,"* says Ethan. *"But why are you telling me this when our arrangement is that I should get out on bail for me to be able to prepare and fight my case"* replied Matthew infuriated. *"Well I just believe I should discuss it with you, because of the overwhelming evidence against you getting caught collecting the drugs"* replied Ethan. *"I am not pleading guilty to a crime I didn't commit!!!"* says Matthew.

Back in the cell later that day, Matthew was sitting on a single chair at his own side of the cell, Peter was sitting at the bottom of the bunk bed, *"that solicitor doesn't want you to get out of here Matthew"* says Peter, *"why would he be telling anyone that might want to help to stand as my surety to contact his solicitor to get legal advice?"* asked Matthew *"what's his name?"* asked Peter. *"His name is "Ethan Ahern"* replied Matthew. Peter quickly got up from the bed and went to get a pen and paper on a table on his own side of the cell, *"Ethan Ahern right?"* asked Peter to confirm the name. *"Yes"* replied again Matthew. *"I can help you to check if you need to fire him and get another solicitor"* says Peter. *"Okay, so I can change my solicitor?"* Matthew excitedly asked. *"Yes, you are allowed to change your solicitor,"* replied Peter.

The next day, Matthew was sitting in the computer room during the final lock out with six other prisoners, Peter opened the only door to the room, gesticulated with his hand to Matthew to come out to the corridor, Matthew quickly got up and met Peter and one other prisoner that is in his early thirties and about six feet tall at the corridor *"this is Liam"* Peter introduced the guy to Matthew *"hi, my name is Matthew"* says Matthew to Liam as he extend his hand in handshake *"I know you, I saw you at the court house in Waterford when you first got charged for the drugs"* says Liam as he took the handshake, *"Peter said Ethan Ahern is your solicitor"* says Liam *"yes, he's my solicitor"* replied Matthew, *"well, if you want to fight your case, you'll have to get rid of him and get a good solicitor that can help you to fight your case because he is not going to do his best to help you win your case"* says Liam *"I think you are right"* says Matthew *"that bastard got me to plead guilty to a burglary I didn't commit"* says Liam *"and why would you do that?"* asked Matthew *"I had to because if I didn't and am found guilty I would be getting eight years, but I got two years for pleading guilty"* says Liam, *"if you want to fight your case, get*

Luke Hoare to represent you" says Liam again. Back in the cell that night, Matthew sitting on the top bed of the bunk bed and Peter standing by his table buttering eight slices of bread *"I don't understand why Liam pleaded guilty to a crime he did not commit?"* says Matthew *"you see, if he didn't plead guilty, he believed that he would have been found guilty because Liam is known in the area that the burglary was committed as a burglar, he has done time in prison three times for committing burglary, so immediately the burglary was committed and the police couldn't find the real burglar, they arrested Liam, notwithstanding that it wasn't Liam that did the crime, and the reason why I believe Liam didn't committed the burglary is because I already spoke to the real guy that committed the burglary, he's right here doing time for another burglary crime he got caught with, he told me in private that he committed the burglary Liam is here for,"* says Peter. *"Well I am not going to plead guilty to a crime I didn't commit"* says Matthew. *"Then you'll have to fire your solicitor then"* says Peter. The next day, immediately after the first lock out, Matthew was in the prison yard on the phone to his wife *"please sweet heart, immediately you get the letters, take the one for Luke Hoare to his office and please deliver the one to Ethan Ahern personally to him"* says Matthew. *"I believe you're definitely doing the right thing, he doesn't want you to get out"* replied Delilah.

Two days later, around 2pm, Delilah carrying Debbie on her back and pushing Samuel in the stroller arrived at Ethan Ahern's office after twenty five minutes' walk from her apartment, ten minutes later, she was sitting in Ethan's office on a chair and Samuel sitting beside her, at the other end of the office desk sat Ethan Ahern. *"I know that it's not easy Delilah for you and the children, but with the overwhelming evidence of your husband getting caught with the package that contained the drugs, if he pleads guilty, he'll get a maximum six years sentence, the police has offered that deal, but if he goes to trial, there is a high probability that he'll be found guilty and he will be getting the mandatory ten years sentence or even more for not pleading guilty"* says Ethan. Delilah starts crying *"but my husband is innocent, he wasn't aware of the drugs in the package"* says Delilah as she sniffles, *"but unfortunately the jury may not believe that, and he will be found guilty"* says Ethan, Delilah sniffled as she brought out the letter Matthew sent to her to give to Ethan. *"Matthew sent me this letter to give to you"* says Delilah. *"Okay"* says Ethan as he stretched his hand over the office desk to collect the letter from Delilah and opened it, it took him just two minutes to read the letter, he looked devastated after reading the letter, *"so, your husband wants me off his case?"* asked Ethan. *"Yes, he wants you to transfer all his correspondence to the new solicitor"* replied Delilah as she stood up, and helped Samuel down from the chair, put him in the stroller and left Ethan's office.

Three days after Matthew fired Ethan Ahern and got a new solicitor, he was sitting in one of the cubicles of the prison truck on the way to the high court, he was dressed in his black suit and black shoe with a checker's short sleeve shirt, he managed to hold his Holy Bible in his hand that was handcuffed to the front, it was going to 10am in the morning when the prison truck finally arrived at the high court in Dublin after about two hour's drive from cork prison. Ten minutes later, one of the prison officers brought him from the prison truck to the entrance door at the back of the court house to the reception desk, two court officers were sitting at the desk, one male and the other female both officers are huge, they are over six feet tall, the female officer stood up from her sit to attend to the prison officer, the prison officer gave the female court officer a piece of paper, she looked at the paper and checks Matthew's name on a piece of paper on the wall, she saw Matthew's name, she removed Matthew's handcuff and took him to the holding cell that already had five other prisoners, Matthew still holding his Holy Bible sat on the only brick bench in the cell with four of the prisoners that were smoking cigarette, the fifth prisoner that is in his early twenties that wasn't smoking cigarette was standing up and had his back to the wall *"what is that book you are holding there?"* he asked Matthew as he pointed to the book Matthew was holding *"it's my bible,"* replied Matthew, the fifth prisoner laughed as the other four prisoners immediately looked at Matthew and started laughing as well. *"Are you a priest?"* the prisoner sitting beside Matthew that is in his late thirties asked smiling. *"I am not a priest"* replied Matthew, *"are you trying to get bail?"* the fifth prisoner asked Matthew. *"No, I am trying to reduce my bail money"* replied Matthew, *"what are you in for?"* the prisoner sitting beside him asked. *"I am in for collecting a package that contained drugs"* replied Matthew. *"Okay, and how much money is your bail money?"* asked the fifth prisoner *"twenty thousand"* replied Matthew *"wow, you must have been caught with loads of drugs!!!"* says the prisoner sitting beside Matthew *"what is the quantity of drugs you got caught with?"* asked the fifth prisoner, *"about nine hundred grams"* replied Matthew *"I think you can get it reduced to twelve thousand, or maybe even ten thousand"* says the prisoner that was sitting beside Matthew. When it was going to 1pm, the cell door opened, the female court officer that Matthew saw at the court reception earlier on that morning stood by a trolley at the door with nylon bags that contain burger, chips and can of coke, she handed one bag at a time to the first prisoner sitting by the cell door to hand over the other prisoners, when the female officer closed the cell door and left, Matthew asked the prisoner sitting beside him if he wants his own lunch bag *"you don't want it?"* the prisoner asked Matthew, *"no, I don't want to eat now"* replied Matthew, the prisoner collected the bag from Matthew, he took the beef bugger from the bag *"does anyone wants extra chips or coke?"* he asked the other prisoners, the fifth prisoner that was standing up took the can of coke, and another prisoner took the Matthew's chips *"are you sure you don't want it?"* the fifth prisoner asked Matthew, showing him the can of Coke *"no, am alright"* replied Matthew, he didn't want to tell anyone that he was fasting and praying. Twenty minutes after the last time the officer brought the lunch for the prisoners, the cell door opened again, this time it was the male prison court officer that opened the cell door *"Matthew Williams!!!"* the officer called. *"That's me officer,"* answered Matthew as he stood up. *"Come with me,"* says the officer. After locking the cell door, the officer handcuffed Matthew to the front and took him to an office down the corridor, they only walked for ten seconds, when Matthew got into the office, he saw a man in his early forties, sitting on a chair by an office desk, Luke Hoare is five feet eight inches tall, he's in his late thirties, dressed in a blue suit and a blue tie to match, *"sit down Matthew."* Luke pointed to the only available sit at the other side of the desk, the court officer stood outside the door to the office *"I am Luke Hoare"* the man extended his hand over the desk to greet Matthew who managed to take his handshake with the handcuff on his hand, they have talked on the phone for about four times in the past two weeks since Matthew got him as his new solicitor *"your bail money has been reduced to seven thousand, so we just need a surety that can come up with the amount, then you can get out on bail,"* says Luke. *"Thank you very much sir"* replied Matthew.

The next day Matthew was walking in the prison yard with Peter and Lucky during the first lock out, *"so your bail money as now been reduced to seven thousand?"* asked Lucky. *"Yes, but I don't know or have anyone that will put down the money or stand as a surety for me,"* replied Matthew *"you have to get someone by all means that can help you to get out on bail and run"* says Lucky *"I hope you get someone Matthew"* says Peter. Marcello came to join them, *"Matthew, have you talk to your wife today?"* ask Marcello *"yes, I spoke to her immediately I came to the yard, my bail money has been reduced to seven thousand yesterday, I am just looking for someone that can stand has a surety for me."* replied Matthew. *"Well, I don't know why you want to go out for a short while and then after your trial come back here again, I believe you should just face everything now,"* says Marcello. *"What do you mean, you don't know why he's going out for a short while Marcello?"* asked Lucky in annoyance. *"Well, for you Lucky, you want to go out and run, you are not going to fight your case, right?"* asked Marcello, *"yes, I am going to run, I can't do one year jail time, not to talk of six years that my solicitor told me I'll get if I plead guilty, so, I am definitely going to run,"* replied Lucky. *"I believe if you want to get out on bail, you should run, but Matthew wants to fight his case when he gets out on bail, which I am very sure that the jury will find him guilty whether he knows about the drugs in the package he collected or not, Matthew will be coming back here, I definitely know that,"* Marcello frankly said *"I won't be coming back here in Jesus mighty name, but I need to get out first,"* says Matthew.

Later that afternoon, during the second lockout, Matthew was sitting in on a chair at the reverend of the prison office talking to Delilah on the phone, *"since morning, I have gone to beg the pastor and three other people to let them know that the bail money has been reduced to seven thousand, but nobody wants to help"* says Delilah, sniffling as she speaks. *"We have to keep praying and have hope that we'll get someone that will help."* says Matthew as tears trickles from his eyes, the reverend stood up from his chair to part Matthew on the shoulder to calm him down, the call lasted for about six minutes. When Matthew got back to the cell, he cried to God holding his bible on the top of the bunk bed as he prayed, he prayed for a miracle for someone that can help to stand as surety for him.

Two days later, Matthew was walking in the prison yard with Peter and Lucky at the first lock out *"you need to tell your wife to try her best to get someone that can put up with the bail money to get you out of here"* says

Lucky, *"it's not easy for my wife out there, she's trying her best to get someone that has the money and can stand as a surety for me"* replied Matthew, *"for me, the guys that sent me to bring the market from Nigeria has given my brother the ten thousand bail money, and my brother has agreed to stand as surety for me, I think I should be out of here by the end of this week or unfailingly next week"* says Lucky again, just then, the only gate to the prison yard opened, and Jude walks into the yard, he first stood by the wall immediately after the entrance gate, then he saw Lucky, he then walked up to him, lucky saw him coming to him *"hey!!! Jude, what happened?"* Lucky asked as Jude started walking with them, *"my brother, I got busted yesterday with Ganja"* replied Jude *"this is Jude, and this is Peter, and this is Matthew"* says Lucky fidgeting has he introduced the guys to themselves, they all continued to walk up and down the length of the yard from wall to wall, *"I am going for my bail hearing in two days' time, and I should be out before the end of the week because my father in-law quickly wants me out"* says Jude, *"you are lucky then"* says Lucky, *"look at this guy"* Lucky pointed to Matthew, *"he has been here for eleven weeks now, and hasn't got someone that will stand as surety for him, even three days ago, he went to the high court and got his bail money reduced from twenty thousand to seven thousand, but his wife is still looking for someone that will come up with the bail money"* says Lucky again *"I heard about him from someone outside"* says Jude *"you are the guy that collected the package with drugs in Waterford city?"* Jude asked Matthew *"yes"* replied Matthew. *"I should have learned from your mistake, I shouldn't have gone to collect the package I went to collect, notwithstanding that our case is different, the person that told me about your case said he believes that you didn't know you were collecting a package containing drugs, but I knew I was collecting Ganja, I actually travelled down to West Africa last month to arrange for the drugs to be sent to me here, and I have successfully done it three times before,"* says Jude, *"you are right, he didn't know he was collecting drugs"* says Lucky *"but he would be found guilty if he goes to trial"* says Jude *"I know, that is the reason why he should try and get out on bail and run"* says Lucky.

The next day, at the second lockout, Matthew was in the prison yard walking with Peter, the entrance door to the yard opened *"Matthew Williams!!!"* shouted a male prison officer, Matthew raised up his hand, *"that's me officer!!!"* shouted Matthew as he quickly walks to the officer.

"Come with me, you have a visit" says the officer. Ten minutes after, Matthew walked into the prison visitors' room, the room was not big as Matthew expected, it was eight feet by length and seven feet wide, there were three other prisoners sitting on a stool by a transparent glass that is used to demarcate prisoners from the visitors, the prisoners had their visitors at the other side of the glass, they were talking to their visitors through the glass, Matthew saw Jude sitting on a wooden stool chair talking to a man in his early sixties and another woman in her early thirties that were also sitting on a wooden stool chair, Matthew sat on the available wooden stool chair beside Jude, who immediately looked at him *"what's up Matthew, so, you too have a visit?"* asked Jude. *"Yes, but I don't know who it is"* replied Matthew. *"That is my father in-law Darren, and my wife Susan"* Jude said to Matthew as he looked from Matthew to his visitors, *"hello"* said Matthew to them as he nodded his head, *"hello"* replied Darren, but Susan was in retrospection as she looked at Matthew. Susan now in flashback vividly remembered when she went shopping at a grocery store with her mother a year earlier, when she they finished shopping and wanted to leave, she tried to start her car, but her car couldn't start, just then, Matthew pushed a trolley filled up with groceries walked with his wife that was holding the hand of a two year old boy, Susan remembered that when she was confused about what the problem with her car was as she was looking at the engine of her car after it wouldn't start, that Matthew asked her what the problem was *"my car wouldn't start"* she replied, *"it might be the battery,"* says Matthew as he immediately went back to the boot of his car and brought a battery cable. *"I can try and help you to jump start it with this cable to see if it'll start"* says Matthew, and that was how Matthew helped her to start her car, the presence of Delilah and Matthew's children that came into the visitors room brought Susan back to reality, she sees Delilah puts Debbie on the table by the transparent glass, immediately Matthew saw Debbie, he was overwhelmed with emotions, Debbie was only three months old, she looked like an angel, Delilah sat on the stool chair directly opposite Matthew, then immediately held Debbie with her hand to protect her from falling off the table, *"I didn't know you were coming to see me"* says Matthew, *"I didn't want to tell you this morning when you called me, I know you will discourage me to come, and we've missed you so much, I actually bought the bus ticket yesterday after talking to you on the phone,"* says Delilah as her eyes wells

up with tears, Matthew looked at Debbie touching the transparent glass trying to get through it to come to him, and his son Samuel stood opposite him looking at him with a confused face, tears trickled from Matthew's face *"I missed all of you so much, I think about you every minute and every seconds"* replied Matthew, Susan and Darren looked at Matthew, Delilah and their children as this was going on. Susan whispered to Darren, looking from him to Matthew *"I know him!"* *"Where do you know him?"* Darren asked her, *"what did you say?"* Jude asked Susan, *"remember last year that I told you that a guy helped me to jump start my car battery when I went shopping with my mum when my car wouldn't start?"* Susan asked Jude. *"Yes, I remember, and we got a new battery the next day after because your car couldn't start again that morning"* replied Jude. *"Yes, it was him that helped me to jump start my car, he was driving a blue Nissan Primera"* says Susan, Jude immediately turned to Matthew *"what kind of car do you have?"* asked Jude. *"What?"* asked Matthew, *"what kind of car do you drive out there?"* asked Jude again, *"Nissan Primera, why are you asking?"* asked Matthew curiously, *"okay, my wife is right, she said you helped her out, jump starting her car last year when she went shopping when her car couldn't start"* replied Jude, as he then looked at his father in-law and wife *"you're right, he drives a Nissan Primera car"* says Jude. One hour later, Delilah was carrying Debbie on her back and pushing Samuel in the baby stroller after exiting the final gate from Cork Prison, at the same time, Jude's father in-law and Jude's wife were driving away from the Cork Prison car park that is directly opposite the prison, *"that's Matthew's wife with his children"* says Susan to her Dad, *"I think they are walking to the bus station, can we help them dad?"* asked Susan, *"okay"* replied Darren. Five minutes later, Delilah was seated at the back of the Red Toyota Corolla with her children, *"thank you very much"* says Delilah *"you are very welcome, your husband is a good man, he once helped me out last year to jump start my car when you guys went for grocery shopping, I don't know if you remember me, I saw you with your son sitting in the car while your husband was helping me out"* says Susan. *"Okay, I think I remember now"* replied Delilah, they got stuck in a traffic because there was a road work going on, Darren looked at the time on the dashboard of the car, it was going to 4pm, *"what time is your bus?"* asked Darren as he looked back at Delilah and then looked back to the front to see if the traffic was moving, *"the next Waterford bus is actually at*

5:30pm" replied Delilah. *"We are actually going to Waterford"* says Susan *"you can come with us if it's okay with you"* says Darren *"ooh!!! Thank you so much sir"* says Delilah *"that will save you from the stress of having to wait for about another two hours at the bus station"* says Susan. *"Thank you so much"* says Delilah again, *"my husband said Matthew has not been able to get someone to stand has a surety for him for over two months now?"* asked Susan as she looked in shock at Delilah, *"yes, nobody wants to help us, not withstanding that my husband is innocent of the crime he's in prison for"* replied Delilah. *"Yes, my husband said so, even before my husband was arrested, he was talking to someone that vouch that your husband was used to collect the drugs"* says Susan *"yes, he didn't know that he was collecting drugs"* says Delilah as she sniffled with tears trickling from her eyes, *"me and my children are really suffering, my husband is a very good man"* says Delilah again as she sniffled and cried *"and how much is the bail money?"* asked Darren *"it's been reduced to seven thousand by the high court three days ago, but I have tried to look for someone that will come up as a surety, but nobody still wants to help"* replied Delilah crying.

The next day, after the first lockout, Matthew was in the prison yard talking to Delilah on the phone, Delilah told him that Susan and Darren are looking into helping them to get someone that can stand as a surety for him, Matthew became elated at the news, immediately after the call, he went to meet Jude that was walking with Peter and Lucky, *"Jude can I quickly talk to you for one minute?"* he gently pulled him aside to the wall away from the path of other prisoners that were doing the walk round, *"my wife said your father in-law and your wife are looking to help me with the surety?"* whispered Matthew to Jude, *"yes, my wife was trying to tell me this morning, but there was not enough time, because she was also telling me about my father in-law going to the court today to stand as a surety for me to get out on bail today"* replied Jude, *"okay, thank God"* says Matthew *"yes, I might be getting out today, if not, first thing tomorrow morning"* says Jude confidently, *"if I get out, I'll see what I can do to help you Matthew, you're not supposed to be here"* says Jude *"thank you so much Jude"* says Matthew *"but if you do get out on bail Matthew, I'll advise you to run if you don't want to come back here, because if you go to trial, you'll be found guilty, and you will be getting long years"* Jude frankly said.

Two days after, Delilah was sitting on a two sitter couch in Jude's house with her children talking to Susan, *"my husband is on his way with the guy that as agreed to stand as a surety for your husband"* says Susan, *"thank you so much, I don't know how much to thank you"* says Delilah as she begins to cry again, "you don't need to continue to thank me Delilah, I believe your husband will do the same for my husband, I believe that is tears of joy that your husband will soon be out" says Susan as she smiled at Delilah. Jude was out on bail from Cork prison the previous day. Ten minutes later, Jude unlocked the door to the sitting room from outside and walked into the sitting room with another man in his early fifties, he's about five feet six inches tall, Jude looked at Delilah, *"this is Jim, and that is Matthew's wife, her name is Delilah"* says Jude as he introduced the guy to Delilah *"good afternoon sir"* says Delilah, Jim looked at Samuel playing with a toy car on the rug and then looked at Debbie *"Hello, are this your children?"* Jim asked as he greeted Delilah that was carrying Debbie *"yes those are her children"* says Susan *"they are beautiful children"* says Jim as he looked at Samuel again *"I told Jude that I will be doing this because of the children, not withstanding that Jude told me that your husband is innocent"* says Jim to Delilah *"thank you so much sir"* replied Delilah as she was immediately overwhelmed with emotions and immediately started crying *"aah, don't worry Delilah, everything will be alright"* says Susan again as she tried to calm Delilah down patting her on the back. The next day, in the afternoon, during the second lockout, Matthew was on the phone in the priest office talking to Delilah, *"so, you are at the court house"* asked Matthew, *"yes, the judge just approved Jim as your surety, Jim just need to transfer the seven thousand bail money into the court's account, then the court will instruct the prison to release you"* says Delilah *"thank you so much sweetheart, I can't wait to see you guys, is Jim beside you there so that I can thank him?"* asked Matthew, *"no, Jim as gone to the bank to get the bail money transferred to the account number given to him by the court, but Jude and Susan are here with me"* replied Delilah *"what's up Matthew"* says Jude after Delilah handed her mobile phone to him *"thank you so much Jude, thank you"* says Matthew *"I think you should be out unfailingly by tomorrow immediately the court sees the bail money"* says Jude. That night in his cell, Matthew and Peter sang Christian songs and prayed as they did most nights, the prison officers on duty that night came and opened the peephole to the cell door to observe them as they sang and prayed, but some other prisoners screamed from their cells, shouted *"Fuck you!!!"* caused and shouted from their cell to tell them to shut up, but that is what happens whenever they sang the praise worship songs and prayed so Matthew and Peter are used to them shouting, but the prison guards are always even more surprised and wondered what was happening and curious to know the reason for their amusement for singing and dancing while being locked up, Matthew and Peter could notice the amusement on their face when they open the flap of the peephole to the cell door to observe them, one of the officers asked them most of the time the next morning if the reason for their amusement was because they've been told that they were going to be released from the prison and going home, but they would just smile and tell the officer that they appreciate been alive *"it's all because we are glad to be alive officer"* Matthew would reply to the officer, and there would be that same gobsmacked expression on the officers face as the same expression seen on the faces of the officers that came to check on them the previous night when they were singing and dancing. The next day, Matthew was completely apprehensive from the time he got up from bed, he couldn't go to sleep, he was overwhelmed with the thought of his potential freedom, he only got about three hours sleep, immediately after the first unlock that he was able to get to the phone in the prison yard, he called Delilah *"you'll definitely be out today"* says Delilah, after the call, Matthew walked with Peter, he was the only prisoner that knew that he was about to be released, Marcello came to meet them that afternoon during the second lockout, *"Matthew, have you talked to your wife today?"* he *asked "yes, I spoke to her this morning"* replied Matthew *"don't worry, you just concentrate on your life here, you need to look out for yourself and stop worrying about them, they are outside, they'll be alright, if you plead guilty, you'll get highest maybe 7 years, before you know it, you'll be out, time flies"* says Marcello, *"thank you"* replied Matthew. That night, Matthew was walking with Peter in the prison yard at the final lockout around 6:30pm when he saw the gate to the prison yard opened, his eyes as been on that gate since morning whenever he came out to the yard, *"Matthew Williams!!!"* the male officer shouted his name, Matthew immediately hugged Peter, and ran to meet the officer who immediately told him to go and park his stuffs that he's been released on bail. That night he was released around 8pm, he was given his belonging and bus ticket to get home.

Matthew opened his eyes, he saw his wife Delilah on the bed beside him, he felt surreal, he thought it was one of those dreams again that he tried to picture every night on the bunk bed in the cell in the prison so that he could fall asleep, and tried to stick to what he thought was a dream, because that was the only way he drifted to sleep while in prison, but he wasn't dreaming this time, it was for real, because he was temporarily released from Cork prison the previous night, he jumped up from his bed when he realised that he was definitely at home with his wife and children for real, he went straight to the baby cot were his daughter Debbie was sleeping, he looked at her, she looked like an angel, she was only three months old, he went into his son's room, he was sleeping too, he sat on the single bed by his side, and just looked at his beautiful innocent face as he slept, he missed his wife and children so much that, being in their life now for real is like having the whole world to himself, *"sweetheart"* his wife called him, he quickly went back to their room, and she said *"it's only half seven sweetheart, come back to bed"* he went back to bed, laid down beside her face to face touching and cuddling her, and both of them cried at the same time as they cuddled up and kissed, *"I really missed you, it was like this day would never come"* his wife said again as she touched his face, Delilah's phone that was on the bed started ringing, she picked up her phone and looked at the screen, *"it's Jude"* says Delilah as she quickly picked the call, *"hello Jude, Matthew is here, he came home yesterday late in the night"* says Delilah as she immediately gave the phone to Matthew *"hi Jude, thank you for everything"* says Matthew *"you don't need to thank me, it's Jim that you need to thank"* says Jude, *"have you called him?"* asked Jude, *"no, am sorry, I will call him now"* replied Matthew as he turned to look at Delilah *"I need to call Jim, do you have his number?"* Matthew asked her *"yes I have his number"* replied Delilah *"Delilah has Jim number, I just need to quickly call him and I'll call you later"* says Matthew. After talking to Jim later that morning, Matthew sat in the sitting room holding her daughter with the left hand, and reading the letter from Bolton manufacturing company asking him and his wife to come down for an aptitude test for the job application he and his wife applied for four months earlier before he got into the ordeal that got him locked up, the letter had been sent a month earlier for him and his wife to ring in to the company to arrange for the date to come in and take an aptitude test, which is the first phase before the face to face interview, notwithstanding that he had the scepticism that it might be too late now to phone the company for the aptitude test since the letter had been sent a month earlier, but he still rang the number on the letter, it was around 3pm now, the voice of a lady came on the other end of the line *"hello Bolton manufacturing company, how can I help?"* the lady asked *"please I got a letter from your company about me ringing in to arrange for an aptitude test for the post of an assembler, that is why I am calling"* replied Matthew *"please can you give me the reference number on the letter?"* the lady asked, and Matthew gave her the number on the letter *"there is an aptitude test to be conducted next week Wednesday at 9am, can you come in with your wife to take the aptitude test?"* the lady asked *"yes, certainly we can come in next week Wednesday at 9am"* Matthew replied *"okay, I have put you and your wife down for that day"* replied the lady again *"thank you very much"* says Matthew, and the call dropped. He called his wife *"Sweetheart"* and excitedly walked to meet her in the room *"I just spoke to someone at Bolton, and they said we should come in and do an aptitude test next week Wednesday"* Matthew said as she hugged him smiling *"ooh, that's good news, but who is going to mind the children"* Delilah asked *"well we have to get someone that can mind the children, we just have to pay the person, it's very important that we don't miss the opportunity"* says Matthew, but he had to go and get his car back from the police, his car was taken from the car park on the Quay to the police station, after it was searched by the police on the day he was arrested with the package.

One hour later, Matthew walked into the police station in Waterford City, his apartment is just about twenty minutes' walk to the police station, it was around 5pm and the reception room was empty, there was a sign with a note on an A4 white paper placed on the wall to press the bell on the reception desk, so; Matthew pressed the bell once, and within two minutes, a policeman opened a door from an inner room to the reception and came out, *"what can I do for you sir?"* he said *"please officer, I am looking for sergeant Keane Grant"* says Matthew *"Ooh, he's gone out with some other officers on an investigation"* the officer replied *"do you want me to give him a message for you?"* the officer asked when he saw the disappointment on Matthew's face, *"yes officer, please can you tell him that I came to collect my car, my name is Matthew Williams"* he said *"okay, if you can come back in another thirty minutes he'll be here"* the officer replied *"thank you officer"* Matthew said and left the building.

Thirty minutes later, Matthew was back at the police station in the car park at the back of the station with sergeant Grant, he gave Matthew the key to his car, it's the same Nissan Primera, Matthew tried to start the car, but the car wouldn't start, *"the battery must be dead, you might need to get another battery to be able to start the car because the car has been sitting down there for the past three months"* says sergeant Grant, *"yeah, the battery is definitely gone"* replied Matthew *"I think I can come back with another battery in another one hour to pick it up"* says Matthew *"yes, when you come, just come here and collect it, you have the key and the gate is always open"* sergeant Grant replied, *"thank you sir"* Matthew replied and left. Immediately after getting outside the police station at the entrance to the car park, Matthew rang Jude, *"Hi Jude, please I need a battery to start my car to collect it from the police station, the car won't start because the battery is gone, please can you help me out?"* *"Which police station are you at?"* Jude asked *"I am at the one by the city centre on Ballytruckle road"* Matthew replied. Thirty minutes after talking to Matthew on the phone, Jude arrived with a battery and helped Matthew to start his car and he took the car immediately to the car wash before going home to his wife and children because the car was very dirty.

Walking through the city mall in Waterford city with his wife and children, Matthew carried his two year old boy and his wife pushed his daughter in a trolley, some of the people that knows them starred at them in bewilderment and some people just waved at them and some came to congratulate him for been a free man again, because it was the third day after he got out on bail, the news of his arrest and incarceration was all over the media, most people thought he was going to be locked up for a very long time because any drug case in Waterford city is taken very seriously and people get overwhelmed with such news and believe that the life of the perpetrator is ruined or destroyed forever, Matthew can't blame them, because so many innocent souls or people have died taking drugs. That is the reason why he believes people like Jim that stood as surety for him is an angel sent to his family by God, Matthew finally met Jim in person the day after he came out on bail after talking to him on the phone, and Jim invited him and his wife to the church he worshipped at after he told Matthew how the police tried to get him disqualified by the presiding judge as his surety during the bail hearing in other for the judge not to grant the bail and for Matthew not to get out of jail because in the past Jim had been charged with drunk driving and had to pay a fine, but the judge accepted Jim as a good surety because he had his own business as a plasterer and could account for how he got the bail money, it was a miracle that he agreed to stand as a surety for him as they have never met in person, the main church that Matthew and his wife goes to every Sunday to worship before he got into the drug ordeal, all the members of the church that his wife went and pleaded to, to stand surety for him refused to stand as a surety for him, notwithstanding that he's been worshipping at the church for almost two and half years, the head of the church, the pastor said he doesn't want to have any involvement with the case, because it's a drug case, the pastor was the same pastor that did the naming ceremony for Matthew's two children, this was the same church Matthew paid ten percent of his weekly wages as tithe every Sundays to, Matthew was utterly disappointed when his wife told him that they all refused to stand as a surety for him, the pastor never visited him even for once during the over three months he spent while incarcerated, but when Matthew came out on bail, he went to see him, and the same reason and explanation he gave Matthew for not getting involved was that he doesn't want to get involved in a drug case, Matthew was more even disappointed that he already assumed he's guilty of the crime even before been convicted by the law court, Matthew said to himself *"It's in the time of trials and tribulation that you know who your true friend are"* so Matthew vowed to himself that he'll never attend the church again and stopped going to the church and has now decided to start worshipping at Jim's church. He remembered standing in front of Jim the previous day, thanking him and hugging him, he said *"you're an angel sent to me and my family from the almighty God"* because, Matthew almost lost hope of getting out on bail has most of the people Matthew helped to get a permanent job with Watchcat security also refused to stand as a surety for him, and the major reason was that they believe Matthew would abscond after getting bail and they would lose the bail money.

The next day Matthew went to sign on at the police station, that was one of the conditions of his bail that he sign on every day at the police station, he met Lucky that also came out on bail a day before Matthew got out, he was caught with four kilos of cocaine at Cork Airport by a sniffer dog that sniffed out the drug from the travelling bag he was carrying, his arrest was also all over the news, the prisoners and officers used to make jest of

Lucky while he was in prison, they called him unlucky, and said the dog's name that caught him is lucky, his wife actually dump him when he got caught with the drugs by writing him a letter that she has moved on with another man, that he should forget about her and their three year old daughter, so when Matthew met him at the police station, he told Matthew that his wife left him, and won't even allow him to see his daughter, Lucky has always told Matthew while they were both still locked up in prison before getting out on bail that if he gets bail he's going to run and leave the country to go to South America or Asia, he advised Matthew to do the same, that if he doesn't run, he'll be found guilty, and will get more than the mandatory ten years sentence for drug offence, Lucky had already gone to court after his bail, and he has pleaded guilty to the drug charges against him, but the judge adjourn his sentencing for another two weeks, because of probationer report that was not ready and the judge wanted to put that into consideration before passing sentence, so; the judge allowed him to continue his bail to allow him to see and say goodbye to his daughter because that was the request by his defence, but Lucky told Matthew again finally at the police station that day *"Matthew, I am leaving this country in the next three days for good, I can't survive a year in prison, I'll be dead"* says Lucky, and Matthew believed him because when he was in Cork prison for about three months when he was first arrested before getting his bail, whenever Matthew came across him, he was always shivering and tells Matthew that *"I am very sick, I can't breathe, I am going to die here if I don't quickly get bail"* so; Matthew wasn't surprised when he got a call from him two weeks later, after that day at the police station *"you know who is on the phone?"* Lucky said from the other end of the line *"Lucky, is that you?"* Matthew asked *"yes it's me, I am calling you from Japan, I told you I was leaving that country"* Lucky replied *"How did you do it, your passport is still with the police"* says Matthew. *"Well, I had to buy another person's passport, a look alike passport that really looked like me to get out of Ireland, I am just calling you to tell you, and if you want to get out of that place, I can connect you to the same guy that helped me to get the passport I used, and you can get out as well, or do you still want to continue to fight your case"* Lucky asked *"I want to fight my case, I can't leave my wife and children, apart from that I didn't know about the drugs in the package"* Matthew replied *"Matthew, they are going to find you guilty, I have said that to you several times, well that is your own business*

- 47 -

if you want to stay and go to jail, I have to go now, please don't ever tell anyone that I called you or that I am in Japan" Lucky replied infuriated, and the call dropped, before Lucky rang him, Matthew heard from Jude that the judge had already sentenced Lucky to six years in prison in his absence for the drug charges, and that Lucky is now declared a wanted person by the court and the police.

After a three weeks outside on bail, Matthew went to Cork prison to try and visit Peter his former cell mate, but he was told that Peter had been transferred to Castlerea prison four days earlier, and apart from that, the female prison officer told him that as a former inmate, he's only allowed to visit a prisoner only after six months that he's left the prison *"ooh, I am sorry officer, I didn't know that"* Matthew apologised, after leaving Cork prison that day, Matthew was happy that Peter has been transferred to a better prison. The next day, Matthew left Waterford city with his wife and kids at 6am to county Roscommon to visit Peter at Castlerea prison, it was about six hours drive to the prison, and they were allowed to see Peter, the visit was a contact visit, so they were able to hug him *"Castlerea is a far better prison than Cork prison"* says Peter *"I have applied for a job with the section that manufactures car accessories so that I can earn and safe some money before my transfer back to the England, but I am still waiting to be called to start the job"* says Peter again, *"that's very good, I am just happy that you are okay, my God, this place is far better than Cork prison, see, I can hug you"* Matthew said smiling and hugged him again, the visit was for about an hour, and it was really worth it, because Peter is a very lovely person, and very charismatic as well, they didn't get back home that day until very late in the night.

Driving to Bolton manufacturing company in his car with his wife sitting on the passenger seat after dropping off their children at the child minders house, they discussed about how they'll have to move to Clonmel if they get the job, because it's about forty five minutes' drive from Waterford city to Clonmel were the company is located, it was 8am, and they were dressed in business attire has advised in the letter sent out to them by the company, they got there at some couple of minutes to 9am, that was the first time they had come to the town of Clonmel, it's not a big town, it's a town with about fifteen thousand residents, but there are loads of manufacturing companies in Clonmel, which includes six multinational manufacturing companies, Bolton company has about four hundred employees, and notwithstanding that the job is a shift work, where you have morning shift and night shift, the car park meant for about almost three hundred cars that morning was almost filled up, Matthew had to drive round for almost five minutes before he could get an available parking space, he had already drove to the front of the building at the front of the reception section and advised his wife to go down to the reception before looking for a parking space. They sat in a room with ten other applicants that also came for the aptitude test, they were given pen and paper and a question paper, about forty objective questions with four option answers to choose from, Delilah sat beside Matthew, they gave them thirty minutes to finish the test, the test included three subjects which was English, Maths and General questions. Immediately they were told to start, Matthew was very fast in answering the questions, and as he was doing that, Delilah was just copying what he wrote, because they sat right beside each other, the coordinator of the test, a lady, sat at the far end of the room typing on a desktop computer, after about twenty-five minutes Matthew was done, and so was Delilah. It wasn't until another two weeks they got a phone call from Bolton company to advised them that they passed the aptitude test, and advised them to come for a face to face interview, and a week after the face to face interview, they got another call that they've been given the job, they later received an official letter in the post that same December advising them that they were to start on January 6th a month after, they were ecstatic from getting the job, because the job came with series of fringe benefit like free healthcare, quarterly bonus payment from the company, pension plan by the company, and loads of other benefits, but the fringe benefits was only given to employees after six months' probation when they become a permanent staff. They looked for a house in Clonmel and got a three-bedroom semi dethatched house that was located just five minutes' drive from the company, they chose to do different shifts in other to be able to mind their children between themselves, so; whenever one of them was at work, the other person minds the children.

A day before they moved, Matthew went and told sergeant Grant that he got a job in Clonmel, and had to move to Clonmel since the condition of his bail was that if he moves to another address, he must notify the police, when Matthew told him, he was shocked that Matthew had gotten a job, and wanted to work, he told Matthew *"so you are starting a job."* *"Yes sir,*

I am starting a job and have to move to Clonmel, myself and my wife already got a house not far away from our work place, this is the new address" Matthew said and gave him a piece of paper that the new address was written on, sergeant Grant was the investigating officer in charge of Matthew's case, he was among the officers that arrested him, and he was the officer that refused to allow the other officers to follow him to the address and the location that the real culprit that sent him to collect the package was waiting for him to deliver the package, and he was the same officer that was very adamant in blocking him to get bail, all he always say whenever he sees him, is that *"what you just need to do Matthew is that, just accept that you knew about the drugs in the package then I would be able to help you, if you are saying that you are not aware of the drugs then you are going away for a long time"* but Matthew had always told him that he was not aware of the drugs in the package, which always get sergeant Grant to be more infuriated *"then I can't help you then"* he would say that and would just walk away. Matthew and Delilah also told their new church pastor, Joseph and Ruth Potter that they had to move because of their new job location, but they still intended to drive down to church on Sundays has they don't work on Sundays. The church is a Pentecostal church and the church service was held in a hall in a big hotel in Waterford city, the church had about hundred and twenty members that attended the Sunday service, most people that came to the church were from the refugee hostel in Waterford City, most of the people that emigrated to Ireland fleeing persecution in their country. Pastor Joseph and Ruth Potter are very lovely people from the United State, they love to help people that are in need, they even sacrifice financially and physically for people, most people that knows them believes that they are angels sent from God to help them because of their true love and generosity towards anyone that comes across them, whenever Matthew comes to the church on Sundays, he worked as an usher for the two hours service ushering and directing people to were to sit, and also helped with arranging the chairs, most of the time, he had his daughter in his hand standing up by the entrance door doing his ushering job, because his daughter always cling to him, always want Matthew to carry her in his arms.

When Matthew's daughter celebrated her one-year birthday, most of the people from the church had to travel from Waterford city down to Clonmel for her birthday, including the mummy and daddy Porter, that is what most members of the church calls them. It was real fun at Debbie's one-year birthday party, there was bouncing castle, face painting for children and lovely food to eat as well. In July that year, after Debbie's party in June, Debbie had chicken pox, that caused her to have a mild fever and a rash of itchy inflamed pimples on her body which later turned to blisters and then loose scabs, then a day after, Samuel his brother contacted it, and a day after Matthew contacted it, Matthew was surprised has he thought he already had it when he was a child, he had to call his supervisor at work that he won't be coming to work because of his sickness, and his supervisor really appreciated him ringing him and told him to make sure that he's hundred percent cleared and certified by his doctor that the chicken pox is gone before coming back to work, because where he and Delilah worked was in a clean room environment in Bolton company, they normally changed to PPE gear whenever they get to work before entering the clean room, they manufacture a medical device called stent, that is used for the artery to help in resolving issues with the heart blockage, normally you can have about seventy people working in one of the clean room in close contacts, and for someone with chicken pox to come into that kind of environment, it would be a total disaster as the disease would spread fast, Matthew was out sick for two weeks before he could come back to work.

In the month of December that same year, they took their children to the Christmas party organised by Bolton company at the biggest hotel in Clonmel, there were about two hundred employees of the company that came to the party, most couples came with their children, everyone had a great time including the children, there was a father Christmas present grotto at the party that guest took pictures with and the children also got Christmas presents, they got nice gifts, Matthew and his wife and kids were really enjoying life and very happy until the first week of January the next year when Matthew got a call from his solicitor that, the court had given a date for his drug offence trial from the 18th of that January, that changed the serene atmosphere of their family, it was now fourteen months since he's been out on bail, he had gotten another job, even a better job, and he had now passed his six months' probation period with his wife at the new company, they were now permanent staffs at the company, and now he just received this horrible news, he now had to face reality again, he and his wife told his pastor, Joseph and Ruth Potter, and they were as shocked as Matthew and Delilah, but they said everyone has to be praying that Matthew shouldn't be found guilty, the Potters said everything would be fine, they encouraged Matthew and Delilah to have faith. A month before the trial before Matthew got the letter for the date of his trial in the post, two teenagers died of drug overdose at a birthday party in Waterford city, it was all over the news, a teenager that sold the drugs to the teenagers was arrested, so; the weather climate for any trial in the law court that has got to do with drugs was very unfavourable for any defendant charged with drug offence, the prosecutor in charge of Matthew's case actually persuaded the court to get his trial date to happen within that period in other to subtly get the jury pressurized and prejudicial in their decision to find him guilty, also during his trial, the prosecutor arranged with a secondary school to bring in some of their students whom were teenagers dressed in school uniform to the trial for the Jury to see them and subtly to remind the jury about the two teenagers that died of drug overdose a month earlier.

The trial lasted for four days, from the first day of his trial till the last day, the Potters were present with him and Delilah, and also a lady called Lorraine from the charity shop that Matthew used to work for was also present every day. His defence tried all they could to explain his obliviousness of the drug in the package, that he was only used to collect the drug, and also explained to the jury how he cooperated with the police immediately he was arrested with the package for them to be able to arrest the real culprit that sent him to collect the package and how the police refused to immediately follow him to the location to arrest the main culprit who was the orchestrated of the heinous crime, but the prosecutor argued that the police went to the location Matthew told them the real culprit was waiting but they didn't find any person waiting for Matthew to collect the package, he argued that Matthew was the sole orchestrator of the importation of the drugs into Ireland from India and also the sole individual in charge of the supply and sale of the drugs, it took the jury about four hours to come up with a guilty verdict on the last day of his trial, Jude was there with Joy, a lady from Matthew's church, after the verdict, Matthew and Delilah cried, Joseph and Ruth Potter had to consoled them that they have spoken to his defence after the judgement, and they said they are going to appeal the guilty verdict, but the problem was that it could take up to over a year before the appeal comes up and Matthew would be locked up until his conviction is overturned.

Immediately he was found guilty, the prison guards came over to where he was sitting at the defendant section of the court and handcuffed him, he had to plead to them to allow him to say goodbye to his wife and pastors. That day in the prison truck that was taking him to prison, it was like his world has been obliterated by his incarceration, but some other prisoners in the truck were singing and excited that they were been taken to prison, earlier that morning before the court started when they got to Waterford city, Matthew and Delilah dropped their children off to the minder's house before going to the court house and they didn't finished until around 6pm, sitting in the prison truck now he wondered if his wife and children were okay, the next day when he rang his wife, she told him that the Porters took them to their home, she said she called Bolton to tell them that she won't be coming to work for some time as she was totally overwhelmed and devastated by his conviction and absence.

Chapter Four

Back to Cork Prison

Matthew was in the prison kitchen upstairs standing with two other prisoners Luke and Nathan by the table in the only dining room that the prisoners use whenever they want to eat and relax, they were opening the bags of slice bread and putting six slices of bread each into several small nylon bags and then tie up the end of the nylon bag like a knot to seal it up, and also putting four teabags and sachets of sugar into a separate small nylon bags as well, each bag of both tea bags, sachet of sugar and slice bread would be served to each prisoner of about three hundred and eighty the next morning for breakfast, they would also serve them corn flakes and small boxes of 500ml milk, it was getting to 5pm, they do this every evening to get this ready for the next morning, they needed to finish doing it before 5:30pm, the last unlock time for the day that prisoners would be allowed out of their cell to either go to school, gym or to the yard, the three of them already planned to go to the gym, they were all in the white prison kitchen uniform and shoe. Nathan is in his middle twenty and doing four year sentence for arm robbery, he was arrested when he went to rob a deli store, what he did before he robbed the store was that, he did some research on the shop to know when it was not busy and without customers in the shop, and that happened to be in the evenings, he noticed from his research that there was only one employee whom was the sales person in the shop at that time of the day, so, one evening, Nathan went into the shop and threatened the female attendant with a knife asking her to empty the cash register into a backpack that he brought with him, which she immediately did, but unfortunately for Nathan, two construction workers, two guys, entered the shop to buy cigarettes, and they wrestled him to the ground and called the cops, he's only done three months out of his sentence, his wife Roberta, yes, that is what he calls her, started seeing another guy called Prince two weeks after Nathan got arrested and locked up in prison, Nathan said his wife is a drug addict, that Prince used to supply him and his wife drugs before his incarceration, they have three children, all boys, because Roberta couldn't pay for the drugs after Nathan incarceration, She offered Prince sex for drugs, and before you know it, Prince moved in with Roberta, Nathan said when he went for his sentence, Roberta came with Prince to the court, he said he was shocked when he was in the prison truck and saw prince standing by his own car, that was parked some few meters away from the courthouse, he said Prince was wearing his shirt, Nathan was only lucky to see Prince because there was a traffic hold up and he got up and saw him through the prison truck small window, when he told his wife that he saw Prince wearing his shirt standing by his car, his wife denied it, but one of his friend that came to visit him after his sentence told him that Prince does not only drive his car and wears his clothes, but now stays in his house, that they see Prince and his wife and children in his car most of the time, Roberta stopped visiting Nathan after the sentence, before he got sentenced, Whenever Roberta is coming to visit Nathan, what he does is that, he begs some other prisoners for money to be put into his prison account in other to be able to give the money to her, when Nathan called Prince from prison after seeing him at the court, Prince hung up the phone immediately he heard his voice, but a month after, Prince was arrested with twelve grams of cocaine and brought to Cork prison, and put in one of the cells in B wing, a different wing from were Nathan and Matthew is *"it's payback time, somebody told me Prince is in B wing, he's in here for dealing in drugs, this is my chance to deal with that guy, I am going to beat him bad that if he doesn't die he'll be spending the rest of his life on the hospital bed or on a wheelchair"* says Nathan *"I don't care if they give me a life sentence for killing him, that bastard is the reason why I am in here in the first place, I tried to rob that store to pay him money for his drugs supplies to me and my wife, and he started fucking my wife when I came in here"* he said again infuriatingly and showed Matthew a tattoo of his wife picture, Roberta, that is on his right shoulder *"it's madness yeah? I did this because I was madly in love with her, and I am still madly in love with her, I tried calling my wife so many times but the call is not going through, it seems she has changed her number, I have written so many letters to her, but she refused to reply to all my letters, just because of that monster that has taken over her life by supplying and enticing her with free drugs"* he said again, Nathan is a strong guy, he's respected in the gym as one of the strongest guy in weight lifting, he weighs about hundred kilos, but he lifts weights of one hundred and fifty kilos, he trains with Luke as his partner, they're are almost the same weight, and they lift almost the same weight, but Nathan can lift a little bit more.

Luke is also in his middle twenty and doing eight years for sale and supply of drugs, he was arrested when he received three single sofa armchairs sent from Amsterdam with twenty one kilos of cannabis at a house in Cork city that was delivered by an undercover police pretending to be a truck driver from the delivery company, he lied to the police that he was not aware of the drugs hidden in the armchairs from the beginning of his arrest, but on the first day of his trial, he changed his plea from not guilty to guilty based on the advised from his defence that he'll be getting three years if he pled guilty, and was advised not to risk getting the mandatory ten years or more if found guilty by the jury, but he was shocked when after he pleaded guilty and the judge still sentenced him to eight years imprisonment, but his defence has appealed his sentence, and he believes his sentence would be reduced when he goes for his appeal.

They were in the gym the next day, when one of the prisoners that had just been moved from B wing to A wing, that knows Nathan from the outside, told him that he knows another prisoner in B wing that can lure Prince to the prison yard, so that Nathan can beat him up. Matthew acts like a big brother to Luke, Nathan and some other three prisoners that works in the prison kitchen, so; *"Nathan, you don't need to put yourself in a more difficult and horrible situation by getting into a fight that can lead to you getting more charges or even committing a murder, think about your children, you are doing four years, before you know it, with good behaviour, you'll be out of here and reunited with your children"* Matthew advised him, *"no no no Matthew, I don't care if I kill that monster and get a life sentence, he's already destroyed my life, I have lost my wife to him"* Nathan said *"but what about your children Nathan, please think about your children, you can't just say because your wife is not talking to you now, you will forget about your three children and don't want to be with them, you are their father, you need to put your children into consideration"* Matthew said again *"I can't just let him get away with what he did to me"* Nathan said again and left the room.

Two days after their discussion, in the prison yard, Matthew was walking back and forth with some other prisoners, there were about seventy other prisoners in the yard, some were playing card games, and some playing dice game, and some were jostling to smoke cannabis or drugs, it was a sunny afternoon in the month of May, and the prison school was closed again, so; Matthew decided to stay in the yard, Luke and Marcella came to join him, *"how is your wife and children"* Marcella asked? *"They are fine"* Matthew replied *"when did you talk to them last?"* He asked *"Just now, immediately I came into the yard"* Matthew replied again, just then, there was an uproar at the other end of the yard, by the toilet were some prisoners smokes drugs, Marcella and Luke ran towards the scene of the commotion, but Matthew walked opposite to the entrance and exit gate to the yard, the door was locked, but that is what he normally does when there is pandemonium in the yard, he knows the prison officers would soon open the gate to come and stop the fight and take the prisoners concerned to solitary confinement, he saw Prince ran out from the back of the small building meant for the toilets, his face covered in blood and he held his stomach which was also covered in blood, Nathan ran at him stabbing him with an object which looked like a shiv, an homemade sharp object made in the prison used as a knife, by the time the prison officers arrived, Prince was lying on the floor covered in blood and Nathan ran back to the toilet, three of the officers picked Prince from the floor, and the other four officers went and picked Nathan from the toilet to solitary confinement, Prince couldn't walk, they had to carry him to the small room in B block, the room used as the prison clinic to administer first aid, he was given a first aid treatment before the ambulance from Cork hospital arrived about twenty minutes later to carry him to the hospital, that was the last time Matthew saw Nathan, and as for Prince, he survived the attack because Matthew saw him four days after in B wing when he went to serve food to prisoners, but he was on clutches and covered with bandage on his face and stomach, he still couldn't walk properly, his cell mate had to come and help him take his food to the cell.

Matthew sat on one of the chairs at the table in the dining room at the prison kitchen with six other prisoners, Luke, Charles, Pawel, Widodo,

Jampe, and Akeem, they had just finished their lunch and talking, Charles is from south Africa, he's about six feet tall and in his late forties, he's got tattoo all over his face and body, including on his bald head, he's doing twelve years for drugs, he was arrested at the Dublin airport trying to bring in two kilos of cocaine, Matthew sometimes wonder why someone that looks like a hoodlum can even think he can get away with bringing in drugs on him through the airport, his appearance alone creates suspicion, and that was not the first time Charles was arrested trying to smuggle drugs into another country, he had just finished a seven year sentence for drug importation for sale and supply two years earlier in England before he was caught with drugs again trying to enter into Ireland, that was why when the police ran his finger print and discovered that he had being in prison in England and told him that he will be going away for twenty years, he changed his story of not knowing about the drugs in his briefcase, he then confessed that he was aware of the drugs and pleaded guilty immediately when he went in front of the judge, but the judge still gave him twelve years which is over the ten years mandatory sentence for the quantity of drugs he got caught with, because of his previous conviction and crime, Charles is very arrogant and a bully, he believes he knows everything and also believes that whatever he says to other prisoners in the prison kitchen should be the final, and he's racist as well, during Obama's presidential campaign against John McCain, he was always causing and swearing whenever there was any news or discussion about Obama winning the election, he said he can bet his life that Barrack would never ever come close to winning the US election, not to talk about him becoming the president of United State of America, he said for Obama to have even defeated Hillary to become democrats presidential nominee against the republican was utterly ridiculous and total disgrace to the democrat party, that they already lost for allowing a black man to represent them at the presidential general election, and the only reason for his disapproval of Obama was that he represent a few black Americans which is just about fifteen percent of the American populace, he was so certain that Obama was not going to win the election that he took a bet of ten packet of cigarettes with Matthew over who would win the election, and he was very upset and totally devastated when Matthew was given the job to be in charge of the store room in the prison kitchen because he was already working in the kitchen for seven months before Matthew started working in the kitchen, he complained to Mr O'Sullivan, the head of the prison kitchen about why he wasn't given the job, but Mr O'Sullivan just told him that he has made his decision and that was the final.

Pawel is originally from Poland, he is doing nine years for robbery which he almost completed because he's done over six years of his sentence, he robbed a jewellery shop in Kerry, which he successfully broke into the jewellery shop around midnight with one other polish guy that was able to disabled the alarm to the entrance door to the shop, but they didn't know that there was another secret Alarm that was concealed in the shelves were the jewelleries were kept, the alarm gets triggered when a conceal button underneath the shelve is not first turned off before opening the shelve, and the alarm when triggered alerts a private security company that can get to the shop within five minutes, Pawel was surprised when one armed policeman with two security guards arrived when he was leaving the shop with his accomplice that somehow managed to evade the capture of the police and the security guards that night, Pawel still wonders how his accomplice escaped that night with the loot from the store, yes!!! he escaped with the backpack that contained the loot from the heist, and has never being caught, Pawel said he knows how to find him when he gets out of prison, but his problem is that he's been told two months earlier that he might be transferred back to Poland to face a criminal charges for another crime he committed twelve years earlier when he was sixteen years old, it was a bank robbery job he did with some other guys, he was arrested and let out on bail, but he absconded to Ireland, lived a crime free life for about six years working as a chef, then met this guy that used to know him in Poland, and the guy convinced him to take part in the jewellery heist, and that heist has gotten him into this mess, it was the same guy that escaped with the loot from the heist. Pawel is now in his late twenties, fighting his extradition, he had an excellent record of good behaviour working in the prison kitchen since the second month of his arrival at the prison, he had become well known in the prison and close to most of the prison guards that worked in the prison kitchen because he's very hard working, and they buy him loads of stuffs that is not available to be bought in the prison shop, one day he showed Matthew a perfume that was bought for him by one of the officers, and just like Matthew, he's loved by most of the prisoners as well because he gives them extra food from the kitchen, but his extradition case has overwhelmed and totally demoralised him for the past three weeks that he got the news, it has affected his hard work morale in the prison kitchen because he has stopped doing most of the work assigned to him, and the officers had to give his job to another prisoner, but he was still allowed to come into the prison kitchen, and was still allowed to wear the prison kitchen uniform, and still got his weekly one pack of cigarette that is given to prisoners that works in the prison kitchen.

Akeem is originally from Nigeria, he's doing four years for possession of drug for sale and supply, he's about the same height as Matthew, and he's in his early thirties, he has just done five months of his sentence, he was arrested when one of his female customers, an heroin addict that was arrested by the police with drugs gave him up, Akeem said she made a deal with the police to give him to them, he said he made a mistake for not following his instinct when she came to buy drugs from him on the day of his arrest, what Akeem normally does was to hide the drugs in a car parked on his street, and when his customers comes to buy drugs, he tells them to wait at somewhere in the area after collecting the money for the drugs while he goes to bring the drug in a car parked around the area, he didn't know that he was under surveillance and monitored by four undercover police officers present in the area, he got arrested with sixty five grams of crack cocaine, he also pleaded guilty dying minute before jury selection for his trial, but he still got four years for the small amount of the quantity of drugs found on him, he was totally devastated when the judge passed the sentence because he was told by his defence that if he pleaded guilty he would get a suspended sentence and won't be going to prison because of the small quantity of drugs involved, but the prosecution argued that since he got caught with crack cocaine, a highly addictive drugs, he had to get a custodial sentence has he as destroyed loads of life selling crack cocaine which the judge agreed to and gave him four years imprisonment, Akeem said his wife has abandoned him, he actually did an arranged marriage with a British girl that came from England to marry him in Ireland, because he came in from Brazil with a fake Brazilian passport he bought two years earlier in Brasilia, and destroyed the passport in the plane on his way to Ireland, and seek asylum when he got to Dublin airport, but while waiting for the decision on his asylum claim application from the department of justice, he met one of his friend that he knew from Brazil that has now legalised his stay in Ireland through arranged marriage, and he introduced Akeem to the drug business, and also to the English girl that came from

England to marry him and got him his residency papers, but the lady just came for the business and went back to England after the business was done, Akeem got his papers to stay legally for three years, which was to be renewed with the presence of his wife at the immigration office with her British passport here in Ireland, but when he was out on bail after his arrest, his three years residency expired, and he got his wife to come back to Ireland for him to renew his residency by paying her some agreed fees which he gave her immediately she arrived at the Cork airport, but when they got to the immigration office, the wife discovered that he had been arrested for drugs sale and supply and out on bail, she actually ended knowing about the drug charges when one of the female immigration officer invited her to a private office when Akeem went to use the toilet, by the time he came out of the toilet she was gone, and when he rang her phone, she started swearing and causing him that she's on her way back to England that she has been told about the drug charges and doesn't want to have anything to do with him and she disconnected the call, Akeem tried to call her back several times, but she didn't pick up his call, that was how he couldn't renew his residency before he was sentenced, he said if he knew that he would be getting a custodial sentence he would have bought a passport and ran away to Canada, but now he's facing deportation to Nigeria after his sentence because he's now illegal in the country because of his expired residency, he has a girlfriend called Mary that comes to visit him every week, Mary has a ten year old son from another relationship before she met Akeem that comes with her, Akeem said he has discussed with Mary about helping him out with his residency permit, he said he believes Mary would help him since she's Polish and an EU citizen, and because he still pays all her utility bills through one of his friend that does credit card fraud, he said whatever bills Mary needs to be paid, all she does is to call his friend, and he would give her credit or debit card details to pay the bill, and Akeem believes Mary loves him and can marry him, but the problem is that he's not currently divorced from his current marriage with the English lady and can't marry Mary, and apart from that, Matthew believes Mary is just using Akeem to pay her bills, because there was a time he told Matthew that his wife and children can sleep in Mary's house in Cork city whenever they come to visit Matthew because Mary's house is just about twenty minutes' walk to the prison, and Delilah, Matthew's wife travels down from Clonmel which is over one hour drive to the prison, so,

Akeem advised Matthew that his wife can come on a Friday to visit him, and then sleepover in Mary's house instead of travelling back to Clonmel, and then she can visit him again on Saturday the day after, so Matthew discussed with his wife, and she agreed, but what happened was that, when Delilah came, her money, about three hundred Euro went missing from her bag when she went to take a shower in Mary's house, and when she told Mary, she only said it might be her ten year old son that took the money, that she would try and get it back from him, but the next day, Mary told Delilah that her son said he didn't take the Money, the stolen money was given to Delilah by Matthew that same day when she visited him earlier at the prison that Friday, it was the money Matthew had saved up for three months from his weekly prison allowance given to him by the prison authority, Matthew was totally devastated when Delilah told him when she came back the next day to the prison to visit him from Mary's house, Matthew had to plead to one of the prison officers in the prison kitchen to give his wife fuel money for her to be able to buy fuel in her car to get back to Clonmel.

Jampe was the guy arrested with Widodo at Waterford City Port, he's about five feet tall, the shortest and smallest man in the prison kitchen, he's also the oldest man, he's in his late fifties, he's also from Indonesia as Widodo, he used to work as chef and cleaner with Widodo in the kitchen on the ship, they prepared all the food that the other crew members ate on the ship, Widodo said it was Jampe that introduced him to the drug business that got him into the ordeal, he said Jampe has done it successfully so many times in the past, and said Jampe is a rich guy and has six houses in Indonesia. They all sat there at the dining table eating their lunch when Mr O'Neill, one of the officers that works in the kitchen came in with another prisoner that looked like a giant "guys, this is Eddy, he'll be working in the kitchen" he said, Eddy is a tall, big guy, he's about seven feet tall and would weigh about one hundred and fifty kilos, he was also dressed in the white prison uniform, but he was wearing a runners "We couldn't find his shoe size because his legs is too big, he wears size sixteen" Mr O'Neill said laughing, Matthew observed Eddy as he stood beside Mr O'Neill at the Door to the room, he looked in his late thirties, Matthew later found out he is in his early twenties, he had some scars on his face which Matthew believes he must have gotten as a result from fights, he reminded Matthew of Frankenstein, and he looked mischievous as well, Matthew later knew that he was in for assaulting two men at a night club, beat them to a pulp because one of the men, the ex to his girlfriend took the seat by the side of his girlfriend that Eddy was sitting on before he went to the gents, and when Eddy came back from the gents, he told the guy to get up from his seat, but he refused, so; Jude threw the first punch, the guy actually spent three weeks in the hospital because of the injuries he sustained from the assault, Eddy got only two years because the presiding judge put his earlier guilty plea as a mitigating factor.

Four days after Eddy's arrival in the kitchen, he started having problems with almost all the prisoners in the kitchen, most especially with prisoners he's paired to work with, one day, upstairs at the dining table, Matthew and Akeem were having a conversation, Eddy told them to shut up, that he doesn't want to hear anyone talking as he was having a bad day, all the three other prisoners that were there were shocked as well as Akeem, but Matthew told Akeem that they should go and continue their conversation in the hallway, which they did, but Eddy came and told them again in the hallway to shut up, Matthew then became infuriated, ignored him and continued talking, but he came into Matthew's face and said *"I told you to shut up!!!"* but Matthew didn't answer him and kept talking, he now stood between Matthew and Akeem, Matthew was so infuriated that he immediately went downstairs and reported him to Mr O'Sullivan *"Matthew, just ignore him, I will see what else I can do, because I know that it's not just you that he's having problem with, like I said just ignore him"* says Mr O'Sullivan, but he did nothing to caution Eddy to stop bullying people in the kitchen, Matthew later found out that Eddy is the brother in-law to Mr O'Neill, and that's the reason why he couldn't be fired and sent out of the kitchen, normally any prisoner that is causing such troubles in the kitchen gets fired immediately, because you have sharp objects like knives in the kitchen that can be used to arm other prisoners, Eddy's relationship with Matthew became worse because Matthew reported him, he continued to get in Matthew's way, one day when Eddy told Matthew to shut up again when he was talking to Luke in the same dining room, Matthew looked at him and looked back at Luke and continued talking, so, Eddy came and stood at his front and *said "I said shut the fuck up!!!"* Matthew felt like telling him to fuck off as well, but he immediately pictured the aftermath of what would happen if he says that, and he doesn't want to get into a physical altercation with anyone not to talk of getting into a fight with a giant, it was not as if he was afraid of him, but he doesn't want to take any irrational action that would exacerbate his ordeal, so; instead of telling him to fuck off, Matthew just went to his locker in the kitchen and packed all his stuff and left the kitchen, he later told the officer on the floor on his way out to tell Mr O'Sullivan that he has stopped working in the kitchen because of Eddy, that he doesn't want to get into a fight with anyone, but later that day, Mr O'Sullivan went to meet Matthew in his cell and told him that he can't fire Eddy, but told Matthew to come back and work in the kitchen, that he shouldn't leave his job because of Eddy, but Matthew refused, so, two days after leaving the kitchen, Matthew was moved away from the cell he shared with Widodo on A1 on the first floor, and moved to A3, he moved in with Michael, on the third floor which is the last floor, Michael actually begged the officer on his floor to let Matthew move in with him, he said he wants Matthew as his cell mate, and Matthew as well was very happy to move in with Michael, because they both knew each other from the prison school, Michael was doing seven years for trying to bring in drugs from Congo in Africa to Ireland, he was arrested at Dublin airport, he's in his middle twenties, he's about Matthew's height five feet, ten inches tall, but he weighs lesser than Matthew, he weighs about seventy kilos, he uses a recommended prescription glasses, and he was born in Africa, but his parents are originally from Belgium, but they moved to Congo for business several years back, they are into agricultural produce, Michael has done almost three years of his sentence, and as put in an application to the prison authority to be sent to Belgium because he believes by right he can be sent to Belgium to finish his sentence because of his parents Belgian citizenship, his elder sister actually works at the Belgium embassy in Ireland, she as visited him several times in prison, before Michael's arrest, he had been coming to Ireland from Congo for the past four years on holiday to spend time with his sister, and has never dealt with drugs not until an acquaintance he met at a night club in Dublin introduced him to the guy in Congo that gave him the drugs to bring to Ireland, he was told by the guy that he would make ten thousand Euros if he delivered the four kilos of cocaine parked in his suitcase, when Michael got caught, he gave the phone number of the person that he was supposed to deliver the drugs to, to the police, but whenever the police rang the number, the number didn't go through, what Michael didn't know was that the people that gave him the drugs put a lady on the same flight with him to follow and monitor him from Congo to Ireland, and the lady saw the whole scenario of when Michael got caught by the narcotics officers at the airport, the lady was supposed to monitor him till he gets cleared by all the security personnel at the airport and approach him outside the airport, then take him to were the drugs would be collected from him and then pay him his money for trafficking the drugs, so, when he got caught, the lady immediately called her associates to give them the bad news, so when the police rang the number Michael gave to them, they got a message that the number is not in service. Michael was a very quiet guy, he was also doing a degree course in Horticulture at the prison through Open University which he's almost completed, the only problem Matthew had staying in with Michael in the same cell is that Michael smoked cigarettes a lot, the cell was always smelling like a tobacco factory, but he tried to reduce the amount of cigarette smoking from two parks a day to one park when Matthew moved into his cell because he discovered that Matthew was uncomfortable and not happy with him smoking in the cell.

One day, Matthew was using one of the machines in the woodwork room, under the supervision of the prison teacher, he was trying to make the last three of the wooden table lamps that he planned to give out to people, Anne Marie, the head of the school came in to ask him to come to her office, he quickly set the unfinished lamp beside the other two lamps that had already been completed, he quickly wrote his name on the unfinished lamp like the other two, it takes one week to finish one table lamp as he only attend the woodwork class twice a week for one and half hour for each class, he had plans to give one to his wife, one to pastor Joseph and Ruth Potter, and also the unfinished one to Joshua, the husband of the lady that minds his children when his wife is at work. Now sitting in Ann Marie's office, she gave Matthew the letter of acceptance from the prison authority approving him to start the degree course in computing and mathematics, he was very delighted, *"I believe in you Matthew, I wrote to them on your behalf that you are a responsible prisoner, and that you will complete the course, now, don't let me down"* she said *"Thank you, thank you so much, I will never ever let you down, you don't know how much this means to my life, it's an opportunity for me to prepare for the outside world when I get out"* tears trickled down his eyes as he replied because he was very delighted and overwhelmed with emotions that he won't be wasting his time locked up *"I understand Matthew, look, you deserve it"* says Anne Marie. A week later, he got his first course materials which included eight test books, five DVD's and some other stuffs, such as a scientific calculator, rulers, pencils and pen, and he was even more delighted after getting his course stuffs, he told his wife on his first call to her the next morning. Outside in the yard after making the phone call, Luke came to him and told him that Eddy had been sent to isolation in C wing for beating up Akeem in the prison kitchen the previous day, he said it was serious, that Eddy also had problems with some prison guards in the kitchen because he refused to do his job, he said Eddy became more difficult and more crazy after his friend came to visit him three days earlier, and told him that his girlfriend as gone back to her ex, the guy Eddy beat up at the night club, and as a result got him imprisoned, he said loads of crazy things has happened within the past two weeks that Matthew left the kitchen, that Charles was given the job to work in the store, but two days after he got the job, four jars of sweet honey meant for the officers in the kitchen went missing, he said Mr O'Sullivan found two of the jars of honey in Charles cell when they went and searched all the cells of all the prisoners that works in the kitchen, but the other two jars of honey hasn't been found , and Luke said he really missed Matthew *"Matthew, you can come back now, Eddy is gone and won't be coming back"* says Luke. On his way back from school in the afternoon, Mr O'Sullivan was waiting at his cell door, he smiled at Matthew as he opened the door to his cell, and followed him into the cell *"I am here to give you good news Matthew, your friend, Eddy, he's fired, and I want you to come back to your job"* he said, *"okay sir, if he's gone, I'll come back then"* Matthew replied, but told Mr O'Sullivan about his degree course *"Well, that shouldn't be any problem, as long as you do your job"* Mr O'Sullivan replied *"I promise you that I will do my job"* Matthew replied *"well I believe you Matthew, I know you always do your job, now get back to work, I'll arrange for you to be moved back to one of the kitchen cell on A1"* Mr O'Sullivan said. When Matthew told Michael that he was going back to work in the kitchen, he was shocked and very sad because he knew Matthew would have to move back to one of the cells on A1 and that meant another inmate would have to move in with him, Matthew tried to convince him to come and work in the kitchen, that it won't debar him from completing his degree course that he was about to finish, but Michael said no, he said he doesn't want to work in the kitchen or anywhere in the prison, so Matthew said okay, that he has to move, and told him that they'll be seeing on the landings and in the school.

One week after moving back to work in the kitchen, Matthew was taking the stock in the store in the kitchen when Mr O'Sullivan came to him with a sad face "you will need to go and park your stuffs Matthew, your request has been granted by the prison authority, you are going to Midlands prison today" he said, Matthew just stood there as he looked at him for about five seconds said nothing as he was overwhelmed with the news, notwithstanding that it was good news for him moving to a far better prison, because at Midlands prison, he would be able to have contact visit with his wife and children, and apart from that he would be able to have a single cell with a built in toilet all to himself, that would mean getting more privacy, so; he could sense the adrenalin rushing in his body, Mr O'Sullivan placed his hand on his shoulder smiling *"I am happy for you Matthew"* he said and smiled *"thank you sir, I am just surprised because I wasn't expecting to get that kind of news until about another one year"* Matthew replied smiling *"look, we are going to miss you, I have contacted the kitchen in Midlands so that you can be given a job in the kitchen over there, keep up your good attitude Matthew"* Mr O'Sullivan said maintaining the eye contact *"thank you again sir"* Matthew replied again *"well, you need to quickly park your stuffs, the prison truck would be leaving in about another two hours"* he said *"please sir, can you just quickly get me to the school, I need to speak to Anne Marie to inform her about how I can continue my course at the Midlands"* says Matthew *"okay, I quickly get you down there"* so Mr O'Sullivan quickly took him to the school, but Anne Marie said she had already been informed and said Matthew's file had already been forwarded to the school in Midlands prison, that he just need to report to the school and should ask for Melanie Brogan, the lady in charge of Open University, *"best of luck Matthew"* she said as she extended her hand in handshake to Matthew. When Matthew told Widodo, his cell mate, he was devastated that he was leaving because, apart from that he would miss Matthew, he had already applied and put in a request to be transferred to the Midlands Prison two months before Matthew put in his request, and he has not heard anything back about his application, he was actually told it would take two years because there were loads of other prisoners on the list, but because Matthew is a role model prisoner, he was able to get it within five months of his application. Now sitting in the holding cell with four other prisoners waiting as he looked at the cell door wandering when it would be opened for the prison officers to bring them to the prison truck to begin the journey to Midlands prison, Matthew wandered into retrospection of how he first met his wife five years earlier.

Chapter Five

Meeting the Unknown

It was on a Saturday, the first week of February, he was off work that day, Matthew sat down in the sitting room of the two-bedroom flat that he shared with Bradley, his friend, it was around 11am, he was drinking a cup of coffee, while listening to the news on BBC from the only flat screen television in the apartment, before then he had taken his morning shower and dressed in a black jeans and white tea shirt. The sitting room had a three sitter arm chair, and two single arm chairs, he was lying down on the three sitter, his cup of coffee sat on the rounded mirror coffee table beside the arm chair, the TV was a Panasonic 40 inch" size, it sat on a table about six meters away from where he was watching it from. Bradley, his flat mate came into the sitting room, he was on the phone talking to someone, trying to describe the way to the flat, he told the person to call him when she gets to the front of the house of blocks of twelve flats which they reside in *"talk to you then"* Bradley said before ending the call. He then looked at Matthew excitedly *"I have a visitor on the way, she's one of my friend from secondary school, she's a big girl, I mean she's got money because she dates this guy that plays in the premiership that gives her money, I want to talk to her to loan me some money to start my photography business,"* says Bradley, that is Bradley for you, he's like a parasite that always wants to prey on other people for his own gain, he's about nine years younger than Matthew, he calls Matthew his big brother, he's almost the same height with him, but Bradley is a skinny guy, and he doesn't contribute to the payment of the house rent, he has two girlfriends that he takes money from, he knows when to get them to come visit him one at a time without them meeting each other at the flat. Bradley doesn't last long in any employment, the longest he's lasted in any job is three weeks, he's always talking about looking for money to start his own business.

Matthew's mobile phone rang as he was talking to Bradley, it was Becky his girlfriend, she said she was on the train on her way to him from Brighton, outside London, she said she wanted to come and spend some few days in London, that she's bored of Brighton, Matthew was shocked because, who can be tired of Brighton with the lovely beach that is not far from Becky's house. Becky is the daughter of a very rich entrepreneur, she likes to hang out with Matthew, but they are just close friends, notwithstanding that whenever she comes around and willing to pass the night in the flat, she sleeps in Matthew's room on the same bed with him, but they've never had any amorous relationship or anything associated with sex, to him they are just intimate friends, Becky is almost the same height as Matthew, she's busty and has a big ass, which is usually noticed by most people that comes across her, but even with are busty chest and big ass, she's still able to walk in a smart manner that makes are figure looks sharp and she also looks snazzy in the way she dresses, she's a sophisticated lady, she wears designer stuffs, her bag, wrist watch, clothes, shoes, even her phone are all expensive, she loves quality designers' stuffs. The doorbell rang forty minutes later, Bradley was in the shower, so; Matthew went and opened the door thinking it was Becky, but standing there at the door was this very beautiful lady, she was sophisticatedly and stylishly dressed like the same way Becky does, she was wearing a Gucci sun glasses, her smiles made her look even more beautiful, her beautiful soft voice brought Matthew out of his fantasy *"please I am asking for Bradley"* she said, just then Bradley came out of the bathroom, and peeped over Matthew's shoulder, *"how are you Delilah, you are already here, I was expecting your call,"* he said, he was still in his bathroom towel and has not finished towelling his body, *"this is Delilah"* he said to Matthew, and *"this is Matthew"* he said to Delilah, *"Hello, you look beautiful"* says Matthew. *"Thank you,"* Delilah replied, Matthew immediately stepped out of the way *"please come in"* he said, and Delilah came into the flat *"did you find it easy to get here?"* Bradley asked. *"Yes, the taxi man was very helpful, immediately we got here and I told him your flat number, he told me to go to the third floor, and here I am,"* she replied. *"Give me two minutes, I have to quickly go and dress up"* Bradley said and disappeared into his room, Matthew showed Delilah into the sitting room, and offered her a drink *"mineral water is fine please,"* Delilah replied. After given her the drink, he handed her the TV remote control *"please feel at home"* he said and smiled and went to meet Bradley in his room, he was wearing his shirt as Matthew came in with excitement *"I really like your friend"* Matthew murmured to him, Bradley was surprised to hear that because Matthew doesn't really show interest in women, he has told Matthew several times to make the move to initiate sex into his relationship with Becky, but Matthew has told him several times that he just like Becky as a friend and his pal, and that he's not interested in having any amorous relationship with her, so Bradley thought if Matthew doesn't want her, he should have her, and he has tried all his best to seduce and cajole her into being his girlfriend, but Becky has always told Bradley that he's a small boy that she can never ever date him, notwithstanding that they are of the same age, but Bradley believes if he kept trying, he would get lucky and get her to change her mind. *"You can't date Delilah"* Bradley murmured to him, *"she's a big girl, she's currently going out with a guy that plays in the premiership, a guy that earns about twenty thousand pounds weekly, that is why you see her wearing those expensive stuffs because the guy spoils her with designer gifts and money"* replied Bradley *"but I really like her"* says Matthew again *"don't even think about it, you only earn four hundred and fifty pound a week from your security job, it's not going to happen, forget it."* He said again emphatically, back in the sitting *"I hope you are alright, or is there any other drink you want me to get you, I can quickly go to the store around the corner and get it for you"* Matthew said as he came back into the sitting room *"no thank you, am alright"* Delilah replied, then Bradley came into the sitting room *"I can see that Matthew is already looking after you"* he said and sat down beside her on the three sitter arm chair, just then, the doorbell rang, Matthew went and opened the door, it was Becky, smiling at him, she wore Gucci sunglasses, a blue Calvin Klein Jeans with a Gucci T-shirt with a white Gucci sneakers to match, her big ass was very obvious from the tight jeans, so also her busty breast from the snazzy tight t-shirt, she had a small travelling trolley which Matthew immediately picked up from the ground from beside her and ushered her into the flat, closed the door and then followed her into the sitting room, there was a look of astonishment on Delilah's face when Becky came into the sitting room, and so also on Becky's, she looked astonished *"my God, is this you, Becky?"* Delilah curiously asked *"yes it's me, I think I have seen you around in the college, but I don't know your name"* Becky replied *"her name is Lilah, sorry Delilah, but I call her Lilah"* Bradley jumped in *"Wow!!!, so you guys know each other from school"* Bradley said again excitedly *"yes, she's in my school"* Becky said as she sat down beside Delilah *"I don't have baileys in the house, do you want me to make you a cup of coffee?"* Matthew asked Becky *"don't worry, I'll drink something else, I'll check the fridge, I am even hungry"* Becky said as she stood up and went into the kitchen, Matthew followed her. *"Wow!!! Becky, I like that girl"* Matthew whispered to Becky, but the angry expression on her face startled him *"I am hungry"* she said again as she opened the tap to put water into the kettle to make coffee *"we actually don't have food in the house, I can quickly order for Chinese rice to be delivered or what would you like to eat"* Matthew asked her *"have you guys eaten at all?"* she asked *"no, I am actually hungry, let me ask Bradley and Delilah what they want to eat, I believe you'll like Chinese fried rice"* Matthew replied and left, Delilah and Bradley were laughing and talking when he got to the sitting room *"I want to order for Chinese, what would you guys like to eat"* he asked *"we were just talking about a restaurant in Peckham, they have nice food there"* says Bradley *"okay, Becky, if you don't mind, there is a nice restaurant that we can eat nice food, maybe we should all just go and eat out there"* Matthew said to Becky as she came back into the sitting room with the cup of coffee *"I don't mind, if the food is good, then we should all just go then"* Becky replied *"I have actually heard of that restaurant but I have never being there before, but I know people says they've got nice food,"* Becky said again. *"Okay then, I'll just quickly change then,"* says Matthew as he quickly went into his room to wear his shoe, Bradley followed him *"I'll look after Becky, while you look after Delilah"* he murmured to Matthew smiling, he took Matthew's Armani deodorant from the table, sprayed it on his chest, neck and shirt.

Twenty minutes later, they walked for about five minutes to the bus stop together in pairs, Matthew and Bradley talking, while Becky and Delilah talking right behind them, they took the next bus from Streatham hill to Victoria train station, and then hop on the train to Peckham train station, they walked another ten minutes to Alpha Afrique restaurant, Matthew continued to chat with Bradley, while Flora continued to chat with Delilah about college. There were about twenty people in the restaurant, they took a table for four people, they all ordered delicious delicacies and drinks which Matthew paid the bill, they were there for about an hour, ate, drank and chatted, it was getting to 7pm, so Delilah said she had to start heading home, so they all headed back to Victoria station together and Delilah said she had to take the train to Hammersmith, but Matthew said he would escort her to Hammersmith train station and then take the train back, that he just felt like escorting her if she didn't mind, so Delilah said okay, Matthew immediately noticed the expression of jealousy on Becky's face again, but she reluctantly said goodbye to Delilah, and Bradley nodded his head in gesticulation to Matthew as a sign that it was a good idea for Matthew to go with Delilah *"I'll look after Becky"* he said. In the train on the way to Hammersmith, Matthew told Delilah that he really likes her and wants to date her *"I am sorry Matthew, you seem like a very nice guy, but that's never going to happen, because at the moment, I am okay, I am not looking for any date, my hands are full"* Delilah said as he looked into his eyes *"no problem, talking to you is more than enough for me"* says Matthew, and they both laughed, they talked about job, Delilah said she works part time as a sales rep in a clothing store, they got to Hammersmith, Matthew came out with her out of the train station, and said if she doesn't mind, he'll like to escort her to her house, to just make sure she got home safe, but Delilah said no, that her house is just about six minutes' walk from the train station. From that night Matthew couldn't stop thinking about Delilah, when he got back home that night, Bradley was on the phone with her, while Becky was on the phone with her sister. Matthew went into his room, and she immediately came in after him, and asked him *"how did it go Matthew?"* she asked *"She said she just wants us to be friends and nothing other than that"* replied Matthew looking devastated *"don't worry Matthew, you just have to keep trying, I believe she's just playing too hard to get"* Becky replied. He went to Bradley after he noticed that he had finished speaking to Delilah on the phone and asked him to give him Delilah's phone number *"I asked her on the train but she forgot to give it to me,"* Matthew said. Bradley laughed, *"nice try, but she already told me not to give you her number, I am sorry, I can't give you her number because she would be very mad with me if I do,"* Bradley replied. *"Okay then,"* Matthew said and left his room. Becky slept in Matthew's room that night, notwithstanding Bradley tried to cajole her to date him and get her to sleep in his room when they arrived back at the flat, she always laughed at Bradley and says that he's a small boy.

Matthew didn't get to see Delilah again until another six days later, and that was on February the 14th which was on Valentine's day, Matthew was totally gobsmacked when he saw her, because he never knew that she was coming to his place, he only knew about Becky coming when she called him as she normally does, and told him that morning that she was coming to spend Valentine in London, Matthew was at home in his flat after telling Bradley that he wanted to go and buy some groceries in the house because of Becky coming over for Valentine, and Bradley said he shouldn't worry that he already arranged for one of his girlfriends to come and cook for them for Valentine *"ooh good, thank you"* Matthew replied, thinking it's one of his usual girlfriends that normally comes to the flat, not until when the bell rang and Bradley went and opened the door, and to Matthew's amazement, it was Delilah standing at the door with her Louis Vuitton travelling hand bag and another nylon bag containing the cooking stuffs that she bought from the store on her way to them, she was dressed in a lovely t shirt, a long skirt and a Gucci slippers, she looked like an angel, Matthew was overwhelmed with excitement that he had to immediately placed his hand on the left side of his chest to calm himself down from the serious palpitation of his heart, it was as if his heart was going to fall out from the ecstatic of seeing Delilah again, he quickly got up and took the bags from her and told her to sit down in the sitting room for him to quickly get her a drink, but Delilah said she had to start cooking *"I want to cook you guys a special meal"* she said *"she's actually spending two nights with us"* Bradley said to Matthew *"great, thank you for coming"* Matthew said as Delilah took the bag containing the cooking stuffs back from him and went inside the kitchen, Bradley collected the other bag containing Delilah's clothes from Matthew and dropped it in Matthew's room *"you stick with Delilah, while I stick with Becky when she comes"* he whispered to Matthew as he came back to the sitting room, Matthew smiled and went into the kitchen *"are you okay? I can help with the cooking"* says Matthew *"I am alright"* she replied, but Matthew insisted that he'll hang around her, that he wants to learn how to cook if she doesn't mind, so, she said it was okay. Becky came in almost at the end of the cooking, it was getting to around 5pm, Bradley opened the door for her to let her in, after saying hello to Delilah and Matthew in the kitchen, she took her hand luggage to Matthew's room, but she saw Delilah's luggage and handbag in the room, just then, Bradley came into the room *"Becky, you can have my room, Delilah is sleeping in this room,"* he said. *"Okay,"* she replied reluctantly with a flabbergasted expression, Bradley took her hand luggage to his room and Becky followed him, the room is seven feet long and four feet wide, there was a double mattress neatly made lying on the rug on the floor, Bradley had quickly cleaned and arranged the room when he finished putting Delilah's hand luggage in Matthew's room earlier on, *"you know what, we'll both sleep in here then, I can't kick you out of your room, but you just need to behave yourself, no hanky-panky"* Becky said to him with a serious expression looking into his eyes after accessing the room *"well, I have always tried, haven't I?"* he said and Becky smiled. When it was around 9pm, after they've finished eating the yummy food cooked by Delilah, they were all watching Grease movie, a 1978 college romantic film *"I feel like we should all just go out to dance and drink, come on guys it's Valentine's day"* says Becky *"why not"* Bradley seconded, so they all agreed to go out to Hippodrome nightclub in Leicester square and then to room 10 nightclub in Covent garden.

Roughly around 10pm, all dressed up for the night out, all looking fresh and snazzy, all four of them walked about ten minutes to the bus station and took the next bus to Victoria train station, and then got on the Northern Line train to Leicester square, it was Friday night, and it was very busy, Leicester square has loads of entertainment nightlife like dancing and clubbing all night, were most of the clubs plays mainstream music and R&B, and you get to see the diverse culture of different people that proofs that London is arguably the most cosmopolitan city in the UK, it's always crowded every night from Thursday till Sunday night, other nightlife entertainments also includes; parties and street lives, live music venues, rooftop bars, theatre shows, jazz clubs, games and esports guide, Lesbian and Gay bars, quirky bars, and even late night shopping, there is so much fun and activities that no visitor will ever get bored. When they got to Hippodrome, Matthew paid the entrance fee for himself and Delilah, while Bradley paid for his own ticket and for Becky, that was the plan between the two of them that Matthew looks after Delilah and Bradley looks after Becky, it was just getting to 11pm, so, the club was half full with guests, they went to one of the three bars and ordered drinks and sat down on one of the couch by the bar, Delilah said she has never been to the club before, but Becky said she was there two months earlier, and said by 12am the club would be jam-packed, and said they should start heading to room 10 at 1am, that there would be much more room on the dance floor over there and they would all like the music as well because the DJ there is one of the best in London, so they all agreed to live at 1am.

Room 10 was not crowded as Becky said, it was getting to 2am when they arrived there, the music was Matthew's type of music, mostly R and B old school from the 80's, it was no surprise, because most of the guest present at Room10 were in their late twenty's and early thirty's, matured and acting mannerly. They ordered another round of drinks, Delilah doesn't drink alcohol, he just drank soft drinks like Coke and Fanta or orange juice, but Becky loves Baileys called Irish cream, and she also smokes cigarette as well with Bradley, Matthew used to smoke cigarette before she met Delilah, but he stopped smoking when Delilah said she doesn't like guys that smokes cigarette, as he drank red wine from the wine glass, it was his fourth glass of the night, he was getting tipsy, he asked Delilah for a dance, but she said she didn't feel like dancing, but she said she liked the music, he told her that he really likes her, but she said she already told him that she's not interested in dating him, he asked if it was because of another guy, she said no, that she was having problem with her boyfriend, that she just wanted to be alone for some time and said she needed to go to the ladies, Bradley and Becky were chatting and smoking in the smoking room, Matthew went and met them, but they were about coming to the dance floor, Becky pulled Matthew aside, *"so, how is it going with her?"* She asked *"well, she said she doesn't want to date me, she said she's having problems with her boyfriend and just want to be alone for now."* Matthew replied *"don't worry Matthew, like I said, she's just playing hard to get, you just keep trying like I said, don't give up,"* she said giggling *"would you like to dance, I like this song"* she said again, it was the song by Culture Club *"Karma Karma Karma Karma Karmeleon, you come and go"* that was playing *"com' on Matthew, let's dance to this song, I don't want it to waste,"* she said again to him as she gently pulled him towards the dance floor and started dancing, Bradley joined them, three of them dancing, Delilah came from the ladies, and joined them, she pulled Becky to herself and started dancing with her, Matthew and Bradley dancing beside them, but Becky held Matthew's hand and gently pushed him between herself and Delilah, making him to face Delilah, and she immediately turned and faced Bradley dancing with him, they danced to the next three songs singing to the lyrics and rhythms, they left the club in a Taxi at around 4am. When they got home, Delilah went straight to Matthew's room and slept on the only double bed in the room, but Matthew took a shower and quietly laid on the bed beside her, not wanting to wake her up as she slept, he looked at her face, she looked so beautiful, like a princess, if only she can be mine he thought, well I think she's going to be mine, "be patient, she definitely likes you" he thought in his head, he smiled excitedly and drifted into sleep.

The vibration of Delilah's phone woke him up, her phone has vibrated more than hundred times from calls trying to reach her since she arrived the previous day, what she does was checked who was calling and she disconnects the call, Matthew has asked her who was calling her, but she just told him it's people she doesn't want to talk to. He looked at the time, it was going to 11am, he had only been asleep for about six hours, Delilah was still curled up under the blanket, Matthew went and checked on Bradley and Becky, he was curled up on the bed in the corner by the wall, Becky took almost seventy percent of the space of the double bed, using her big ass to barricade Bradley into the small space left on the bed, Becky opened her eyes as Matthew wanted to leave the room *"how did it go"* she said smiling to him and then closed her eyes again, it was very obvious that she still wanted more sleep, because she had too many Baileys from the night out, Matthew and Bradley had to half carried her from the taxi to the flat when they got back. Delilah left the day after, and they didn't see again until another three weeks when she called Matthew and told him she would be coming to spend the weekend, prior to that, Matthew texted her almost six times daily, telling her how much he loves and misses her, but she never replied to his text, for him to have now received her call all of a sudden about her coming to spend the weekend was just too overwhelming excitement for him, he was supposed to work the next day, but he gave an excuse to his boss for the reason why he won't be able to come to work that weekend, Bradley was starting a new job in Manchester the next day, and already told Matthew that he's going to be staying in Manchester for the week because he couldn't be travelling down from London every day to work in Manchester, so Matthew would be having the flat to himself and Delilah for the two days.

They sat down in the sitting room eating the delicious food Delilah brought from Hammersmith, she said she cooked the food before coming, it was fried rice and fried plantain with fried beef stew, it was very delicious, this made Matthew to even love her more, he thought "she's not just pretty face but also a very good cook". That night, it was romance from the foundation of romance to everything that has got to do with two people truly in love, and guess what? it was Delilah that initiated it from the start to the end, she was in charge, Matthew was just the instrument. Matthew ended up taking two weeks off work because, the day after Delilah arrived at his flat, they both went to the grocery shop after Bradley left for Manchester, they bought loads of food items and drinks, and for the next two weeks they didn't step a foot out of the flat, it was both of them together like a conjoin twins, and within the first three days, they both told themselves the story of their life, Delilah told Matthew that she's going to introduce him to her mum and dad, and said she's finished with her fiancé and her rich boyfriend. The first day after cocooning, Matthew followed Delilah to get her stuffs in Hammersmith and she moved in with him, and after a month, she told him that she was pregnant, and said she has never been pregnant before in her life, and said she thought she was never going to have a biological child of her own, she said she's going to keep the baby, that she has vowed that if she ever gets pregnant, she's never going to abort the pregnancy, Matthew was very delighted. They got married five months after, in October that same year, it was a sensational wedding that showed two love birds seriously in love, after signing the marriage certificate at the registry of marriage, they were both asked to kiss themselves, as they kissed they both cried, it was very emotional, some other guest at their wedding laughed and cried tears of joy as well, and exactly a year after they first met, they had their first child, a boy, and then had their daughter twenty eight months after, Matthew has always thought that he has met his soul mate that he's going to spend the rest of his life with till eternity, but he never knew or thought that there can be challenges in his life that would change the true love Delilah has for him to a demon lying in waiting, that would come into manifestation after waiting for several years to confront him in his darkest time.

The prison truck came to a stopped, Matthew back to reality as he opened his eyes, managed to stand up in the cubicle, it was very uncomfortable for him because he was in handcuffs, he peeped from the small window above him in the cubicle, and discovered that they have stopped at Limerick prison, he never knew that they would be stopping there, he thought they were going straight to the Midlands, Limerick prison has got a female section and also a male section for it prisoners, Matthew has heard a lot about Limerick prison, it's a very dangerous prison for prisoners like him that is not in a gang, you'll have to be in a gang if you don't want to be bullied and attacked by other prisoners all the time, and even if a prisoner is in a gang, he'll be very lucky not to be attacked by other rival gangs, most of the prisoners are aggressive carrier criminal that are always looking for a fight, the only thing that makes the prison better than Cork prison is that it's got inbuilt toilet in the cell. The truck stayed there for about forty minutes before proceeding to Midlands, it took another one hour ten minutes before it finally arrived and stopped at the first entrance gate of Midlands prison, Matthew stood up again as he looked through the small window, and thinking that this would be his new home for another couple of months before going for his appeal, the door to his cubicle opened and the officer told him to get up, his heart palpitating as he followed him to the reception desk of Midlands prison.

Chapter Six

Midlands Prison

The cell was a four man cell, it had two double bunk beds that sat on each side of the room that is eight feet long and six feet wide, the only toilet and wash hand basin in the cell sat on the right hand side by the door, and the only TV in the cell stood on top of a shelf at the top of the wall at the middle of the cell, before he was brought to the cell that same day that he arrived at the prison, he was taken to the office on the first landing on B block and given a pack, which contains tooth brush, tooth paste, bathing soap, a towel, a plastic cup, bowl and cutleries, he was also given a bedspread and pillowcase. He told one of the two officers that he wants to work in the prison kitchen that he was working in the kitchen in Cork prison before his transfer, the officer said he knew *already "we have your file, you've already being assigned to resume work in the prison kitchen, one of the officers from the kitchen will come and get you"* says the officer. There are six buildings on the precinct of Midlands prison, four blocks A, B, C, and D houses the prisoners, each block has three floors which has fifteen cells on each side of each floor, so you have thirty cells on each floor, there are thirteen single cells on each side of each floor, and two four man cell on each side of each floor, so; you have about one hundred and twenty prisoners on each block A and B, but block C has fewer prisoners because that is the section used for solitary confinement and also used to house people that doesn't want to be in the general population because they believed they might be attacked by other prisoners, such prisoners are in that block for their own protection and safety, most of the time, they are on twenty three hours lock up and only allowed to come out for one hour to take a shower, but block D is mostly used to house sex offenders, like child abusers and rapist, they are segregated in that block because they are vulnerable to be attacked by other prisoners in A and B block, they have their own schooling in that same block, they are also not allowed to use the gym and the Library with other prisoners from A and B block, all this is done for their own protection and safety. Matthew took the available top bed of the bunk bed, it was going around 8pm, so; all prisoners had been locked in for the day about fifteen minutes earlier, he told the officer if he could quickly take a shower, that he finds it very hard to sleep if he doesn't take a shower before going to bed, but the officer said no, that it's against the prison rule, that he'll have to wait till the next morning during shower time, and he told him were he'll have to quickly queue up to take a shower, there are four shower rooms on each floor for forty two prisoners.

The next morning around half past 7am, the cell door opened, an officer called his name *"Matthew Williams"* he climbed down from the bed. "Yes officer," he answered. *"You want to work in the kitchen right?"* the officer asked *"yes sir"* he replied *"well it's time, let's go"* says the officer, he quickly dressed up, came out of the cell, the officer locked the cell door back, and pointed at the gate at the end of the hallway which was about eighty meters away from his cell to join three other prisoners waiting at the gate to be taken to the prison kitchen. Ten minutes later, an officer wearing a white long sleeve shirt and black stripe trouser unlocked two gates to get to them, and counted *"one two three, four"* and said *"are you Matthew?"* pointing to him *"yes officer"* Matthew replied. *"Okay,"* says the officer *"follow me,"* so they all followed the officer through about four locked gates, the officer unlocked and closed each gate after them before unlocking the final gate to the kitchen and then locked the gate back after the prisoners and himself. The kitchen was bigger and more modern than Cork prison which looked dilapidated, the reason why is because, Cork prison is the oldest prison in Ireland, it was built over hundred years ago, but Midlands prison was built about twenty-five years ago. The officer introduced himself to Matthew *"my name is Mr O'Dwyer"* he then called one of the other prisoners already in the kitchen *"this is Paddy"* he said pointing to the guy and then looked back at Matthew *"and this is Matthew"* he said as he introduces both of them to each other *"Paddy will look after you, please show him around"* he said finally to Paddy and walked away. *"What are you in for Matthew?"* Paddy asked as he started to show Matthew around the kitchen *"I am in for drugs"* Matthew replied *"I am in for drugs as well, how long are you doing?"* asked Paddy *"I am doing ten years,"* Matthew replied *"whoop, it must have been loads of coke, what's the amount of coke you got caught with?"* Paddy asked again *"well I got caught with less than a kilo of drugs"* Matthew replied *"that judge must be a fucking prick to have given you ten years, is it your first time getting caught with drugs or do you have previous conviction?"* asked Paddy again *"No, it's my first time, I was used to collect a package containing drugs"* Matthew said. *"Oooh you pleaded not guilty, right?"* Paddy asked *"yes, I pleaded not guilty because I wasn't aware I was collecting drugs"* Matthew replied *"you see, no judge will buy that, you should have pleaded guilty, well you've made the mistake"* Paddy said, he took Matthew into an inner room, and pointed to some white kitchen uniforms inside two big basket sitting on the floor, *"those are washed, you just get your size"* he pointed to another door, *"that's the shower room and toilet, you can change in there, and chose your own locker from one of the empty lockers over there,"* he said as he pointed to a metal wardrobe that sat on the left hand side of the entrance door with about twenty small metal lockers with keys dangling in the keyhole of about six empty ones. *"Can I quickly take a shower?"* Matthew asked *"I didn't get one last night, and I feel very uncomfortable,"* says Matthew *"sure you can, just meet me outside on the floor when you're finished"* Paddy replied and left.

Twenty minutes later, Matthew came out to the kitchen floor dressed in the white uniform, the kitchen was almost empty with just one prisoner wearing the same type of uniform that he was wearing, Matthew went to him *"please where is Paddy"* he asked *"my name is Matthew"* he said *"you are the new guy, my name is Liam"* he said and extended his hand in handshake. *"Paddy is gone with the others to the landings to serve breakfast,"* he said and looked at the clock on the wall, *"they should be back in about another twenty minutes, but you can go and speak to Mr O'Dwyer in the office,"* he pointed to a small glass room on the kitchen floor, Matthew could see three officers sitting through the transparent glass, talking and laughing. He went and knocked on the door, one of the officers, a female officer, with a blonde hair looked at him and signalled to him with her hand to come in, immediately he came in, Mr O'Dwyer stood up and said *"this is Matthew"* the other officers said *"hello Matthew."* *"Good morning,"* Matthew replied bowing his head in courtesy, Mr O'Dwyer went around him, *"follow me"* he said, he followed him into another inner smaller office, there were two chairs sitting under a table which had a desktop computer sitting on it and also a printer sitting on another smaller table by the corner *"sit down Matthew"* he said as he sat down on one of the chairs at the other end of the table, he smiled at Matthew *"you were working in the store at Cork prison kitchen"* he asked him *"yes Mr O'Dwyer"* he replied. *"We are ready to give you the same job here if you want it, and you will also help sometimes with cleaning the trolleys as well if that's okay"* he asked *"that's absolutely fine by me, it's just that I am currently doing a degree course with the Open University and I will have to be going to the prison school, actually I need to go and see the head of the school to get the time table for my class,"* Matthew replied. *"You see Matthew, you'll have to discuss that with Mrs O'Neill, she is the head of the kitchen, she's not in today, but I think she'll be definitely in tomorrow, but you can go to the prison school in the afternoon today, but before then, I will get the officer in charge of the store to show you how to take the stocks that comes in and how to manage the store, and she would be supervising you sometimes when she's not busy on the kitchen floor cooking, so if you just follow me again"* he said as they went back to the kitchen floor, Mr O'Dwyer beckon to the same female officer that signalled Matthew to come into the glass office earlier on to come and meet them on the kitchen floor, has she got to them, *"this is Mrs O'Connell"* he said as he looked at the female officer *"this is Matthew, you know what to do"* he said to the officer. *"I can show him now if that's okay"* she said *"yes, if you want to show him now please, but he also said something about going to school, but I have told him to discuss that with Mrs O'Neill tomorrow"* Mr O'Dwyer *said* *"okay, I'll just show him the store room and what to do at the main time"* she replied *"okay"* he said and walked back to the glass office *"have you had your breakfast Matthew?"* she asked *"No, I haven't"* he replied *"you quickly go and grab your breakfast and come back to me later"* she said *"Am sorry Miss, please I need to fix my PIN number to be able to call my wife and children"* Matthew said to her *"you'll have to get Mr O'Dwyer to sought that out for you, I'll tell him to come back to you"* she said as she went into the glass office and briefly told Mr O'Dwyer about Matthew looking to activate his PIN *"I'll get you the form to fill out and get that processed for you"* Mr O'Dwyer said to him as he came back to him.

Standing in the store room with Mrs O'Connell twenty minutes later was Matthew, she was showing him how to arrange stuffs and take stocks in the store, Mrs O'Connell is about five feet and ten inches tall, she has long strawberry blonde hair and blue eyes, she's slim build, she's a beautiful lady, she looked like she's in her early thirties, she was wearing the prison kitchen uniform like all the other officers that works in the kitchen, the store room was twice the size of the one in Cork prison, so; more spacious, *"I heard that you're doing ten years Matthew"* she asked *"yes Miss"* he replied *"and you said you want to go to the prison school ?"* she asked again *"yes, I am doing a degree course in Computing and Mathematics, it's a four year course which I have to get 360 points to be able to have the degree qualification"* he replied *"and who pays for that? is it the government?"* she asked *"well, I don't really know who pays the fees Miss, but it was approved by the prison authority, I only started two months ago"* he replied. *"Wow, you guys get everything for free, I wanted to do a course with the Open University, and they said I have to pay four thousand euro for the first year, and I don't have that money"* she said in annoyance, *"sometimes I think it's not fair, and I don't think Mrs O'Neill will allow you to work in the kitchen and as well be going to the school, so; you might have to choose one"* she said again with an angry face. *"Well I'll have to discuss that with her and see what happens."*

By the time he came out of the store room to the kitchen floor after arranging all the stuffs on the shelves it was getting to 10am, and all the other prisoners, about twelve of them, were back from the landings from serving breakfast to other prisoners, some of them were playing cards, some were playing chess and scrabble game, some were standing in pairs talking. He went to Join Paddy and three other prisoners that were playing scrabble, Paddy introduced him to the other three guys, Francis, Mick and Dee, Paddy was doing twelve years for possession of drugs for sale and supply, he's in his late thirties, he's five feet, nine inches tall like Matthew, and medium build guy like Matthew, he's done seven years of his sentence and has two more years to be released on parole on good behaviour, he was the longest prisoner that has been working in the kitchen, but that was not the first time that he's done time in prison, he was previously given five years sentence for sale and supply of drugs, which he did three and half years and got out on parole for good behaviour, but he was only out for two months when he got arrested and got caught with four kilos of cocaine which got him this current sentence *"do you know how to play scrabble?"* he asked Matthew *"yes, I know how to play Scrabble"* he replied, right then the officers came out of the glass office, about six of them, one of them shouted *"it's time to prepare for lunch guys, let's go!!!"* all the prisoners got to action, they all knew what section they would be working, the menu for that afternoon was rice and curry stew with chicken, the officers do the cooking while the prisoners help with washing the utensils and cleaning the floor and four massive ovens used to do the cooking for over five hundred prisoners, it takes about one hour thirty minutes to make the food, and another thirty minutes to dish it into about six hundred plastics plates and covers, then load it unto four trolleys, before it's then taken to the four blocks A, B, C and D to be distributed to prisoners that would queue up on the landings to get their lunch, Paddy asked Matthew to follow him to C Block with another prisoner, they would be assisting one of the officers, each trolley is accompanied by one officer with three or two prisoners, the officer is there to supervise most of the time. Most of the prisoners on C Block don't really look like criminals, most of them looks innocent and clean, you get to wonder why or if they really committed the crime they've been charged or convicted for, but the real truth is that, most of them pleaded guilty to the crime, but most of the time they claim that they are mentally deranged and say they don't know what made them to commit heinous crimes like rape, child abuse and paedophilia, and it's like some of them, their face looks like they have mental illness issues, some of them don't even want to come out of their cell, the officer had to try and convince or cajole them to come out and get their food or get some exercise.

Fifty minutes later they were back to the kitchen, and immediately they got back Mr O'Dwyer came to Matthew in the recreation room that is meant for the prisoners, *"Matthew, your PIN number is activated and the numbers on your list has been approved"* he said immediately he opened the door. *"Thank you sir"* Matthew replied excitedly *"please when can I make a call, I need to phone my wife and children"* he asked as My O'Dwyer was about to leave, *"that's the phone on the wall there,"* he replied pointing to a telephone box that hung on the wall by the entrance door to the room, *"oh, thank you sir"* Matthew said excitedly as he quickly went to the phone, his heart palpitating as he dialled the PIN number and chose the number that has his wife's mobile number waiting in complete anxiety as her mobile rang, he has been looking forward to hear her voice again since the previous morning that he last spoke to her before he left Cork prison. *"Hello sweetheart"* she said, *"my love, the queen of my heart"* Matthew replied, she laughed, *"I knew it is you"* she said, *"I got a call from Midlands prison to ask me if I would like to receive calls from you about thirty minutes ago, and I immediately said yes, how is the place, and how are you?"* she asked. *"This place is far better than Cork prison, it's cleaner, you have toilet in the cells, it's a new building, but the big problem is that I miss you and the kids every minute"* he said as his eye immediately welled up in tears. *"We miss you too"* she said *"we have to visit you as soon as we can, maybe tomorrow, we can't wait to touch you, I think we are allowed to touch you?"* she asked. *"Yes it's a contact visit here, no glass blocking us, you just need to call the prison, and tell them you want to come and visit me, and they can give you the clearance and time to come"* he replied *"How are the kids? "They are fine, I am starting work today at 4pm, I am waiting for the child minder to come in the next twenty minutes, then I can start going"* says Delilah *"okay, I am calling you from the prison kitchen, I started immediately today, but I have told them that I also need to go to the school to do my Open University course, but one of the officers I spoke to said I need to discuss it with the head of the kitchen, I can't wait to touch and hold you and the kids, it's been ten months now that I touched you and the kids,"* Matthew said emotionally. *"I will call the prison now to arrange the visit"* Delilah replied, the phone started beeping to give the last warning that it was the last thirty seconds of the three minutes call *"I will have to call you tomorrow morning cause the phone is beeping, that the signal that the phone is about to cut off, I love you so much, you are the queen of my heart"* Matthew quickly said *"I love you too"* Delilah replied as the phone disconnected. He felt very relieved at the end of the call, his mood changed, talking to his wife boosted his morale to survive, but his serenity only last for about twenty minutes most of the time, then he's dismally mood thinking about being away from his wife and children kicks in after that, and he start looking forward to talking to them again.

Mrs O'Neill is in her early fifties, she has a blonde hair, she's about five feet, six inches tall and has a small stature, her kitchen uniform is different from the other kitchen officers to show that she's the kitchen boss, her uniform as a black stripes on the white top, so also is her hat, she came into the storeroom at around 10am the day after to introduce herself to Matthew, he ceased the opportunity to discuss about him going to school because of his Open University degree course, and she said, she doesn't see any problem with that as long as it doesn't affect him doing his job in the kitchen, so; Matthew promised that he would make sure he does his job properly, so; Mrs O'Neill said, notwithstanding that no other prisoner has been allowed to take full time education while working in the kitchen she would give Matthew the chance since he already started the course from Cork prison before coming down to the Midlands *"we'll see how it goes"* she said "thanks a million, I will never disappoint you" Matthew replied as she left the store room. Later on that day, Matthew was cleaning the trolley that was used to serve lunch on B Block when one of the officers at the reception office came into the kitchen, and called for his name *"Matthew Williams!!!"* he immediately looked towards the entrance door at the officer *"that's me officer"* he answered *"you have a visit"* the officer said *"thank you officer, please I'll just quickly change"* he said and then ran towards the bathroom.

Fifteen minutes later, he walked following the officer, he had quickly brushed his teeth, changed into a white tea shirt and jeans pant with blue sneakers after quickly washing his head and face, he had to clean up has he hasn't seen his wife and children for the past three months and has not even get to touch them since January since his incarceration, he was seriously overwhelmed with the excitement of the contact visit, he had called his wife that morning and she had told him that she would be coming that late afternoon, and that was the first time he would be receiving a visit at the prison, when they got to the visitor's room, the officer pointed to one of the available rows of seats with a brick table for him to go and sit down to wait for his visitors, Matthew sat on the first seat by the entrance door to the left, there were other four seats left on that row, and there were other two rows of seats and tables behind him that had been occupied by other prisoners and their visitors, they were smiling and talking, some of the prisoners were holding their children and another prisoner held unto his wife's hand, the atmosphere of the room was totally different from the visiting room in Cork prison, it was more relaxed and no prison officers standing by the prisoners telling them what to do and what not to do, but at the end of each row with seats and table, there were prison officers seating on a chair and resting their hands on the long table to see through the middle of the table to be able to detect or notice if any illegal substance or unapproved material is been passed from the visitor to the prisoner, if they noticed any substance is been passed from the visitor to the prisoner, the visit would be immediately ended and the visitor would be immediately escorted out of the visiting room and the prisoner sent back to his cell, but in a more serious situation like if a large amount of drugs or mobile phone is discovered to be involved, the police would be immediately contacted and the visitor would be arrested and prosecuted. After waiting for another ten minutes, Delilah came into the room carrying his daughter and his son walked behind, they were trying to look for him in the middle of the other prisoners and visitors that were sitting behind him, but he waved his hand in gesticulation for them to see him and for them to come to his table, by this time, the table on his left and right side had been taken by other prisoners, his daughter jumped on the table from his wife's hand and came to him, he carried her held her tightly with his left hand while he also held his son with his right hand and kissing both of them as tears of joy trickled from his eyes, he reached across the table to kiss his wife. *"I am sorry to have put you and the kids through all this stress and mess"* he mumbled to her, *"are you okay"* she replied as she managed to smile, *"yes am a little bit alright now that you and the kids are here"* he replied. *"How was the journey from the house to here?"* he asked. *"It's not bad, about one hour ten minutes' drive, I am just happy that we can touch you"* she replied and hugged him again. *"How is the prison?"* she asked, *"the prison is far better than Cork prison, most especially because of the contact visit, and I would be having a single cell to myself very soon, the problem is that I miss you and the kids every seconds and minutes, I love you so much"* he said this with his eyes welled up with tears *"I know, and we really miss you too"* she replied, her eyes welled up with tears as well, but she immediately tried to smiled again saying *"at least we can touch you"* he gave his children the two bars of chocolates that was given to him in the prison kitchen earlier on by one of the kitchen officers when he said to her that his wife and children were coming to visit him, the visit lasted for one hour, when the visit finished they hugged again and smiled, he told his wife that he left some money for her at the reception, that she should ask for the money on her way out *"thank you, I will use the money to pay off some of the debts I owe the childminder"* says Delilah, she carried Debbie and held unto Samuel's hand has she left the room.

Back in the kitchen *"how was the visit"* Mrs O'Rouke, the female officers that gave him the bars of chocolate to give to his children asked him *"it was great, I got to touch my wife and kids for the first time since my incarceration, it was great,"* he replied smiling because he was still exhilarated from the visit. *"Ooh, that's so sweet,"* she said cheerfully, *"but I am missing them badly already"* he said. *"Ooh, before you know it they'll be back again"* she said, patting him on the shoulder *"please whenever the kids are coming again, you tell me, and I can give you chocolates to give to them"* she said *"thank you Miss"* he said as she walked away. It was getting to 5pm, and all the prisoners in the kitchen were getting the stuffs for breakfast for the next morning ready and cleaning the kitchen because at 5:30pm, in about another thirty minutes, they would all be finished for the day's job and taking back to the landings.

They were all told to queue up by the entrance and exit door to the kitchen at 5:35pm, and from the first prisoner at the front of the line was searched and frisked by one of the two officers while the second officer moved on to the next prisoner on the line, and each prisoner is let out of the door to wait by the next locked gate which was about six meters away, after all prisoners had been searched and cleared, they were all taken to their different block A or B. Immediately Matthew got back to B block, the officer told him that he's been moved to a single cell number 28, the officer went with him to unlock the door, when Matthew looked into the cell, it was dirty and untidy, but the excitement of having a cell all to himself and having his privacy overwhelmed him, he smiled, *"thank you officer"* says Matthew as he smiled. *"Since you work in the kitchen, I'll leave your door open, I won't be locking it, you can go and get your stuffs from the four man cell,"* the officer said again *"thank you officer"* Matthew replied and ran to the four man cell, but the door was locked, *officer!!! Officer!!!* he called out to the officer that was on his way back to the officers room at the end of the landing by the entrance door *"the cell is locked"* he said to him has he looked back at him curiously *"okay, I'll open the door for you"* the officer said and immediately walked back to him and unlocked the door, there were two other inmates in the cell, one was lying down on the bottom bed of the bunk bed Matthew was assigned to the previous evening, and the other inmate sat down on the chair smoking and watching the TV, the officer told Matthew to immediately get his stuffs that he wanted to lock the cell, *"are you going home"* the guy that sat at the bottom bed of the bunk bed asked him as he was quickly packing his stuffs *"going home? No"* he replied *"I am moving to another cell"* he replied, then quickly got out of the cell, the officer asked the prisoner in the cell if they wanted to go to the yard, they both said no, so, the officer closed the cell door to lock it. Apart from his cell, there was just one other cell that was left opened on the floor, and that was Frank's cell, he was the cleaner on the landing, when Matthew went to tell the officer that he needed sweeping brush to clean his cell, the officer called Frank to take him to where to get a brush, and Frank took him to the utility room and told him to get one of the four brushes there, Frank is about Matthew's height but slightly bigger than Matthew, he's in his middle twenties, he was doing four years for possession of drug for sale and supply, it was his first time in prison, it was getting to 6pm and the final lockdown for the day would be at 7:45pm, so Matthew had a enough time to quickly clean his cell, the cell was "8 by 4" meter size, with a single bed, with a toilet and a hand wash basin and a table and a chair, the cell also had a window that Matthew could look through to see the prison yard for B block, notwithstanding that he already took a shower in the kitchen before coming down to the landing, he quickly took another shower in one of the four showers on the landing before the final lockdown because by the time he finished cleaning his cell he was sweating, he finds taking a shower therapeutic, that night he felt some freedom for having the cell all alone to himself since his incarceration, he had the TV to himself, and the first time that he held the TV remote in his hand and changed channels without having to ask another inmate what channel they'll like to watch, the mattress on the bed were two mattresses that he met in the cell, he just put the clean bedspread and pillow case that he was given the previous night when he arrived on the mattress and pillow, it felt very comfortable for him, it was his best night since his incarceration, first day since his incarceration that he was able to have a physical contact visit with his wife and children and first day having a cell all to himself, he thought about the prison school that he'll be starting the next Monday in another two days, he wondered how it's going to look like, it's definitely going to look better and more modern than the one in Cork prison he thought as he drifted to sleep.

The next morning he stood by the locked gate to the exit from second floor of B block waiting with nine other prisoners for the officer that would come and take them to the prison school, it was half past 9am, Matthew was excited, five minutes later, a male officer arrived at the gate with about fourteen other prisoners from A Block, he unlocked the gate and they all followed him to the school after locking the gate after them, they had to go through three more gates that was unlocked and locked back again by the officer before getting to the final gate that got them to the school. Matthew went to the female officer that stood on the corridor to tell her that he was new to the school after other prisoners had disappeared into their various classes, he told the officer that he was looking for Melanie Brogan, that she's in charge of the Open University, the officer told him to take the next turn on the left on the corridor and to go to the extreme end and knock on the door to the school offices for the teachers, and to wait for an officer that would come and open the door, then he can then ask for Melanie. After knocking on the door a male officer unlocked the door *"please officer, I am looking for Melanie Brogan"* he said *"and what do you want?"* the officer asked. *"I just came from Cork prison, my name is Matthew, I believe she's expecting me"* he said, the officer told him to wait and closed the door back, after about five minutes, Melanie came out to him, she was short, small lady, about 5 inches tall, she has a blonde hair, she looked like she is in her early forties, she smiled and extended her hand in hand shake, *"Hi, Matthew?"* she asked him in curiosity waiting for him to confirm if she got his name right, *"yes my name is Matthew"* he replied, she was carrying a small box *"I can help you with this"* Matthew said as he offered to carry the box for her *"it's actually for you, this are your Open University stuffs"* she said as he handed it to him *"oh thank you"* he said *"so, you came from Cork prison?"* she asked as she walked towards one of the rooms on the corridor and Matthew followed her *"yes, I came last Friday"* he replied, she was holding a file with documents to her chest, as they entered the next available room on the corridor *"I have your file, you can open the box, I just want you to check if there is any other thing you need for your course"* says Melanie, after quickly checking the stuffs in the box *"I think I have everything I need for now, but I'll be needing help from the school sometimes when I am struggling with the course"* Matthew replied *"okay"* she said as she looked through the file and brought out a paper, looked at it, and handed it to Matthew *"this is your time table, are you in B Block?"* she asked *"yes"* he replied *"there is another guy in your block that does Open University, the same course that you are doing, and he's in his first year as well, his name is George"* she said *"very good, I haven't met him yet"* Matthew replied with excitement. Melanie took him to the Maths class further down the corridor, and introduced him to the tutor, *"this is Mark, and this is Matthew, he just came from Cork prison, he's doing Computing and Mathematics with the Open University"* she said *"ooh, the same course with George"* Mark said, as he looked at George sitting at the back of the class, he smiled as Mark introduce him to Matthew *"I'll leave you guys now"* Melanie said and left the room. There were five prisoners in the class room including Matthew, the other three students were trying to do there leaving cert, and one of the major subjects was in Maths *"I think you work in the kitchen"* says George as Matthew came and sat down beside him *"yes, I work in the kitchen, Melanie said you are also in B Block"* Matthew asked *"yes, I am on B 3, I think I saw you yesterday afternoon, you were serving food on the landing"* George sceptically said *"yes I was"* Matthew replied, George is in his late twenties, he's about five feet, seven inches tall, a skinny and baldhead guy, he was doing eight year for drug possession for sale and supply, and was just seven months into his sentence, he worked at the prison laundry, it was his first time of incarceration. The way Mark teaches his Maths class is that, any prisoner that has got problem with their maths studies comes to the class and ask him for help, so what he does is take questions from each prisoner, one at a time, and because the class only last for two hours, sometimes he goes very fast in explaining the solution to the problem by solving it on the blackboard, but sometimes he takes his time and thoroughly does the solution if there are not much students in the class, most of the time the class doesn't have more than three students because most of the students don't really come to class, some of them only come when they have problem and need his help.

One hour later, Matthew stood on the line with other prisoners, they were on the way back to B Block from school, he was talking to George about the course, they were talking about an assignment that was needed to be finished and submitted to Melanie unfailingly in about a week's time *"I haven't started the assignment, I just quickly looked through the questions"* George said *"well, I am almost finished with the assignment, but I tell you George, it's not easy, I'll advise you to start doing it because of the deadline, but I want to get mine out of the way and submit it in two days, hopefully am done by then"* Matthew replied *"I will see if I can do mine this week, if I am struggling, I'll get Mark to have a look at the question"* says George. Four officers at the final door to the exit from the school frisked each prisoner with a hand held metal detector, and some stuffs were ceased from some prisoners, foods like cakes were ceased as well from some prisoners, Matthew had the box of the stuffs he collected from Melanie, the officers allowed him to go with the box after they finished searching him, he waited for George, they walked with other prisoners, followed the officer that was taking them back to B Block whom unlocked the door to the second landing, allowed them to go into the landing before locking the gate back. George said he'll see him later. Matthew went to his cell to drop his school stuffs, he had to quickly get back to the kitchen to help with the lunch, but on his way back to the kitchen, he discovered that the team of two prisoners and one officer that would be serving the lunch on B Block were already there at the location were the food is served, he quickly continued to the kitchen, he had to change to his white kitchen uniform, when he got back to the kitchen he only saw two other prisoners cleaning the large cooking pots and utensils used for cooking the lunch, so he quickly changed and joined them in the cleaning, but they told him that he should get the brush and mob to clean the floor, it was just gone past 12pm, he quickly brushed and mobbed the floor, the teams from the landings came in with trolleys with about seven hundred plastics covers to plates used to serve food to prisoners that was needed to be watched, Paddy came to Matthew as he was about to get his lunch, *"you disappeared this morning, were where you?"* he asked *"I went to school"* Matthew replied. *"You went to school?, but you can't go to school while you work in the kitchen"* says Paddy *"well, I got permission from Mrs O'Neill"* Matthew replied *"and she said you can go to school while you work in the kitchen?"* asked Paddy again looking curious *"yes, she said I can go, she said that as long as I finish my work in the store room I can head to school"* Matthew replied. *"Well, that has never happened before,"* he said, *"we've been very busy while you were gone, you'll have to wash the three trolleys that was used to serve the food on the landings then"* he said, *"okay,"* Matthew replied. It took him about fifty minutes to clean the trolleys and by the time he got his lunch, it was too late for him to go back to school that afternoon because it was going 2:30pm, and the officers that comes to the landings to get prisoners to school comes at 2:15pm, so he concluded they were definitely gone, and he still needed to clean the store room.

Two days later, Paddy and one other prisoner Ahmed were playing scrabble, Matthew stood by one of the tables in the kitchen watched them as they played the game, it was in the afternoon after lunch, Ahmed was doing six years for drug possession for sale and supply, he's a slender guy, about six feet tall, he asked Matthew, *"do you know how to play scrabble at all?"* before Matthew answered, Paddy said *"definitely he has never played it before, I think he wants to learn, I think he has no idea of what we are doing,"* says Paddy again, *"well I do know how to play the game Paddy, you've asked me before, and I told you that I do know how to the game,"* Matthew replied. *"Really?"* Paddy said, *"how about me and you bet a pack of cigarette on who wins between you and me"* says Paddy *"okay, one park of cigarette then"* Matthew replied accepting the challenge. They started playing, Matthew had the confident that he was going to win the game, notwithstanding that sometimes winning the game can depend on luck with the help of picking the right tiles at the right time, but from watching how Paddy played with Ahmed for the first ten minutes that Matthew stood there, he knew that he should be able to beat Paddy, even if he's not lucky in getting the right *tiles "I will be the referee, I'll take down the score"* says Ahmed, during the game when Matthew was leading by almost seventy points, about three other prisoners joined up with Paddy, helping him to arrange his tiles, telling him which word to play to get the highest point, it was like four people against one, but Matthew didn't care or complained, he kept on playing, and eventually won the game, Paddy was utterly livid that he lost the game. Another day Matthew was watching two other prisoners playing chess, Paddy tapped him on the shoulder *"I can beat you in chess, do you know how to play chess"* he asked *"yes I can play chess"* Matthew *replied "so you can play chess as well"* says Paddy gobsmacked, *"well I can bet four packs of cigarettes that I can definitely beat you"* Paddy confidently *said "well if you think so, let's play then"* Matthew replied accepting the bet, because he had watched Paddy played chess some couple of days earlier, notwithstanding that he won, Matthew knew that he can still beat him, and ten minutes into the game, Matthew checkmated him within nine moves and won, Paddy was really pissed off again. The reason behind Paddy coming after Matthew was basically because he was very upset that Matthew was allowed to be going to the prison school while working in the kitchen, and when he complained about it to Mrs O'Neill *"as long as Matthew does his job in the store room, I am okay with him going to the school"* she said to him, so Paddy said he too would start going to the school *"as long as you are able to do your designated job Paddy, I don't have problem with you going to the school"* Mrs O'Neil replied, so, he started going to the school to learn cooking at the cookery class, but he was still not happy that Matthew was spending his time judiciously in the prison by doing a degree course and going to school.

In the third week in December, four days to Christmas, Matthew was in the kitchen, it was going to 2pm, he had just changed into his clothes from the kitchen uniform and wanted to tell one of the officers in the kitchen to take him back to the landings to join the other prisoners that would be waiting on the second floor on B block to be picked up by officers that comes from the school, but Mrs O'Connell came to him, *"Matthew, I was at the Mass on Sunday, and the way you sang really made my day, you have a very beautiful voice Matthew"* she said. *"Oh, thank you Mrs O'Connell"* he replied, as he was about to ask her to take him to the landing, another officer came into the kitchen and called out his name *"Matthew Williams!!!"* *"Yes, that's me officer,"* he answered him, *"you have a visitor,"* he said, Matthew was gobsmacked because he wasn't expecting any visitor *"Enjoy your visit"* Mrs O'Connell said as he went towards the exit door from the kitchen were the officer was waiting for him. Ten minutes after, he was sitting in one of the three special visitors room that is only meant for one prisoner and their visitors, a female officer came in with pastor Joseph potter, his wife Ruth and their daughter Pamela, they bended over the table that separated them from him one after the other to hug him, this was the fifth time Joseph and Ruth Potter has come to visit him at Midlands prison, but this was Pamela's first time at Midlands prison, she visited him once at Cork prison with her parents, the Potters visit Matthew almost every month since his incarceration, whenever they come, they pray with him, they encourage him that he would get a fair trial at his appeal, they always tell him to have faith that he would soon be out of prison, as they prayed, the female officer that sat by the door behind Matthew looked amazed, the prayer lasted for about five minutes *"how are you doing brother Matthew?"* daddy Potter asked *"well I am hanging on, trusting in God that this ordeal will soon be over"* replied Matthew *"we are all praying for you, the church is praying for you, we all love you"* says daddy Potter *"thank you very much, your prayer and support is definitely keeping me strong, I really appreciate your love"* says Matthew *"we shall overcome brother Matthew, just believe, hold onto your faith"* pastor Potter said *"thank you sir, thank you mummy Potter, thank you sister Pamela"* Matthew replied, they hugged him again when it was time for them to leave to say goodbye, he thanked them again, the whole visit lasted for about thirty five minutes, it was going to 3pm, the school finishes at 4pm for the day, so, Matthew told the officer to take him to the school instead of going back to the kitchen because he had a problem with his Open University course assignment that he needed to discuss with Mark. George was the only prisoner in the class, he had problem with the same assignment, so; Mark was explaining the solution to him on the blackboard, from the way Mark was acting, trying to solve the equation, writing the solutions of the question and robbing it off the board back and forth for about four times after arriving at four different answers, it was very obvious to Matthew that he was struggling as well and that he doesn't know how to solve the question, so when Mark turned to them *"you know what guys, I am not supposed to be solving the solution to questions that has been given to students as assignment, I will be breaking the rules, I will just give you guys an idea of how to go about getting to the final answer, I am sorry, that's all I am allowed to do"* he said to both of them *"come on Mark, help us out with this one"* says George *"I am sorry George, that's not going to happen, I am only supposed to teach you guys the topic, which I already did"* he said again, Matthew wasn't surprised, Mark finally gave them a bogus idea of the solution to the equation, and told them to solve the equation themselves, Matthew and George later laughed about Mark struggling and not knowing the answer to the equation on their way back to B block after school *"Matthew since you work in the kitchen, you get me special food like cakes or pie, and I can look after your clothes at the laundry for free, I normally take a pack of cigarette weekly to look after someone's clothes but for you it'll be free, if that's okay"* says George *"yes definitely, I am down for that George, my clothes has not been properly washed by the laundry guys, sometimes some of my clothes get missing when I get them back from the landing after sending it to the laundry, I had to go to the laundry myself most of the time to wash my clothes myself, so if you are going to look after my clothes you are doing me a great favour George, I'll definitely look after you too, you just let me know the type of food or fruits you want me to get you from the kitchen"* asked Matthew *"if you can get me cake, fruits like apple or if you can make me a pizza, that would be great"* George replied laughing *"you don't worry my friend, I'll look after you, but pizza, I can't guarantee that"* says Matthew as George went into his cell and he continued walking down the staircase to the first floor *"Matthew, Matthew"* he heard Amuda called his name as he came down to the second floor *"what, I need to quickly get back to the kitchen, I'll see you later"* says Matthew, but Amuda told him to wait as he quickly walked to meet him at the staircase *"there is a guy that just came in today, he was caught with the same type of package that you were caught with, drugs concealed in a package that contained mobile phones, I was talking to him in the yard some few minutes ago, but he said he knew that he was collecting drugs, I think he works for the same guy that you collected the same type of package for, if you can come to the yard this evening at the last unlock, he said he'll be there because I told him about you, and he said he heard about you, that he'll like to see you"* Matthew was flabbergasted but excited that he might be able to have a chance to get the guy that used him to collect the package arrested through this guy Amuda is talking about *"I will definitely be coming to the yard this evening, what floor is the guy on?"* Matthew asked *"he's actually on the third floor, his name is Jason, do you know him?"* Amuda asked *"no, I don't know him but I'll like to speak to him, I'll see you in the yard"* says Matthew again as he continued down the staircase.

Later that day when he walked into the yard, there were about forty five other prisoners, some were playing card game, some were standing in group of three and four smoking cigarette and talking while some were doing the normal walk in circle going round the yard which is like a rectangular shape, sixty metre by length and thirty metres wide , Matthew saw Amuda walking with a new guy that he has never seen before "that must be Jason" he thought, he immediately went and joined them "what's the crack?" he said as he tapped Amuda on the shoulder *"Matthew this is the guy I was telling you about"* says Amuda *"Matthew, right?"* the guy said as he looked at him *"yes, and you must be Jason?"* Matthew replied extending his hand in handshake *"yes"* the new guy replied as he accepted his handshake *"he got caught after collecting the same type of package you collected"* says Amuda to Matthew as they all continued to walk *"where did you get caught?"* Matthew asked Jason *"I got caught in Cork, I was stupid to have gone to collect that package after hearing the news of how you got caught"* Jason replied and told them the story of how he got caught with the package. Jason is about six feet tall, medium build, he's in his early thirties, he's married and has three daughters, this was not the first time he's been caught with drugs, two years earlier, he was caught dealing in drugs while trying to sell four grams of cocaine to a woman who was an undercover police, he was lucky when he got two years suspended sentence by the presiding judge, notwithstanding that the prosecutor wanted him to get a custodial sentence, but the judge agreed with his defence and put his early guilty plea and also for the mare fact that it was his first time in front of a judge, and also the small quantity of the drugs was used as a mitigating factor for the reason why the judge decided to give him a warning which was the suspended sentence, but this time around, Jason said he was approached by one of his friends that was initially supposed to collect the package whom intentionally missed the delivery guy, but the delivery guy dropped a slip for the package to be picked up at a post office in Cork, Jason friend showed him the slip left by the delivery guy *"I will give you three thousand euro Jason if you can collect the package"* Jason agreed to go and collect the package, when Matthew asked Jason to describe the main guy that promised to give him three thousand euro, it fit the description of the same guy that used Matthew to collect the same type of package that got him into the ordeal that he's presently in, Jason said when he got to the post office, he acted as the owner of the package, and he was given the package after signing for it, but what he didn't know was that the post office staffs had already called the police who were waiting for anyone that would come and collect the package, when Jason came out of the post office with the package, he noticed that there were three undercover policemen following him, so he started running with the package, but it was not easy for him to run with the package, so he dropped the package and ran towards the car that the same guy that got Matthew to collect the same type of package was supposed to be waiting for him to come with the package, but Jason said the guy drove off when he noticed that the undercover policemen were chasing him, he said he almost made it to the car before the guy drove off, but he only got caught because the guy drove off, but when Matthew asked him the name of the guy, he gave a different name to the name Matthew knows the guy as, Jason said he was only on transit at Midlands prison, that he went to the high court to get his bail which was granted, he said he has to get someone that would stand as a surety with ten thousand euro deposit, he said his friend that told him to collect the package as given the ten thousand euro to his wife, that they just need to give it to someone that would stand as a surety, then he'll be out on bail, Jason said he believes he'll be out on bail within a week, but said he'll be leaving the country because he knows if he stays for the sentence he'll be going away for at least eight years even if he pleads guilty, because he got caught with two kilos of cocaine, he said he's not ready to be locked up for that long, Matthew got his contact number, that night in his cell, Matthew ruminated about what he should do to try and get the police to apprehend the guy that got him to collect the package, he thought he might be lucky that the guy confess about his obliviousness of the drug in the package that he sent him to collect in other to proof his innocence, he thought about discussing it with his pastors, the Potters, he thought he would try and cajole Jason to give him his friend address, but from the way Jason spoke in the yard, because the guy put down ten thousand euro for his bail, he doesn't look like he would want to give him the address, and him wanting to live the country after getting out on bail proofs that he'll definitely not give the guy up, but Matthew thought he should at least try.

Chapter Seven

The Devil Neighbour

It was in the evening after he came back from the kitchen, after the day's work, Matthew stood at the front of his cell, all the other cells were just opened for the final unlock for prisoners to either go to the yard or gym, John Dunne, his neighbour in cell number 27 immediately to the left side of his cell came out of his cell smoking cigarette *"hey Matthew, father Freddie's son, you still alive yeah?"* He asked *"am still alive"* Matthew replied, they don't really see much during the day because most of the time, Matthew leaves his cell every morning at 7:30am to work in the kitchen seven days a week, but they see themselves once in a while during the day when Matthew is assign to come and serve food on B block with two other prisoners from the kitchen, Matthew remembered as he stood there smiling at John when three months earlier when he first saw John, the day after moving into the single cell, when he greeted John, and John scowled and then went ballistic *"if you ever fucking say a word to me again, I will fucking hurt you badly, I am not your fucking friend, you stay out of my way or I will fucking kill you"* John said, the expression of rage on his face showed his sadistic nature and proved that he really meant what he said, Matthew backed up into his cell, and immediately after then, another prisoner, Amuda, came into Matthew's cell, he's a small short guy, about just five feet tall, he's in his early thirties, he was doing eight years for drug trafficking, he's a bald headed guy, he was arrested at Dublin airport on transit to Canada, he swallowed about eighty five small tiny balloons that contained about eight hundred grams of cocaine, he was apprehended by the narcotics officers at the airport, he said when he finished walking through the last security checks on his way to go to the gate number for his onward flight to Canada, one of the narcotics officers, a lady that looked at his passport said he should come with her after checking the black backpack he was carrying and after also a frisk search on his body, so he followed her, he said he thought it would be a quick interrogation about the Canadian Visa on his Nigerian passport, which he said it was genuine and since his connection flight was leaving about two hours after he was stopped, he thought it would be something quick, but he was surprised when he got into a room with the narcotic officer, two other officers were waiting in the room, the first question they asked him was *"are you carrying any drugs in your stomach"* he said his reply was *"no, what do you mean if I am carrying drugs in my stomach?"* so; they asked him to step into a machine, which he did, and after about one minute, he was told to step out of the machine *"what have you eaten today sir?"* one of the officers asked him, he said it was going around 2pm. *"I have only had my breakfast, I had cereal"* he replied *"but you have some tiny balls of something in your stomach which looks like you might have ingested drugs sir, so; you would need to go through further checks, but we need you to sign a document to agree to swallow a laxative pill that will quickly purge you of the stuffs in your stomach within thirty minutes and if it is clear that you are not carrying any drugs, then you will be able to get on the next flight and continue your journey to Canada sir"* one of the officers said to him, but Amuda said he was told if he refused to sign the documents to agree to take the pill, he would have to go and use a special toilet to excrete what he has in his stomach, which would be examined and if it was found not to be drugs, he can continue his journey, or the final option would be for him to miss his flight if he can't excrete the stuff before the next flight to Canada lives, and he would be put on the next flight after he excrete the stuffs if it's discovered that he's not carrying drugs, he said he tried to convince them that he doesn't feel like going to the toilet and that he was not carrying drugs, so he said they decided to put him on the third option, which he said he later excreted the drugs after trying not to pooh for sixteen hours, but he was getting really sick so he had to excrete the drugs in a specially made toilet that couldn't be flushed and immediately about after ten minutes he excreted the drugs, a narcotics officer came into the room, he read him his rights and told him that he's been charged for drug trafficking, he was then taken to another room were three other officers were waiting with the excreted drugs, he was transported to the nearest prison, he said *"I have always query or complained about the reason why I was stopped and arrested in Ireland when I was only on transit here, and the drugs I was caught with was not to be sold in Ireland or meant for the Irish market or people, and one more thing Matthew, you need to be very careful of John, your neighbour"* he murmured to him *"do you know the reason why he's doing four years?"* Matthew looked at him in curiosity *"of cause you don't know, he's only doing four years sentence because the police couldn't find enough evidence to prosecute him for two murders that he committed, he was only caught with six grams of drugs which is adjudged by law in this country to be a quantity considered to be for personal usage, but he was given four years for a crime that most people would just get a suspended sentence or maximum a six months custodial sentence for, he's supposed to be doing life imprisonment for sending his gang to kill his wife's father and his wife's best friend while he was locked up here in prison, but the Gardai couldn't find any concrete evidence or proof that he killed them or locate the bodies, so; they couldn't prosecute him for their death, most of the prisoners know that he's diabolical, you need to stay away from him Matthew"* says Amuda. *"Thank you for telling me this, at least now I know, I don't want any trouble from anybody"* Matthew replied *"you are very unlucky to be put in a cell beside him, before I go Matthew, please can you get me extra fruits from the kitchen since you work there, you should be able to get me extra fruits"* he said *"I'll see what I can do, notwithstanding that we get searched before living the kitchen every time"* says Matthew.

It's now three months since Matthew has been John's neighbour, and they have become friends, they play chess board game together in the evening most of the time during the final unlock from 5:30pm when most prisoners go out in the yard to take a walk or do some other activities, or when some prisoners go to the gym, most of the time it is John that comes into Matthew's cell to play chess because Matthew's cell is always left opened by the officer because he just came back from work from the kitchen, and the officers allows John to stay in Matthew's cell. John confided in Matthew that when he gets out of prison, he's planning to kidnap and torture his ex-wife *"can you imagine that fucking bitch is fucking the guy that set me up, and when I confronted the slut when she came here to visit me, she stood up and walked out on me, and two weeks after, I got a letter and documents for devoice for me to sign, I can't fucking wait"* he said, and the way he said it Matthew believes hundred percent that he meant what he said and going to do it *"and you know what, I already killed the bitch's father, cause he was taking my hard earned money when I was out there, but when I called him to tell him that his daughter was asking me to sign a devoice papers, he supported his daughter to abandon me here, he even had the guts to tell me that I am going to die here in prison and hung up the phone on me, the bastard thought because I am locked up in here I can't do anything to him and his daughter, you know what I did Matthew?"* he asked. *"What did you do?"* Matthew asked not withstanding that he was uncomfortable with what he was saying and not happy with his ominous plan to kill his wife. *"I got my boys to kidnap him, he was tortured to death, and you know what? I watched every pain that he went through, I watched as he screamed before he died, I saw it all live from a video link sent to me, I mean live Matthew, whenever I remember the way he screamed and begged for his life before he died it makes me relaxed that I did something great, I find it therapeutic, and you know what again Matthew, I also kidnap the bitch's best friend, another bitch, the reason why I haven't got my boys to kidnap my ex-wife is because I want to be out there when that happens, so that I can looked into her eyes and watch her scream and beg for her life when I torture her, it's going to be special torture, Matthew, I want to show you something on my chest"* he said as he removed his shirt, Matthew looked startled, *"trust me, I am not going to rape you, I am not fucking your father Freddie that stick his cock into boys ass"* John said and laughed, he pointed to a big tattoo on the left side of his chest, and said *"do you know what this is?"* It was a tattoo of a person with two horns and written immediately below the tattoo is *"I am the devil." "Can you see that I am the daddy devil, I have got just about seven months left to finish my sentence, I can't wait to look into that bitch face and see her eyes and hear her voice screaming begging for her life when I am torturing her before I set her ablaze to go and meet her father in hell"* he said with a sniggering laugh, Matthew put on a poker face by smiling as he spoke *"John, I really want you to come with me to the church on Sunday, you are going to love it"* says Matthew *"you're crazy Matthew!!! How many times have I told you that I don't believe in God, and apart from that, I don't want to be around that priest, father Freddie or what's his name? I believe he sticks his dirty cock into boys ass, most especially children"* says John. *"How do you know that John?"* asked Matthew *"well I know from his face, he wears make up and walks like a woman, and the way he looks at people, you'll know he's looking to get closer to guys to stick his cock into their ass, and if he comes near me I will reap his head off,"* John said frantically with his face suddenly the expression of a monster. *"I have a plan John, all the officers and most guys here believe you are the devil, I just want you to see the shock on their face when they see you going into the church, the devil coming to church,"* Matthew said *"is that what you think Matthew?"* John said as he laughed. *"I think I like to see that Matthew, the daddy devil in the church, when are we going?"* John asked. *"8am on Sunday, but you'll have to put down your name with the officer on the landing at 5:30pm Saturday evening at the final unlock, so that the officer can let you out on Sunday morning when it's time for Mass,"* Matthew replied. That night in his cell, lying on his bed after the final lockdown, Matthew thought about what he can do to stop John from committing another murder when he gets out, he thought about speaking to the governor of the prison in private about it, or consulting with his solicitor about what to do with the information divulged to him by John, he was restless with the overwhelming thoughts of stopping him from killing his ex-wife, he doesn't know his wife, but he felt that her staying alive and not getting killed is in his hand to stop John, and he only had seven months to do it, he said to himself that he'll first discuss it with pastor Potter when he comes to visit *him "there has to be a way to stop him"* he said to himself reassuringly.

He was arranging the cooking stuffs that was just delivered that afternoon to the kitchen, he couldn't go to the prison school because he was told by Mrs O'Connell that he needed to be around when the delivery comes in, so that he can help her to bring it into the store and arrange it immediately on the shelves, as all the other officers and prisoners would be going to serve food on the landings if the delivery arrives late, he was arranging the stuffs when Miss O'Connell stealthily came into the store room *"hello Matthew"* she murmured to him smiling as she quietly locked the door, and immediately unbuttoned her shirt exposing her bra *"we only have about fifteen minutes"* she said as she hurriedly came forward and kissed him on his lips, hugged and caressing him, Matthew was shocked for about twenty seconds and got carried away as he stood there motionless, he has not had sex for about the last ten months since his incarceration, and here comes this beautiful woman in her late thirties, almost the same age as him, submitting herself to him in this cage, this is a miracle!!! Something screamed in his head, he could feel the rush of adrenaline and his heart palpitating as he subconsciously kissed her back, but not holding her, his hands drops by his sides in a nosey standing posture, he remembered his appeal and his devotion and determination to stay out of sin for his prayers to be answered, this is adultery!!! Something ringing that word in his head, adultery!!! If you do this, it will be catastrophic for your appeal!!! He immediately stop kissing her back and gently backed off from her *"please Miss O'Connell, am sorry, I can't do this"* he said reluctantly *"but everyone has gone to serve lunch on the landings, no one is in the kitchen, just you and me,"* she said as she grabbed him and started kissing him again, but he quickly backed up again saying, *"I am sorry Miss O'Connell, I just believe it's very wrong for us to do this"* she started buttoning back her shirt in utter shock *"you'll regret this Matthew"* she said. *"Please I promise you that I'll never discuss this with anyone, it will stay between you and me, I promise miss"* he said *"please I don't want to get into more trouble please, I am begging you, it's between us"* Matthew pleaded again fidgeting *"okay it's between us as you promised, I want you to know it's because I really like you Matthew, and if you change your mind you let me know"* she reluctantly replied *"okay miss, I'll let you know, it's just that I am really stressed up with my appeal coming up"* replied Matthew *"okay Matthew"* she said, still in shock that he refused her, she then went and unlocked the door and left the store room. Matthew stood there confused and restless, he thought to himself, what is she going to do? Is she going to frame me for rape? He thought, he quickly went out of the store room, there was no other person in the kitchen apart from Miss O'Connell who he could see through the glass office sitting on a couch, she smiled at him, and he smiled back. He quickly went back into the store and quickly finished arranging the stuffs on the shelves, at the same time thinking about if he should stop working in the kitchen or not, he had been missing classes in the school lately, and he had an Open University exam coming up on programming that he needed to spend more time using the computer in the school to check if the HTML , the machine language for the program on Lotto Draws assignment he wrote in his cell overnight for several nights is correct, he thought, I might just have to concentrate on my degree course, he decided that he will have to live his kitchen job in another week, he felt that he should live immediately, but he doesn't want Miss O'Connell to think or suspect that he left because of her.

He reluctantly managed to get up from the bed, he checked the time on the screen of the fourteen inch television that stood on a shelve about one meter away from his bed in his cell, it was past seven in the morning, he makes sure that the television is always turned on whenever he's in his cell, even when he's going to bed, Matthew needed the sound from the TV to be able to fall asleep, he finds it therapeutic and relaxing, and whenever he wakes up in the middle of the night and the TV has turned off itself, he immediately gets overwhelmed with the rush of negative thoughts of been locked up in prison away from his wife and children and his heart immediately starts palpitating, it's only when he manages to quickly turn on the TV and hears the sound coming from it that he becomes a little relax and calm to focus on what he needs and wants to do, but there are also some programmes that comes on the TV that immediately unsettles him, most especially cartoon programmes like Bob the builder that he used to watch with his son before his ordeal, and also programmes like the Tweenies that his daughter really loves and Matthew watched with her, what he does when such programme comes on the TV, Matthew will quickly turn the TV to another channel, he has tried to watch this two programmes when they come up on the TV but he finds out that he get overwhelm with the thoughts of not been physically present in the life of his children and that completely unsettles him and he starts crying, so he has decided that whenever any of such programmes comes up, he'll quickly switch the telly to another channel, which he has been doing, now he needs to quickly do his thirty minutes yoga stretch that he does every night before going to bed immediately after the final lock down and first thing in the morning after brushing his teeth and washing his face when he gets off from bed, the officers would be unlocking the cell doors for breakfast in another forty minutes at 8am for about thirty minutes for prisoners to get breakfast and lock it back, then open it again at 8:45am for the prisoners that put their name down for Mass to be taken to the only church service in the prison that starts at 9am and finishes at 10am.

At 8:45am when the officer opened Matthew's cell, he immediately told the officer about John wanting to go to Mass, the officer looked at him, gobsmacked, and immediately looked at the A4 paper with the list of names down for people going to Mass, he said *"okay, his name is on the list"* looking even more surprised as he looked at Matthew, before finally opening the flap to the small window to the cell door to be able to see inside John's cell, *"John are you going to Mass?"* he sceptically asked. *"Open the fucking door, daddy devil wants to go to Mass today,"* John replied smiling, the officer unlocked the door, John came out with a cigarette in his mouth, he was dressed in Jeans, t-shirt and wore a white sock and slippers, he looked at Matthew who was smiling and happy thinking that he's managed to get him to church at last, Matthew said to him, *"we have to go to the gate on the second landings to wait with the others for the officers that will come and take us to mass,"* there were about twenty one other prisoners waiting at the gate when they got there, they all looked flabbergasted to see John, two prisoners came to him smiling, *"John are you going to Mass?"* one of them asked. *"Yes, daddy devil is going to Mass to kill that father Filly, or what's his fucking name?"* John asked, the guys laughed, just then two officers arrived at the other side of the gate, one of them unlocked the gate, the officers also looked astonished to see John, they walk through two other gates which was unlocked by the officers, it only took about three minutes' walk and they arrived at the hall in the prison school used for the Mass, there were about twenty six other prisoners sitting on single plastic chairs in the hall and five other officers waiting by the entrance door, Matthew went and said good morning to the priest at the altar and they both had an handshake, he sat down beside two other prisoners, Paul and Stephen, the three of them sang in the church choir together for mass, they practise twice during the week on Tuesdays and Thursdays evening with the priest to get the songs that would be sang on Sunday ready, Paul plays the guitar while Matthew and Stephen sang, but Matthew is the head of the vocals, sometimes an elderly lady called Ger. in her late sixties comes in from her house that is not far away from the prison for mass to play the piano. John sat at the back of the hall with the two guys that first spoke to him at the first gate at B block when they were waiting for the officers to come and bring them to Mass, that Sunday they sang a song by Gabrielle, called Sunshine, it is a lovely song, most of the prisoners and officers hum along while they sang the song, Matthew and Stephen sang *"Sunshine through my window, That's what you are."* The singing only took about ten minutes, but immediately after the song was finished, when the priest started to say the sermon which the topic was on forgiveness, John stood up, and went to one of the officers by the exit door and asked him to take him back to his cell, the officer said he should wait that the mass would soon be over and they would be taking all prisoners back, but John said if the officer doesn't take him back right away, that whatever happens next would his own fault, he was fuming, so one other officer said he would take him back to his cell, and immediately told him to follow him. John later told Matthew later that afternoon in his cell when Matthew went to say hello to him that, something was telling him to reap off the priest head, that he had to quickly get out of the Mass in other not to do that *"but I would gladly really love to reap that your father filly's head off if there is a way I can do it and not get caught"* says John with sniggering laugh, Matthew smiled back shaking his head to gesticulate his disappointment and walked out of his cell.

The next day in the prison kitchen *"I am sorry Matthew, we're going to miss you"* Mrs O'Neill said to him in the glass office in the kitchen, it was going to 9am, he had told her five minutes earlier that he had to leave the job in the kitchen to concentrate on his degree course at the prison school that he's been finding it hard to cope doing the job and his studies together that he's not been able to complete most of his assignments and his exams is coming up in some couple of days that he needed to fully focus on his studies, which Mrs O'Neill said she fully understood and wish him best of luck, as they both came out of the office, the other prisoners and officers that went to serve breakfast on the landings came back into the kitchen, Mrs O'Neill said to one of the three officers *"Mr Egan, Matthew is leaving us for now because he needs to study for his degree course that he's doing in the school, please can you get him back to the landings?"* Matthew was just happy that Miss O'Connell was not around to see him leave and he was also restless and quickly wanted to get out thinking she might come in at any moment, he quickly went to his locker to clear out his stuffs, Paddy came to him *"so you are leaving because of school?"* he said flabbergasted and looked infuriated *"you are crazy Matthew"* he said *"but I have to go and concentrate on my exam coming up in some couple of days"* he replied *"well you go then, but watch your back on the landing"* he said furiously as he walked away, Matthew was gobsmacked by his reaction and also for Paddy to say that he should watch his back on the landing, he thought to himself, for what, this guy has always bullied him, trying to intimidate and dehumanise him most of the time he comes across him, but he has proved himself that he's smarter than him, beating him in all the challenges he throws at him, which most other prisoners and officers in the kitchen has come to respect Matthew because of his personality and the way he relates to them, most prisoners in the kitchen and prisoners on B block doesn't really like Paddy, they know he's a bully, Matthew has been told by Amuda that he sells drugs in the prison, that the drugs is brought into the prison to him by one male officer that works in the prison and that he peddles the drug for the officer and that he makes loads of money from the deal, that the way the business is done is that, before Paddy sells drugs to any prisoner, he arranges with the prisoner to get their family or friend outside to pay the money for the drugs to an associate of his outside which is organised by the prison officer that brings in the drugs before he now hand over the drugs, but sometimes he gives the drugs to some of his top customers on credit to pay later, and if the prisoner doesn't pay the money, he arranges with other prisoners by giving them free drugs to beat up the prisoner that owes him, now been told to watch his back, Matthew thought to himself that he needs to be more careful and thought he should consult with the psychologist that he sees every Wednesday to help him to move to D block were people that wants to be put in protection are moved to, well first of all he had to get out of the kitchen, then he would know what to do, he thought maybe he should just beg Paddy or get someone that can talk to him and convince him to leave him alone.

Chapter Eight

Unexpected Windstorm

He heard the sound of keys dangling and cell doors unlocking, he was already dressed up and ready to go and see the prison psychologist called Sarah Lennon, he sees her on every Wednesday afternoon during the unlock period, immediately his cell door opened, he picked up his folder from the bed and quickly got out of his cell, looked to the left and then to the right side of the landing, then closed the door to his cell, he has been more cautious and vigilant in his movement around the prison since Paddy threatened him to watch his back, it's been two days now, and he has discovered that immediately the cell doors are opened for the final unlock at 5:30pm three other prisoners from the third landing comes down to the first landing walking up and down past his cell several times, all three of them looking at his cell talking, it was very obvious that they were planning to jump into his cell to attack him, and he knows two of the guys are junkies, definitely Paddy's customer, so Matthew decided he has to quickly do something to stop the attack, he was looking forward to discuss his situation with Sarah, he was absolutely certain that she can help him get transferred to C Block which is a very quiet and more secured section of the prison for prisoners that needs protection, all he's after now is safety, he thought to himself, being locked up is very harrowing for him, but getting beat up and seriously injured would be more harrowing, and for almost two years that he's been locked up, he's never being in a physical altercation with any prisoner, he has been in verbal altercation or argument with some few racist and low life bullies that he has come across and wanted to intimidate him, but he has never ever gotten into a physical altercation with any prisoner, the worst that has ever happened to him was when he was back in Cork prison when he was standing in the yard with about twenty other prisoners waiting to be taken to the prison school, a new prisoner that just came in the previous night kicked him from behind without any justifiable reason, immediately the guy kicked him, four other prisoners jumped on the guy and started beating him, Matthew had to step in to stop the guys from beating him further, the next day after the incident, Matthew was in his cell, it was during the time he had stopped working in the kitchen when he had problem with Eddy, the guy that kicked him the previous day came into his cell and apologised to him, and said he was sorry for what he did, and asked Matthew if he wanted him to buy him anything from the prison store, but Matthew said no, that it's okay, since then before he left Cock prison, the guy always greet him whenever they passed each other, and for having never been in any fight or trouble with the prison authority since his incarceration, he has become well known in the prison precinct and respected by most prisoners and officers, most of the prison officers try most of the time to help him make extra phone calls to his wife and children, most especially the officers in the kitchen where he previously worked, and even now that he has stopped working in the kitchen, at least twice a week, he goes to the governor of the prison for extra calls, and the governor always authorised the officer on his landing to give him an extra call in the evening, because most of the time he always wants to talk to his wife and children, because he's always missing them and thinks about them every minute which he gets overwhelmed making him extremely depressed, but after hearing their voice, he becomes relaxed for some couple of hours, and apart from always missing them, because of his claustrophobic nature, he gets easily overwhelmed with depression, but he has discovered what to do in his cell that can help him to calm down and reduce his fear and restlessness of confinement, things like yoga which he does in his cell most of the time and also with a group of about six other prisoners and a yoga tutor for one hour twice a week at the yoga class in the prison school, he finds doing yoga very therapeutic, he always thought and say to himself he has to do everything he can to stay alive, even when he's in despair thinking that his wife must be having an affair when she doesn't pick his calls for several days, he would summon courage to do whatever he can do that can help him to stay positive and not lose hope in getting out of his incarceration ordeal successfully.

Matthew was sitting in the Maths class twenty five minutes later, he was the only student in the class, Mark was complaining about not seeing George for over a month and asked him if George was okay, he said that

Melanie the lady in charge of the Open University has been complaining to him that George didn't submitted the previous assignment, that maybe he's looking to quit the course *"I didn't know that, I'll talk to him, I have not seen him for a while now myself,"* Matthew replied, a male officer came into the class to get him to see Sarah, the psychologist. He quickly packed his stuffs in his folder and left with the officer, the walk to where Sarah was waiting for him was another five minutes through three locked gates unlocked by the officer as they walked along to C Block, she was seating in a room with two single couch facing each other, immediately he came in Sarah extended her hand in hand shake and told him to sit down on the single couch that was directly opposite the couch she was sitting on, he immediately sat down, and Sarah beckon to the officer to wait outside the room, which the officer did, but the door was left opened. Sarah is in her early thirties, a slender build woman and about five foot nine inches tall, almost the same height as Matthew, he has been seeing her now off and on for therapy since he came to the prison, Sarah as discovered that the major reason for his trauma is because he's missing his wife and his kids, and his wife hasn't made things easy for him as well, she hasn't been replying the several letters Matthew sent her since over six months now, and most of the time when he calls her from the prison he could hear a man talking underground in the house, and whenever he ask her who the man in the house was, his wife always says is the voice from the TV, and there was a time his wife screamed at him when he called her that she told him to forget about her, that she has started seeing someone else, that he should stop calling her and hung up the phone, and for about a week she didn't pick his calls whenever he rang her, he was in utter despair and suicidal, she stopped visiting him, and also stopped going to pastor Potter's church and also stopped taking Joseph and Ruth Potter's calls as well, Matthew believe that his wife already told pastor Potter about her new relationship and that she has moved on with her life when she stopped going to the church, but when the Potters came to visit him, and he told them what his wife said that she has moved on with her life, they told him to concentrate on looking after himself and continue to pray about his appeal that was coming up, it wasn't easy for him to cope, he was so overwhelmed with the thoughts of his wife bringing another man, another stranger into his children's life, he wrote her a very passionate letter pleading to her to remember their marriage vows and begged her that she's made a very big mistake by bringing another man into their children's life, and also told her to make the right decision to stand by him in their ordeal, and told her that he's absolutely certain that when he goes for his appeal, his conviction would be overturn and he would be set free, he told her how much he loves her and their children, and how looking forward for them to reunite was the reason keeping him alive and determined to continue fighting for his freedom. He is entitled to two letters to be written and sent out weekly from the prison, and he wrote two letters weekly to his wife, and not withstanding that she stopped picking his call, he still called her every day, sometimes calling her over twenty times a day hoping and begging God to make her pick his call, Sarah knew all this, because when Matthew comes in for his therapy, he tells her everything, and cried a lot when telling her, she sometimes get emotional and cries with him as well, and she tried her best to be professional and get him to understand that the reason why his wife is behaving the way she did might be because she herself is very traumatised with his incarceration and couldn't cope, that's the reason why she said all she said, so; now when he was telling her about how Paddy threatened him to watch his back when he was leaving the kitchen, she felt that she had to do something, she told him that she can get him transferred to C wing were he can be save, but she said he won't be able to go to the prison school because the attack can also happen in the school, that the rules that goes with putting people in C Block for protection is that the prisoner can't be allowed to go to the prison school and can't also work in the prison as well, so Sarah asked Matthew if he's happy with the conditions behind moving to C Block for his protection, then she can arrange that with the governor of the prison, but Matthew said she should give him till the next meeting which would be the next Wednesday, to see if there is another way he can go about the situation because he doesn't want to miss going to the school because he needs to be using the computers in the school for his degree course assignments.

That evening they all stood by the gate, waiting for the officer that would come and take them to the gym, Matthew stood impatiently with them, they were about fourteen prisoners from B Block, it was around half past 5pm, they had about one hour fifteen minutes to use the gym because by 7:20pm the officer would have to bring them back to the landing so that anyone of them that wants to take a shower can do that before the final lock down at 7:45pm. The walk to the prison gym is about four minutes, and most of the prisoners tried to be at the forefront of the group while going to the gym because immediately the officer opens the entrance door to the gym, most of the prisoners scamper and jostle for the equipment that they'll like to use first, so Matthew tried to stay at the front to be able to get to the cross country machine that he likes to go on first to do thirty minutes workout, and then go unto the rower machine to complete a 5km rowing that takes about another twenty minutes and then finally go on the treadmill to do a fifteen minutes run on level seven, but starting with a five minute walk on level four, but that day he had plans to speak to Ronnie Clark about helping him to resolve his problem with Paddy. Ronnie is in his late thirties, a British guy, averagely built about six foot, he's on the same landing with Paddy on the same B Block as Matthew, he was arrested for importing about three tons of cocaine from south America with three other guys, it was the largest drug seizure in Ireland, he's doing twenty five years, Matthew and Ronnie knew themselves back from Cork prison from three years ago, but they became friends in Midlands prison when they started playing scrabble game together, most of the time they play scrabble twice a week in Ronnie's cell, mostly on weekends, Ronnie would tell Matthew to come up to his cell during unlock times, and it was during one of this games that Ronnie told Matthew the full story of how the drugs importation was arranged and shipped from south America to Ireland that led to his arrest and incarceration, not withstanding that he pled not guilty and denied ever been part of the importation of the drugs, but he told Matthew all about how the deal went wrong. Four years earlier Ronnie was sitting in a meeting with his elder brother Ed Clark, he was one of the superintendent of police in charge of drug law enforcement in London, also at the meeting were four other men, a Colombian guy Carlos Blanco sent by the Medellin cartel from Columbia, he is in his late thirties and dressed in a stylish suit, and also sitting at the meeting were three other British guys, Alex Mulvey in his early twenties, Francis Warren in his late thirties, a bulky guy, about six foot tall, he just got out of prison five months earlier after doing seventeen years for murder, he was given early release from prison because of his exceptional behaviour, he actually completed two degree courses in prison, he was adjudged by the parole board to be a complete rehabilitated man and no more a menace to the society, and also at the meeting was Danny Beeton, he is in his early fifties, about six foot tall as well, and has done time in prison for drug offence twice in South

Africa and also in Italy, each of this men sat there at the meeting represented their organisation in the drug deal, they discussed how the shipment of the drugs would be shipped from Colombia to Ireland, then unloaded onto a truck, stored in a warehouse and then finally transported to the final destination in London, they also discussed expenses and logistics which was decided and agreed to be taken care of by the organisations in England, they also discussed the payment for the drugs one month after arrival at the final destination, so; the cartel in Colombia agreed to sell the drugs on credit. Three days after the meeting, Alex, Francis and Danny boarded a flight from London Heathrow airport to Colombia, they all travelled as separate passengers, while Ronnie boarded a flight to Dublin, he had to buy the truck that would be used to transport the drugs from the Dunlough Bay, Cork, to a warehouse in Cork city which he'll also have to arrange, he had three weeks to do all this in other to be ready for the drugs that would arrive in a yacht at Dunlough Bay from between three to four weeks. What he first did was, he rented a two-bedroom holiday home at about three kilometres away from the shore of Dunlough, he has been to Cork City several times, his mother is from Cork, and he used to come and spend holiday with one of his aunt during his teenage years, within the next three weeks he'll buy the truck, rent the warehouse and get himself accustomed to Dunlough area and people.

Outside Eldorado International Airport in Columbia, Francis, Alex and Danny put their travel luggage into the open booth of awaiting car, it was going to 11am, they had just arrived from a twelve hours' flight from London via Madrid, the taxi drove them to an airfield about fifteen minutes away to get on awaiting private jet that took them to a farmhouse in Medellin to meet Daniel Blanco, the head of Medellin cartel. They were ushered into a big house on the farm house that was surrounded by about twenty armed men most of them carrying AK47, they were told to wait in one of the sitting room, and were served drinks from the big bar in the sitting room, four men with AK47 waited with them in the room, five minutes later Daniel came out of the inner room with two other armed men, he is in his late thirties, a short guy, about five inches four feet tall, he's pot belly as well. The three men stood up, Daniel went to the bar and served himself a glass of brandy, he gulped it all up in one go, he came towards them *"welcome to Colombia"* says Daniel *"my name is"* Francis wanted to introduce himself to him *"I know who you are Francis, and you are Alex, and you are Danny"* Daniel interrupted him politely smiling as he extended his hand in handshake to each one of them as he mentioned their name *"I also believe you guys know who I am"* he said with a sniggering smile *"follow me"* he said, he walked towards four SUV cars at the front of the mansion and got into one of the cars, two arm guards each took one British guy with them to one of the other three SUVs, separated them and blindfolded them with hood face cover, twenty five minutes later they arrived at another farmhouse surrounded by about thirty armed men each carrying AK47, the blindfolded clothes was removed from their face, and they were brought out of the cars, they followed Daniel round to the back of a big house to a massive hall used as the laboratory and production of the drugs, the roof was covered in canopy and then trees to hide the building away from the sky, there were about forty men and women working, cooking, mixing and weighing drugs, they walked on to another massive hall used as the storage *"that is your product"* Daniel said pointing to three thousand brown packages each package contained one kilo of cocaine *"the reason why I am giving it to you guys at four thousand euro per kilo is because you guaranteed my money within three months, I have your boat arranged, and also guarantee your safety in Colombia, any problem outside Colombia is your problem, and I'll still get my money or"* he stopped talking and looked at one of the eight armed men in the room, he nodded his head to him and the guy came forward with a laptop which he set upon a table in the middle of the room, and played a live video, sitting on a chair tied up from the video was a British guy which is well known to Francis, Alex and Danny, he was covered in blood from head to toe as a result from the torture he had received from the three men standing beside him in the video, one of them was Carlos, the guy that sat at the meeting in London with Danny, Alex and Francis before they left for Colombia, he brought out a gun from his jacket and shot the guy sitting on the chair right in the head, his brain splatter has he shot him, the horrific look on Alex, Francis and Danny's face proved that they got the message Daniel wanted them to get *"He was delayed paying for his shipment since last week"* Daniel said as he looked at the three British guys that were still overwhelmed with the shock that Hugo Brown, the head of the drug organisation in Manchester had just been executed *"I expect that we won't have to get to that stage guys"* Daniel said has he pointed towards the lab top looking at their face *"You get us out of Colombia with the product, and leave the rest to us, and we'll fulfil our own side of the deal, hundred percent"* says Francis as he looked at Alex and Danny, who nodded their head to Daniel to affirm what Francis had just said.

Sixteen days later the three British guys were on the boat loaded with three thousand kilos of cocaine, they had sailed for about four thousand nine hundred miles and had about another quarter of a mile to get to Dunlough shore when the boat came to a stop, it was around 8pm, it was very windy and raining heavily due to a windstorm that they had been battling with for the last three hours, Francis discovered that the boat was out of fuel, Alex the youngest volunteered to quickly go and refuel the fuel tank, but he mistaken refuel the tank with diesel instead of petrol, so the boat wouldn't start and the boat capsized after drifting further three hundred metres towards the shore, then leaving about thirty bales of cocaine floating around the bay, each bale contained hundred kilos. All three guys swam for the shore, but Danny started screaming that he's hurt and can't make it, Alex and Francis both held his hand on each side and managed to swim to the shore with him, by this time Ronnie was already waiting with the truck at the shore, he had been waiting there impatiently for over four hours, it was on a Thursday, and before coming that day, he had gone to receive the key to the warehouse were the drugs would be kept, he had also investigated and made sure that the water police won't be around in that area that evening to obstruct their mission, he had his contacts and connections in that section, which he paid for and had also promised his informant that more money would be coming his way after mission accomplished. Ronnie saw three people swimming towards the shore, they were about fifty meters from the shore, he looked at them in curiosity as they swam towards the shore, he wondered why there would be anyone in the water at that time of the night, he had been coming to the shore of Dunlough every evening from between 5pm to 9pm for the past three weeks to monitor the activity around the shore, and he had never come across anyone or found anybody swimming on the ocean around that particular time, he looked at the three people closely and nervously, now they were about five meters to the shore, he discovered that it was Alex and Francis swimming ashore pulling Danny with them, he immediately ran towards them, by the time he got to them they were at the shore, he helped Alex and Francis to pull Danny further to the shore, Danny was unconscious and unresponsive as they called his name, Francis tried CPR on him, mouth to mouth, but he was still unresponsive, Alex and Francis told Ronnie what happened and how the boat had capsized, Alex told Ronnie to call emergency number for help, but Ronnie discovered his phone and the key to the truck and his wallet was gone, he thought he must have lost it while running to them at the shore, Alex said he had to go and get help and ran towards the road, but discovered that there were some cabins at the other side of the road, he ran to the cabins he first got to knocking on the doors, a man opened the door to the third cabin that he knocked on, he told the man to call the emergency number that his friend is unconscious by the shore, the man called the emergency number and gave his phone to Alex, he told the person on the phone that his friend is unconscious by the shore, the person on the line said help would arrive in another about fifteen minutes. Ten minutes later, Ronnie and Francis could see three bales of the drugs floating on the ocean about fifty meters from the shore, *"Ronnie, Francis!!!"* Alex shouted, they looked back, and they saw Alex running towards them and at the same time they heard the sound of helicopter and also the sound of ambulance closing in, Alex shouted that he has called for help, Ronnie looked at Francis, and they both looked at the bales of drugs on the ocean again, they both immediately stood up from Danny and started running away from the shore past Alex, then past the road and disappeared into the jungle on the other side of the road.

Ronnie had been running in the jungle for over fifteen minutes and thought that Frances was behind him, but when he looked back he discovered that he wasn't behind him, he continued to run towards the jungle towards a rural village on the south western tip of Ireland called Goleen, he had rented a property there and had been staying underground for the past two weeks, it is about eight miles East from the shore of Dunlough bay, and it would take him about fifty minutes to get there, he could hear the sound of helicopter not far away, it was going half past 8pm, but it was still bright, he reassured himself that if they've started looking for him they won't be able to see him from above because of the trees that covered the area, he could hear the whirling sound from the helicopter, he thought about the bales of cocaine floating on the ocean, he thought about Alex, his heart palpitating as he ran and walked, he had to quickly get to the house that he rented in another name, lay low for some days, and then get out of Ireland and make his way back to England he thought. He turned on the TV after taking a shower and changed into a new pants and tea shirt, all over the news was the story about the bales of cocaine found at Dunlough bay, Alex in handcuffs and Danny on a ventilator, on a stretcher taken to the hospital, the news further said that the police are looking for two men, and showed a sketch picture of him and Francis, Ronnie thought to himself, he has to move first thing the next morning because he felt unsafe around Cork area, three hours later, the news of Frances arrested at Barleycove area, three kilometres east of Dunlough bay completely devastated him, from the news on the TV, Francis was handcuffed and put into a police car with four armed policemen, the news says that the police continued to search for him, showing the sketch of his face on the TV, the news further says that the police have surrounded the whole Dunlough Bay area and that check points had been created by the police in strategic places in Cork that they believe he can escape through. Ronnie couldn't sleep that night, he stayed in the house for three days waiting for the search on him to calm down, but by the third day he was very hungry and had to go out to get some food and also see if he can make his move to get out of the area. Ronnie walked to the mini grocery shop which was five minute walk from the house he has been hiding, he was wearing a face cap to try and look a little bit different from the sketched picture of himself that he saw on the news, there were three other people in the shop including a man at the till, he got bread, milk and butter, but when he was paying for the grocery, he saw two posters of the picture of himself one on each side immediately before the exit door of the shop that says *"have you seen this man, he's a dangerous man, he's wanted by the police"* and also the poster has a number for anyone that has seen him to immediately contact, as he looked at the poster apprehensively, the man at the till looked at him suspiciously, and asked him *"you're not from here, are you?"* which Ronnie replied *"I am here on a visit to my mum"* he tried to smile putting on a poker face and quickly paid for the groceries, but when he was leaving, the man was still looking at him suspiciously, looking at the poster and at him, back and forth, and immediately put his hand in his pocket to reach his phone, Ronnie believed he was going to call the police, so; Ronnie thought that he had to quickly get out of the village.

Five minutes later, Ronnie was back in the house eating the slices of bread and drinking the milk restlessly, standing, walking up and down in the sitting room thinking about his next move, the weather wasn't great, it was very windy and raining heavily as well, he didn't know that the man from the grocery shop didn't only called the police but immediately Ronnie left the shop, the man called the attention of one of the two other men in the shop to see the poster and pointed at Ronnie leaving the shop, so the man immediately followed and trailed him to the house he was staying, but Ronnie was utterly perturbed with the thoughts of how he'll get out of Ireland that he didn't noticed that the man was following him, so, Ronnie now eating fidgety, a loud knock came from the door *"open up, it's the police"* Ronnie looked through the closed windows he could see shadows of people and knew that the house had been surrounded by the police, the knock on the door persisted, but he kept quiet, gently placing the bread and the one litre box of milk on the table, he went and hide under the bed, the police kicked down the door after two minutes of no reply, they ransacked the house and discovered him under the bed, they pulled him out, handcuffed and arrested him. During interrogation at the police station, he discovered that Alex had pleaded guilty, and that the police had discovered how he rented a warehouse and bought a truck for the haulage of the drugs from Dunlough bay to the warehouse, but he pleaded not guilty and chose to be uncooperative with the police, after four months of more investigation, and after trial in court, he got twenty five years sentence each with Danny and Francis that also pleaded not guilty, but because Alex pleaded guilty, he got ten year sentence for the same drug offence. During the over two years that Matthew has known Ronnie in prison, they've become close friends because of the scrabble game and also because they are both family men, and they discussed about their wife and kids with each other, which in the past, he told Matthew that he's got a lovely wife and four children, and said he already told his wife to stop coming from England to visit him because he's utterly certain that his wife would move on with her life if she finds another man she can replace him with, that he's absolutely sure that it would get to that stage, and if it gets to that stage if his wife tells him or give him the news he won't be able to handle it then if he's not prepared, so by telling her to move on with her life is the only way he can prepare himself for the worse, that's the reason why he decided to stop his wife coming to see him because he believes that their relationship as husband and wife is over, he told Matthew that after he's appeal, he would put in a transfer to go and do the remaining of his sentence in England in other to be closer to his children *"I will talk to Paddy"* Ronnie said smiling as he took his water bottle from the exercise bicycle that he had just finished using *"please Ronnie, I don't want to get into any fight with anyone, I just want to do my time in peace"* says Matthew *"I promise, I'll talk to him tonight, and if he doesn't listen, me and you will beat him up"* Ronnie said smiling, Matthew laughed, just then the officer called *"time to go back, come on come on, let's go!!!"*

The next day during the afternoon unlock on the way to school, Ronnie told Matthew that he spoke to Paddy about his malevolence to harm him, and Ronnie said Paddy has decided to back off the hit on him, *"thank you Ronnie, and what should I get you from the shop for helping me out with that?"* Matthew asked. *"You can buy me the whole shop, because he already put a heat on you, and I really had to be persuasive in telling him to call it off,"* Ronnie replied smiling, but as he noticed the shock expression on Matthew's face. *"I am only kidding, you owe me two weeks scrabble game starting from tonight"* Ronnie said smiling again *"okay Ronnie, I'll make it a month"* Matthew replied. *"Good"* said Ronnie, and they both went their ways into different classes. On his way back from the school, Matthew climbed up to the third landing, went to George's cell and opened the flap that covers the small transparent glass that prison officers look through to check prisoners in their cell, he saw that George was lying down on the bed watching TV, he banged on the cell door *"George!!!, George!!!"* he called his name to get his attention, George came to the door *"what is happening George? Melanie and Mark said you've not been coming to the school, and you've not been submitting the course assignments"* Matthew asked *"Matthew, I have stopped doing that course, I couldn't cope with doing the course, I want to go back to bed, I'll see you later"* he said and went back to lie down on the bed. *"Matthew, he's on too much drugs, he's crazy"* the guy in the next cell beside George mumbled to Matthew as he released the flap on the cell door to leave *"he hasn't been coming to the school"* Matthew mumbled back to him, Matthew knows the guy when he used to work in the kitchen, Matthew was disappointed that George gave up finishing the course, but he was not surprise, eight out of ten prisoners given an opportunity to complete a degree course ended up quitting the course half way or even in the first three months doing the course, but to him, he is determined to complete the course, notwithstanding that he finds it difficult doing a computer course when he doesn't have enough time to access the school computers, most of the assignment has got to do with writing programmes, code writing using

- 121 -

HTML which he needs to enter the codes called machine language into a computer to check if the programme is properly written, it hasn't been easy for him as well.

Four weeks later, after the first unlock, Matthew was on his way to the print shop, another section of the prison that prisoners go to study foundation in computer, the course is supervised by a prison officer called Mr Roach, he's been going to the class now for three weeks since he finished from the kitchen, and he has managed to complete and passed the ECDL computer course, but at the print shop, Mr Roach also does loads of printing stuffs for the prison, stuffs like letter headed paper, memos, stickers, envelopes and loads of other printing jobs, he uses the help of another prisoner called Dave that comes from D block, but Matthew has been told by Mr Roach and chief O'Reilly that he can start the cleaning job that is now available at that section, the previous guy that was doing the job would be leaving in another two weeks because he's been given an early release for good behaviour, his name is Stephen, he was doing two years for drug possession for sale and supply, he used to be a taxi driver, he was caught with about four hundred grams of cocaine in his taxi, Stephen told Matthew that he told the police that he was oblivious of the drugs in his car when he was stopped in Dublin during routine checks one evening by the police, he said he told them that a passenger must have forgotten the package that contained the drugs in his car, but dying minute before his trial, his solicitor advised him that he has discussed with the prosecutor and he has been advised that if he plead guilty, he would get a suspended sentence since it was his first offence, so he changed his plea and pleaded guilty, but he was gobsmacked when the sitting judge sentenced him to four years suspending two years, but he also said his solicitor told him after his sentence that if he had pleaded not guilty and gone to trial and found guilty, he would have gotten ten years because of the quantity of the drugs found in his car that is worth over ten thousand euro, so he consoled himself that he's only doing two years and not ten years, he's on the same wing and first landing with Matthew, they play scrabble together sometimes, and his wife comes to visit him with their daughter almost every week since his incarceration, but now that he's about to get out, he said he can't wait to leave the prison precinct and finally reunite with his wife and daughter. Matthew was looking forward not only to start his new job, but also to see the governor of the prison at chief O'Reilly's office to discuss what John the daddy devil told him about killing his wife when he gets out, Matthew had confided in Mr Roach four days earlier immediately after completing the computer course, and he told Matthew that he would discuss it with chief O'Reilly that has his office beside him, and later that day they both discussed with Matthew that they would arrange for the governor to see him for them to decide on how they can stop John from hurting or killing his wife when he gets out, Matthew couldn't wait in apprehension to know how they would stop John that is very adamant about his despicable mission, he wonders if they are going to put a secret cancelled recorder on him to get the confession off John to use to prosecute him or will they just prosecute him, he's been ruminating about this for the past four days, well he thought again that he has done his own part by telling them, whatever happens it won't be his fault. Ten minutes after, he was in chief O'Reilly's office with Mr Roach, one of the three governors of the prison and also with one other person who they introduced to him as superintendent Browne, a superintendent of police, he was in casual wears, a jeans and t-shirt, whom first thanked Matthew for bringing the information to them, Matthew looked at them in jittery and worried what might happen if John finds out he ratted on him, something told him that he must be very stupid to have not shut up his mouth and mind his own business, but another thought came to his mind that he has gotten himself into it this far, and it was too late to back out.

Chapter Nine

Mission Stop Daddy Devil

Superintendent Browne stood in one of the meeting rooms with three other undercover police officers at Clontarf police station, on a white board on the wall was the picture of John Dunne the daddy devil in the middle of two other pictures of missing people believed to have been murdered by him which is the picture of his ex-father in-law and his ex-wife's best friend, the reason for the meeting was due to the information given by Matthew about John's contemptible revenge lethality pursuit to kidnap and kill his ex-wife after his release from prison in another four months. Superintendent Browne told them that they have to start investigating and monitoring were John will be going to when he's released from prison, he also told them to investigate his closed associate that he's still communicating with, he also advised that they need to monitor the movement of his ex-wife in other to keep her safe from the attack, he said he would arrange to get in touch with John ex-wife Cathy, to let her know that her life might be in danger after John's release from prison, in other to let her know that the police will do their best to stop John and put him back behind bars. The police have listened to the calls John makes on daily basis to his father, but there is no discussion of him committing any crime, his father is the only person he calls from the prison phone and he's the only person that comes almost every week to visit him in prison, and they've not heard any discussion about is revenge pursuit. It's now been three months since Matthew started the cleaning job at the print shop, he comes there mostly at the first prison unlock between 9:30am and 12pm, he sweeps the two classrooms were the prisoners come in to do the computer study, he also cleans the two offices used by Mr Roach and chief O'Reilly, and also cleans the corridors and the kitchen, he also mobs all the floors after finish sweeping it, then finally empties all the bins. He has been given kudos several times by Mr Roach and chief O'Reilly for doing the job better and cleaner than the previous prisoners that was doing it in the past, there were sometimes he went and clean their offices and there was a concealed video camera in the office to monitor him if he would take or steal something like the pack of cigarettes intentionally placed on the table by chief O'Reilly in his office, or to see if he'll take the pile of money on Mr Roach's table, or to see if he'll try to make a phone call from the telephone on the office table, but what Matthew does is just clean the two offices, empty the bins and out he goes, so; he has earn the trust of this two officers, and most of the time Mr Roach gives him a park of cigarette to buy stuffs in the prison shop, but there are loads of other advantages Matthew gets from working at the print shop and for his civility for the officers, he has access to the laminating sheets used for laminating photos, so what he does is, he takes photos from other prisoners on B Block that doesn't come to the print shop to laminate it for them, and the prisoners gives the laminated photos to their families when they come to visit them, they also collect ordinary photos sent to them by their families which they give to Matthew to laminate for them, but Matthew charges one pack of cigarette to laminate five photos, most times in one week, he ends up laminating twenty photos and gets four parks of cigarettes, he doesn't have to pay any money at the print shop to laminate the photos for the prisoners because the laminating sheets at the print shop is always replaced by Mr Roach when it's about to finish, Matthew also do the premier league betting game for football in England which each prisoner that wants to participate puts one park of 20 cigarettes as a bet and complete the form given to them by the prisoner in charge of the bet, which is Ronnie Clark in B Block, the same guy that helped Matthew to speak to Paddy to desist from attacking him when he left the kitchen job, it's a weekly bet, Ronnie gives out the form for the fixtures on Mondays to all participants, and everyone has to fill out their predictions of the team that they think would win the march or if it's going to be a draw, and hand back the form to Ronnie before the deadline which is a day before the first march kick off, which is most of the time on a Thursday, because the first march kick off is normally on a Friday, but Ronnie has to put in the predictions of every participants on a sheet of A4 paper and then make several copies and give one copy each to each participant for them to be able to use to monitor the score and for them to know which participant got the highest point after all the marches for that week has been played and the winner can then claim their price, which is the pack of cigarettes put in by the other prisoners, but Ronnie goes in for free because he's the organizer, so if it's twenty participants, the winner gets nineteen packs of cigarettes, so every participants is always looking forward to the game from the first march kick-off to the last march which is normally played on Sunday evening, Matthew has won the price twice in the past four months, which he takes to the prison shop and buys the things he wants like boxers, socks, good quality peanuts and chocolates, he believes it's a good investment, not withstanding that after putting in cigarettes week after weeks and he doesn't win, but by the time he wins, he wins nineteen packs of cigarettes, so winning twice in four months is thirty eight parks, which works out as investing sixteen parks of cigarettes to make thirty eight parks of cigarettes, so that's a gain of twenty two packs of cigarettes for him, he also participate in the same game done at D block which is organised by another prisoner in that wing called Dave who walks with Matthew at the print shop, he helps Mr Roach out with the printing with Matthew, and they have become very good friends, he hands in the form for the fixtures to Matthew at the print shop and he collects it from him and also gives Matthew the completed sheet of all the predictions of other participants including Dave himself before the first march kick off, and Dave is very good in predicting the right outcome of the matches, so; he gets to win the price once every two months not wit standing he has nothing to lose as he goes in for free as the organiser, but the number of participants in D block with Dave is not much, they are about thirteen prisoners because another prisoner organises the same betting game on D Block who most of the prisoners prefers to participate in, but in B Block it is only Ronnie that organises the bet, Matthew has also won twice in the past three months that he has been doing the game with Dave, and Dave brings his winnings to him at the print shop, so with the packs of cigarettes he gets from doing the game and doing the laminated pictures for other prisoners, there was a time he was able to save up forty two packs of cigarettes which he kept with Mr Roach at the print shop, because it's not save for him to keep the pack of cigarettes in his cell because most of the time during the unlocks before he comes back from the print shop or from school, his cell is always already unlocked by the officers on his landing, and he has discovered several times that his cell had been ransacked and this always happened a day after he had just won the packs of cigarettes for the soccer game for that week, also, there was a time a prisoner asked him to laminate forty five pictures and gave him eight packs of cigarettes instead of nine because he gave him a discount for doing loads of pictures, a day after, when he came back from the print shop he discovered that his cell had been ransacked, and whenever he discovers that his cell has been ransacked, he knows that some other prisoners had come looking for the packs of cigarettes, not withstanding that sometimes the officers search cells to detect if any prisoner is hiding contra band stuffs like hooch, a locally made alcoholic drink, or shiv, which is a homemade like weapon normally used by prisoners to hurt other prisoners, or officers come looking for drugs, but Matthew knows when it's an officer that came to search his cell, because the cell would be completely turned upside down, and the officers just don't go searching a cell, there has to be a concrete reason or based on information that the prisoner has something illegal before prison officer goes searching the prisoner's cell, and for the fact that Matthew has a good relationship with the officers and serves as a role model prisoner with no bad record, the officers won't be looking to search his cell, they've only searched his cell once due to a wrong information given by another officer, because Matthew gave the officer a letter to give to Dave in D Block, the guy that works with Matthew at the print shop, the reason for the letter was because Matthew discovered that he had won the premier league betting game for that week after the last game on that Sunday, Dave didn't come to the print shop the previous Friday, but Matthew saw him last at the print shop when Dave gave him the copy of the betting of all the prisoners at D block, that participated for that weekend on Thursday, when Matthew asked Mr Roach why Dave didn't come to the print shop that Friday, he told Matthew that Dave said he was not feeling okay, so Matthew thought Dave won't be coming again on the following Monday, so Matthew wrote in the letter that he discovered that he has won the trophy and said in the letter that Dave should try and come with his trophy the next day, the officer that Matthew gave the letter to on B Block, instead of the officer delivering the letter to Dave when he got to D Block, he went straight to the two officers on Dave's landing to show them the letter, because Dave has a bad record in the prison because he was caught with one stick of cannabis and a bottle of hooch for personal use in the past, the officer thought the trophy meant something else like drugs, so; the officers rummage through Dave's cell, searching it thoroughly to see if they can find any contra band, Dave was shocked, and later that evening on that Sunday when Matthew came back from the yard, he discovered that his cell too had been ransacked by the officers, Dave later came with Matthew's winnings to the print shop the next day and warned Matthew never again to send such letter to him, and also told Matthew that the officers later asked him that evening after ransacking his cell to explain the meaning of the trophy Matthew wrote on the letter, he said he started laughing and told them about how Matthew had won the football betting for that weekend and entitle to the pack of cigarettes, that the trophy meant the packs of cigarettes Matthew had won, and he immediately pointed to the packs of cigarettes on the single chair in his cell and told them that *"that's the trophy"* he said the three officers looked at one another in utter dismay, because before the search they were absolutely certain that something illicit was definitely going on between him and Matthew and were determined that they were going to crack it *"we're watching you"* he said one of them said to him pointing his finger in gesticulation at him as they left his cell.

Two weeks later, four prisoners sat in the common room, each of them on a single plastic chair playing scrabble, there were five other prisoners playing snooker on two snooker tables, Matthew and Amuda has played scrabble several times in the past, when Matthew won the first six games, they both agreed that before the start of the game, Amuda gets fifty points as a head start, but Matthew still wins the game, sometimes he allows Amuda to have hundred points head start before the game, but most of the time Matthew still ended up winning the game, but today, Amuda is pissed up with Matthew's wife, because the money his elder sister sent to her bank account for her to bring down to the prison and for her to give to the prison officer at the reception to be deposited into Amuda's account for him to buy some stuffs that he needed in the prison shop as not been deposited in his account because Matthew's wife has not come to the prison since she received the money, and for the past three weeks, whenever he ask Matthew when his wife would be coming to visit, he would tell him at the weekend, and she has not turned up, but what Matthew hasn't said to Amuda is that his wife already told him that he has used the three hundred and fifty euro to balance up the house rent for that month, and doesn't have the money, so this afternoon with the way things are, Matthew has to find a way to pay Amuda the money, so what he decided was that he would give him the twenty nine packs of cigarettes in his possession which is valued at two hundred and ten Euros, and then would ask him to give him about another two or three weeks to pay the balance, so that was what he did, and he told his wife not to worry about the money that he has paid the money to Amuda, but he just wants her to bring his children to visit him, but his wife still refused to come down to the prison to see him, and also refused to reply to his letters as well. The next day during the second lockout, Matthew sat on a chair at a table in Mr Roach office, sitting at the other side of the table was a slim lady about five feet eight inches tall, her name is Breda, she had started working in that section of the prison for the past two weeks as a probationer officer, the officer that advise and help prisoners that are about to be released from the prison on how to gain employment, or how to get ongoing therapy if they need one, or advise them on how to get training or complete ongoing training outside the prison after release, she has come to know Matthew as a role model prisoner because she has heard about his impeccable record in the prison from other prison officers, she believes also like most officers that he is not a career criminal but naive of the actions he took that got him incarcerated, as they sat at her desk that was moved into Mr Roach's office two weeks earlier by Matthew and Dave the day she started at that section, for her to be able to have an office to come back to after going to see prisoners on the landings, Breda advised Matthew to look after himself and not to worry too much about his wife, Breda had just helped Matthew to place a call to his wife from the telephone in the office and his wife didn't answer her phone after three calls, he was in tears as he told Breda, she consoled him again. *"Matthew, you are a good man, this things happens when you are in this kind of situation, you need to be strong for your children,"* she emotionally said *"yes I know, I have to be strong for my children, but it's just that it's not easy when she's not picking my calls and not allowing me to talk to my children"* he replied as tears trickle out of his eyes, she held his hand, her eyes well up with tears as she looked into his eyes, she felt the huge temptation to hug him, but something came up in her mind that she should comport herself, so; she released his hand, sat upright *"Matthew if you need anything that I can help you with, please let me know"* she said to him.

A knock came on the door as she stood in the kitchen, it was going to about 4pm, Cathy, John ex-wife puts the glass of water she was drinking from on the dining table, she is in her early thirties, about five feet, eight inches tall, and has a model body, John the daddy devil used to call her sexy when they used to be together and in good terms, because she has a ginger hair that makes her looks unique and very attractive, but now she calls her a bitch, Cathy went to the door, she looked through the door eye spy, she could see two people at the door, a woman and a man, not withstanding that they were dressed in mufti, she knew immediately that it was the police, as she was thinking *"why would the police be knocking on her door?"* she has been on the social welfare for over four months now, and she has not gotten involved in any dodgy or illicit deal, another knock on the door brought her out of her imagination and she subconsciously opened the door *"good evening, you must be Cathy Doyle"* the female police officer asked *"yes"* Cathy replied *"how can I help you?"* she asked, *"can we come inside, I am inspector Julie, and this is my colleague, inspector Barry"* the female officer said and showed Cathy the police badge she brought out of her jacket and inspector Barry immediate showed her his own badge as well. *"Sure you can come in"* Cathy immediately replied, and stepped out of the door way for them to come into the house. Ten minutes later, they were on their way out after telling her that they got concrete information that John would be coming after her after he's released from prison in another two months, they told her that he confided in another prison inmates that he killed her father and her best friend, they told her that they would be on his tail to make sure that he doesn't hurt her, and also to try and get him to lead them to where he put or buried the body of Cathy's father and her best friend, they gave her a number to reach them in case of any emergency or if she has any information about John.

Two days after the visit from the police, Cathy was talking to Chris Murphy, her childhood friend, a top professional martial arts specialist, she has just told him about her predicament and how she needed to learn his skill for self-defence, as they stood beside the four square ring in one of the rooms in his house, Chris has agreed to train her five days a week for her to be ready in three months that John would be out, but he has told her to be ready for the hard work she needs to put in the training if she really wants to be ready within that three months, she promised to put in all her best in the training, and she did, learning all the self-defence stuffs in kickboxing, wrestling, judo, taekwondo and boxing, by the end of the tenth week of training, Chris was so amazed by her new acquired skill and determination that he said to her *"Cathy you are definitely ready, hundred percent"* Cathy busted into tears *"I have to Chris, unless he's going to kill me, if there is anything else I need to learn, please teach me, please,"* she said as she cried again. Two weeks after, John walked out of the Midlands prison, it was around 4pm, waiting outside the prison gate beside a car has he walked out of the final gate and exited the prison precinct was two of his associate, one of them took the two bags with his stuffs from him and opened the car boot and put it inside, twenty-five minutes after, they were seated in a pub drinking beer *"Snake, when was the last time you saw that bitch?"* John asked. *"I saw her just yesterday, I have been keeping tab on her since you told me to, I don't know why you stopped us from taking her out"* John looked into his face frantically *"you know why Snake, because I want to see her scream, now it will soon be time that bitch screams, I can't wait, but we'll do it next week, in another six days, I have a plan,"* he said and sinisterly smiled at the two guys. Immediately the prison authorities notified superintendent Browne a day before John's released from the prison that he was going to be released, he told the same cops that went to see Cathy about John's mission to assassinate her to inform her of the new development, so, they called her that same day to tell her about John's release and also told her to meet them up at a house twenty miles away from the city in order to give her more information on what the police have planned to do.

That evening of the same day, Cathy was seated at the table with the two officers and superintendent Browne, who extended his hand in handshake to introduce himself *"Good evening"* Cathy reciprocated *"I believe you've met inspector Julie Kilmurray, and inspector Barry Foley"* he said to her looking at the two officers. *"Yes I have"* she replied and extended her hand to greet the two officers. *"I understand you've been told that John, your ex-husband will be released tomorrow from prison, and you've also been informed of his plans of coming after you"* he asked her. *"Yes I am fully aware of that sir"* Cathy replied, *"well we have a plan not only to stop him from hurting you, but also to nab him to make sure he pays for your father and friend's disappearance, but we really need your help,"* says superintendent Brown, looking from Cathy to the two officers who nodded their head at Cathy to agree with superintendent Browne that they do need her help *"please I am the one that needs your help to stop this monster from killing me, anything you want from me or you want me to do that can help to put this monster away for life, please tell me, I am ready to do it"* Cathy replied *"Okay"* says superintendent Browne, *"we have a plan to insert into your body a microchip GPS tracker that can help us to locate your movement or were about, we also have plans that you contact us every one hour from getting off from sleep in the morning until when you are about to go to bed in the night, are you okay with that"* chief Browne asked, *"where are you going to insert the chip?"* Cathy asked curiously as she looked from superintendent Brown to the two officers, *"it's a very small microchip, like the size of a grain of rice, it can be inserted in your thumb, and it's done within twenty seconds, and no health issues or any adverse consequence, it's just to use the chip to locate your whereabouts when we don't hear from you at expected time"* officer Julie said to Cathy as she looked from officer Barry and superintendent Browne who nodded to Cathy to assure her that there's no problem with her getting the chip inserted. *"Okay, I'll do it, I'll do anything that can get that bastard pay for what he did to me and my family and get him locked up for life"* she said. That same day around 8pm, she was lying down on a stretcher in one of the rooms in the same house that the meeting was held earlier on, a doctor that works for the police was called immediately by superintendent Browne to come down to the house and insert the microchip into Cathy's thumb after she agreed for the chip to be inserted. It took just about ten seconds for the chip to be inserted into her skin just above her thumb, the doctor used a syringe used for vaccination to insert the microchip, they showed her how her whereabouts can be monitored on a tablet computer, they took her on a walk of about thirty meters away from the house to text the chip, she smiled as her new location was shown to her on a small hand held computer device.

The night before John was due to leave Midlands prison, Matthew sat with John on a chair in his cell, between them was another single chair which they placed the scrabble board on, playing scrabble, John was restless, he barely concentrated on the game, he drank from the locally made alcohol hooch from a plastic cup, he had earlier offered Matthew the drink, but he refused because he's very conscious of what he eats and drinks, he has heard that the process that the local drink is made from can be very unhygienic and can cause serious sickness, mostly diarrhoea, most of the time during processing the drink, the drink is hidden from the officers, it is stored in the bucket used to mop the landings, or hidden in the black inlet for water in one of the toilets on the landings were everyone goes and pee or take shit during unlock when the cells are locked, but John insisted that he must have a drink with him on his last night, so Matthew drank almost half of the hooch from the plastic cup John handed to him, that night John bragged about his hideous plan about how he's going to torture his ex-wife *"you'll be watching the news of that bitch disappearance on the TV very soon Matthew"* says John, he said his associates are stalking her to know where she is when he's ready to give them the go ahead to kidnap her *"do you believe the bitch moved house six months ago, but my boys know where the bitch moved to, I can't wait to set her ablaze and watch her scream, and you also know what Matthew?"* *"What?"* Matthew asked with a poker face smiling, "I am going to torture her for at least three days before I end it for her, I want her to scream and beg for her life many times and for days before I finally end it for her, ooh I can't wait to get started" shaking his head and clasping his hand apprehensively as he spoke, from the way he wrongly placed the tiles on the scrabble board, Matthew knew that he was drunk from the hooch, *"I like you Matthew, I think I should give you a number"* he tore a piece of paper from the notepad booklet used to record the points from the scrabble game and wrote a mobile number on it and handed it to Matthew. *"You will get out one day Matthew, you call me"* he said. *"I'll definitely call the daddy devil,"* Matthew said smiling, he felt tipsy from the hooch as well, it tasted like orange juice, he hasn't drank anything alcoholic in the past three years before that night. The next morning Matthew saw John for the last time when he was going to the print shop. When Matthew resumed at the print shop and was moping the kitchen floor, Mr Roach approached him to ask him if he has any new information about John's hideous mission, he told Mr Roach about what John told him the night before to let him know that he's still excited to carry out his devious act, he also gave him the mobile number John gave to him to reach him when he's released from prison, Mr Roach thanked him *"you're a good man Matthew"* he said *"I will give this number to superintendent Browne"* he said as he walked away.

It was going to 9pm, John sat in the passenger sit of a car at the car park behind Dumbo pub the day after he got out of prison, he was smoking cannabis, there were about nine other cars at the car park, it was not a busy night at the pub because it was Wednesday night, just about eleven people in the pub including two of John associates, one of the two guys was Snake, he was speaking to Glenn, the owner of the pub in a corner, he invited Snake into his private office, Glenn is in his early sixties, a tall big guy, about six feet three inches tall, he's pot belly, Glenn is the guy most bad guys comes to when it comes to looking for information, he has ears everywhere in the city and knows how to look after his informants *"the police are watching that bitch, I think they know John will come after her, my information is that they put a microchip on her thumb to be able to find her if she goes missing"* Glenn said, *"they were talking to her two days ago, you really need to be careful"* Snake nodded his head to show that he got the message *"where is John, I thought he said he's coming with you?"* asked Glenn, *"He's waiting in the car at the car park at the back, it's part of being careful, he doesn't want to come in here because he doesn't know who'll be here"* Snake replied, *"okay, just tell him to lay low for a while, well I think I'll just go and tell him myself"* Glenn said. Two minutes after, Glenn came out to the car park and walked to the car were Snake, John and the other guy seated at the back seat talking, John stepped out of the car immediately Glenn got to the car and hugged him, they both smiled *"I told Snake, you have to back off Cathy for now, he's been watched by the cops, that's the bad news, but the good news is, I think I know how you can get Casey"* he said *"that bastard set me up Glenn, and after I was locked up, he started fucking Cathy, it's like they both set me up together, he needs to pay with his life"* John said quietly with the look of utmost rage obvious on his face *"you just give me twenty four hours, and I let you know where exactly he is, okay?"* Glenn said *"okay, I have waited thirty six months already, why not another twenty four hours"* John said smiling *"now you leave that bank job information for me to finalise, remember the take is about two million, and I don't want the hit on you to fuck it up"* Glenn said, *"okay Glenn, if you can handle the arrangement alone, that's fine by me, you just tell me when you want my boys to do the job, I mean give me two days' notice before the job, for me to arrange the boys"* John said, *"okay then"* Glenn replied, *"remember, no discussion over the phone, and in two weeks we'll be ready to go"* says Glenn again. *"Okay"* John replied, and Glenn walked back to the pub, while Snake started the car, they were on their way to a farm yard, their secret hideout were they planned to bring Cathy after she's kidnapped, *"Glenn said the cops are watching that bitch, he said they put a microchip in her thumb to track her were about if she goes missing, I think we should just put a bullet in that bitch's head"* Snake said looking back and forth from John to the road as he spoke to him, *"no, no , no, that bitch has to beg for her life, she has to suffer, okay, we'll cut out the thumb then, yes that's what we'll do and we'll put more men on the job if you think you and Froggy can't do the job alone"* John said as he looked from Snake to the other guy sitting at the back seat of the car, *"Froggy, what do you think?"* John asked as he looked at the guy sitting at the back seat, *"I think, that bitch needs to suffer before she goes, we'll get ready to remove the microchip immediately we put her in the van before we bundle her to the farm yard, I think we'll need just one more guy, Mark has to come with us then"* Froggy replied, *"You see, that bitch has to scream"* John said again to Snake as he patted him on the shoulder laughing. They arrived at the farm yard twenty-five minutes later, a bulky guy in his early thirties, about five foot eleven inches tall opened the door to the house, he smiled as he saw them, he hugged John *"Hello boss, good to see you"* he said. *"Where is that bitch?"* John asked him as he released him from the hug, ooh!!! *"she's down in the hole"* he pointed towards the kitchen as he spoke, John, Snake and Froggy followed Mark to the kitchen, he pushed the table supposedly the dining table to a side, removed a rug covering the door to an underground basement, he opened the door, the four of them climbed down on the ladder and went through a corridor which is just about nine meters long and three metres wide, Mark unlocked a door, right there in a cage that is six metre long and four metres wide and with the height of seven metres was Lucy, Cathy's best friend, sitting on the chair by a single bed, she is in her early thirties, she was in a short jeans pant and a blue tea shirt, she looked malnourish, there was a small section in the cage which had a tap, bucket and a latrine basin on the floor, she's been there for over a year since she's been reported missing by her father while John was in prison *"surprise!!! Surprise!!!I am back bitch"* John said to her as he moved closer to the cage looking into her eyes. *"Please John, please, please, please"* Lucy begged and sobbed, *"I don't want to die, please let me go, I won't tell anyone about you, I promise, I swear, please I am begging you, I have really suffered"* she cried *"No bitch, I'll send you off soon, I'll put you out of your misery soon, but it's not going to be easy for you, so; be ready"* he laughed as he spoke looking at the other three men as they all laughed as well *"and you know what?"* he looked back to Lucy in the face again *"Cathy will be joining you soon, she's going to watch you scream, before she gets it as well"* he said as the three guys in the room laughed again, and just then Snake's phone rang, he answered the call *"he's here with me, okay"* he said and handed his phone to John *"it's Glenn, he said he knows where Casey is hiding out."*

Ben Foley walked into Clontarf police station, it was going to be 9am, he is in early sixties, a tall guy about six feet, he was casually dressed in shirt and trouser with a sweater and black shoe, he's Lucy's father, he has heard of John's released from prison the previous day, he came to see superintendent Browne to know if there is any information about his daughter's body, because it has gotten to a point within the past one year that he has come to accept that Lucy is dead, he's been very unsettled and more determined to locate her body or remains in other to be able to give her a befitting burial, he has come to tell superintendent Browne that he wants to go and look for John to confront and beg him to tell him where Lucy body is or to beg him to tell him what he has done with her body. He went to the front desk immediately at the entrance of the station, *"please can I see superintendent Browne"* he asked the two officers, one of the officers knew him very well because Ben was almost in the station every day for six months when Lucy first went missing, so; he the officer pointed towards one of the desk in the room where superintendent Browne was sitting talking on his mobile phone, he went past three other desk over to his desk, superintendent Browne saw him coming, so; he immediately pointed to the two available seats at the other side of his desk as a signal for him to sit down, *"I'll call you later"* he said to the person on the phone, and extended his hand in handshake to Ben *"please sit down"* he said pointing to the two single chairs at the other side of his desk *"I was looking to call you today, I know you must have heard of John's released from prison because it was on the news two days ago that he would be released yesterday"* superintendent Browne said *"yes, but still, you should have called me personally to tell me, if you have forgotten about my daughter, I haven't,"* says Ben. *"Of cause, I haven't forgotten about your daughter, and I apologize for not notifying you of John's released, but I was waiting for us to get a concrete information that will interest you before I call you because we are putting a surveillance on John to see how to get information about your daughter's whereabouts"* he said again *"I am thinking of going to confront him to beg him to just tell me where the body of my daughter is"* Ben said, *"No no please don't do that because we have a plan that might help us this time around to crack the case, please just give us some couple of weeks or even days"* says superintendent Browne. *"Okay, I'll be expecting your call"* Ben said, stood up and left.

Casey O'Donnell pulled the handle to the microwave to open it, he brought out the crack cocaine out of the microwave. He is in his late twenties, a slightly built man, about five foot and nine inches tall, he was in white singlet and pant, he just got out of bed from having sex with a lady called Sabrina, most of the time he has a junkie that comes home with him to his trailer because they don't have money to pay for their drug supplies, he gave the lady a bit of the crack cocaine, and also gave her the pipe and lighter to use to smoke it, they both drag the drug from the pipe one after the other, Sabrina is a young skinny lady in her early twenties, Casey has brought her back to his trailer with his car from the city about six times now when she couldn't afford the money to pay for her drug supply, John's ex-wife, Cathy was also one of the women that has been taken advantage of by Casey because of her addiction to cocaine use in the past, but what Casey doesn't know is that a day before this particular trip, Sabrina was talking to Glenn about Casey, and she was offered one thousand euro to give him the location of the trailer, which was parked in a secluded mountain side about thirty minutes' drive away from the city, but because there is a signpost on the major road that gives the direction to Trim castle which the mountain where Casey's trailer is located is two minutes' drive from, Sabrina was able to give Glenn the right description of locating the trailer, she also told him when Casey would be at the trailer which was this particular night they were smoking the drug, the time was going to about 11pm. Snake, Froggy and John were sitting in the car, Snake at the wheel driving while John sat at the passenger seat, John was seriously agitated and anxious as well, the flashback of when he was arrested by three undercover policemen that cornered him that night before he entered his car where Cathy was waiting for him, because Casey disappearance from the scene that night immediately aroused John's suspicion that he set him up, which Glenn later confirmed to him through a policeman that is on Glenn payroll, he said Casey gave John up as a bargain to get a good deal not to go to jail for peddling drugs when he was arrested a week earlier before John's arrest because John came to buy one hundred and twenty grams of cocaine from him to be smoked by himself, Cathy and Lucy, they were all addicted to drugs then, and he was even more angry when just after four months in prison when he heard from another prisoner through Glenn that his wife and Lucy were sleeping with Casey for free drugs, and his wife then wrote him a letter to tell him that she was leaving him with the divorce papers for him to sign, which he did immediately as he was very angry, and when he called Lucy from prison, she told him to fuck off, that he should forget about Cathy, since then he had his plans to kill Cathy, Lucy and Casey, he first wanted to do it from prison, he had access to a mobile phone supplied to him by one of the prison officers that he used to communicate with his associate like Snake and Glenn, he wanted Cathy to be there to witness the torture and death of Lucy and Casey, but Cathy he planned to torture and kill himself, but when Snake and Froggy planned the kidnap over a year earlier when John instructed them from prison, they planned to kidnap Cathy and Lucy together to be taken to the farm yard, but only Lucy turned up at the location they planned to take both of them, that was the reason why John told them to put Lucy in the cage till he returns from prison, now as they walked stealthily to Casey's trailer, it was very dark, but they could see a bulb light from the trailer about eighty metres away, and could see the shadow of Casey's car, when they got to the trailer, they could hear Casey's voice as he was talking on the phone *"I'll come and get it tomorrow, I'll call when am on the way"* he said and finished the call, immediately Casey finished the call, Snake brought out a pistol from his pocket, held it in his right hand and kicked the trailer door, it went flying because the door was unlocked, he immediately jumped in with John and Froggy, by this time Casey was going for his shot gun that was under the bed, but it was too late, Snake fired a shot to his left leg, Sabrina screamed from where she was sitting on the bed as she dropped the pipe she was smoking from *"shut the fuck up bitch!!!"* John shouted at Sabrina, Froggy plunged the needle with the sedative drug into Casey's neck as he was whining from the pain from the gun shot and holding his left leg, he looked at John in tremor *"what do you want from me"* he screamed, John spat on his face *"you fucking rat, I have come to play with you"* John replied, Casey passed out from the sedative drug *"I'll go and bring the car closer"* Snake said as he walked out of the trailer, ten minutes later, he and Froggy put Casey in the boot of the car, while John escorted Sabrina to the car, *"if you say anything about this to anyone or the cops, I am going to find you and cut your throat,"* John said to threaten her, she nodded her head apprehensively as he spoke to let him know she understood what he meant. They let her off at the city near her house, and drove to the farm yard with Casey that was still unconscious in the boot of the car. Cathy came out of the bathroom in a white towel after taking a shower, it was going to 10pm, she had been very busy since morning from martial arts training for self-defence, which she has been training vigorously since she was told about John's vindictive mission, she picked up her mobile phone from the coffee table in the sitting room, went to the window, pulled the window blind aside to the left a bit to look outside the bungalow house that is a two bedroom house, she's been restless and unsettle since John's released from prison and checks or look around anywhere she goes being extra ordinarily cautious, knowing that her life is in danger, the neighbourhood is a quiet neighbourhood, she just finished six months therapy recuperation from drug addiction a week before inspector Julie and Barry knocked on her door for the first time on the day they gave her the information about Johns hideous mission, after finishing therapy she made up her mind to stay off drugs forever, she got a call from a solicitor while she was still receiving therapy after her grandmother died to tell her that she willed the house to her since she is the only child of her late mother who died when she was just eight years old and with no sibling, she had moved into the house immediately after finishing therapy hoping that she has started a new life and now she has to deal with John madness again, she saw the message from inspector Julie checking on her to know if she's okay and asking her to ring in to confirm that she's alright, this she does every hour from 8am when she gets up from bed in the morning to the last hour before going to bed, that was the arrangement since John released from prison at the meeting the police had with her after inserting the microchip tracker, Cathy rang her to tell her that she's okay and about to go to bed for the night.

The next morning when Casey came back to consciousness, he discovered that he is tied up to a chair, his hands tied to the back of the single chair he was sitting on, and his legs tied up as well, he looked around the small room which is six metre long and four metres wide, there was no one in the room, he felt serious pain on his left leg, he had the flashback of the gun shot to his leg, he froze as Mark came into the room, *"you bastard, you're back"* says Mark, then John came into the room, looked at Casey ominously, he walked up to him, crouch at his front holding him by the throat *"you piece of shit, you set me up, and you enjoyed fucking my wife while you sent me to prison"* he furiously said as he spat on his face, Mark brought out a pistol and handed it to John. *"No, he's not going that way, he's not going out the easy way, I am going to send this guy to hell by burning him alive, I am going to douse him with petrol and light him up and watch him scream"* he said angrily looking at Mark's face and then over to Casey's, who glanced back at him apprehensively. *"If you want to do it that way, then we'll have to move him out of here, we can't do that in the room"* says Mark, looking from John to Casey, who looked at them in utter jittery *"please John, am sorry, please don't kill me"* Casey begged and cried, *"you are not going to die now moron"* John said to him as he punched him in the face again, *"I want to see Cathy's face when you burn!!!"* he shouted at him, enraged, spat on his face again and then punched him in the face again sending Casey with the chair tumbling on his back to the floor, Casey squeals in agony with his face covered in blood. Mark went over and pulled him up with the chair not knowing that the rope used to tie his hand to the back of the chair has loosen up, but Casey pretended that the rope was still firmly tied to his hand to the chair as he continued to squeal *"You, Snake and Froggy must get that bitch here tonight!!!"* he screamed at Mark as they both walked out of the room, I can't wait to get the party started.

Chapter Ten

Trip to The Farmyard

A white van was parked round the right corner of the street that Cathy lives, about sixty meters from the bus stop that Cathy gets off the bus and walks another ten minutes to her house, it was going to 9pm, it was dark and raining. One kilometres away, Mark sat inside a forty sitter passenger commercial bus at the back row watching Cathy that sat at the front, five rows away from him, he had watched Cathy go into a grocery shop forty minutes earlier, and stealthily followed her and quietly talking on his mobile phone to Froggy and Snake, giving them the information of her movement, they were first parked at the alleyway not far from the shopping mall that Cathy did her shopping earlier on, they knew Cathy would walk past the alleyway to get to the bus stop, but it was a busy night since it was Friday night and many people were present on the alleyway that also came from the shopping mall, there was also a police car parked on the alleyway with a police officer sitting in the driver's seat talking on a mobile phone, so they skipped the plan to snap her at that location, and decided that Mark should get on the bus with her, then they'll figure out another location that'll be safe for them to grab her successfully, so they discovered that the new location that they are now parked at, that is quiet at this time of the night to kidnap her. Cathy was dressed in a blue track suit and white runners, because she had gone to Chris earlier that day to do her normal day to day martial art training, but the information Glenn gave Snake was that she shopped at that grocery store every Friday night, so they waited in the van from 7pm that day until Cathy arrived at around 8pm, Snake immediately told Mark to follow her into the store because she doesn't know Mark, but she knows Snake and Froggy as Johns boys and if she sees them, it'll blow there cover and jeopardise their mission. After coming down from the bus, Cathy walked with her hand bag slung on her left shoulder and held two nylon bags full of groceries with each hand, she looked around, most especially at the back as she walked hurriedly to get home, she saw Mark, she immediately recollected seeing him on the bus seating at the back, *"he must be following me"* she thought as she immediately increased her pace, walking faster and looking behind her and then to the front, but as she made the right turn into the final street to her house, Snake seated at the driver seat saw her from the left side mirror of the van *"the bitch is here"* he quietly said to Froggy that was sitting at the back of the van as Cathy got to the van *"now"* Snake mumbled as they both jumped out, Snake hit her on the head with the butt of his gun, while Froggy ready with the syringe with the sedative drug, plunged it into her neck as she fell on the floor dropping the nylon bags, but her hand bag still hung to her shoulder, they quickly picked her up and put her in the van, Froggy jumped into the van with her at the back quickly closing the door, immediately cut off the tip of the left thumb with the microchip, and quickly applied an antiseptic liquid to the thumb, and immediately bandaged it up to stop the bleeding, *"do you have it out"* Snake asked as he drove off the van, Froggy checked the piece of skin he was holding in his left hand using his right index finger to check for the microchip, he saw the chip, *"yes"* he said *"give to me"* Snake said, he gave it to him, he immediately threw it out of the window, just then a sound came from Cathy's phone in her handbag, *"what's that?"* Snake asked, Froggy quickly opened the handbag and brought out the phone that the sound came from, and could see on the screen, it was a message that says *"call me Cathy"* the message was from inspector Julie, *"it's a message from her phone"* says Froggy, *"give me that fucking phone!!!"* Snake said, he handed it over to him, he immediately threw it out of the window as he continued to drive the van. Three hours later, inspector Julie checked her phone, it was going to 12am, no message from Cathy, she called her number but it went straight into voice mail, she tried again and again, it went into voice mail, she waited another thirty minutes, she rang the number again, but was the same voice mail answer, she got the tablet computer to try and trace the microchip to know were Cathy is, the location of the microchip showed that she's about two kilometres away from her house, she immediately called inspector Barry, who was already at home sleeping, but he managed to take his mobile phone that was on the bedroom table right beside the bed and picked her call, he later met up with her at the police station, both of them got into one of the undercover police car, with inspector Barry driving, with inspector Julie holding the tablet computer and giving the directions, they followed the trace on the tablet for the microchip, tracking the trace to the front of a house about two kilometres away from Cathy's house, after managing to use a touch light to search and locate the microchip that was on the floor outside a bungalow house, they both looked flabbergasted as they looked at each other, they went to the house and pressed the doorbell twice ready waiting at alert to defend themselves from any attack that comes from the house, nobody came to the door, it was very late in the night going to 2am, they knocked on the door after waiting for five minutes, then they heard *"who is there!!!?"* a voice shouted from the house *"police"* inspector Julie replied *"what do you want?"* the voice of a lady asked, *"we just want to talk to you"* inspector Julie replied again, the lady peeped through the peephole. Inspector Julie showed her badge for her to see that it was the police, she opened the door, she was an elderly lady in her late seventies, *"is there any problem officers?"* she asked curiously and fidgeting, they both looked at her, and looked back at each other and back at her, *"is there anyone else in the house?"* inspector Julie asked, *"no, I live with my daughter, she's currently at work, she's a nurse, is there any problem with my daughter? Is she okay?"* the lady asked. *"No it's not about your daughter, please can we come in, just to have a look?"* inspector Julie said again, *"yes come in, but what are you looking for?"* the lady said as she stepped aside for them to come into the hallway, the two officers quickly looked through the two bedroom house, and went to the back garden, it took just about five minutes, they apologised to the lady and got back into the car, *"we should go straight to her house"* inspector Julie said, and drove straight to Cathy's house, on the way, inspector Julie rang Cathy's phone again, it was going straight into voice mail again, when they arrived at Cathy's house, inspector Julie jumped out of the car, ran to the door, pressed the door bell and also knocked hard on the door, but there was no answer, she went round the house trying to look through the window with a touch light *"Cathy, Cathy!!!"* he shouted, but no one answered, they both decided she was not in the house, they decided they'll have to discuss the next action to take in the morning with superintendent Browne as they drove back to the police station.

Cathy laid flat on a single bed in one of the three rooms in the basement in the farm yard, it was going to 7am in the morning, she was still unconscious from the sedative drug injected into her body the previous night during the kidnap, she was tied up with a rope to the bed, John came into the room with Mark, he turned on the switch button to the only light bulb in the room from the wall and walked aggressively to the bed, he saw that Cathy's eyes were closed, he thought she was sleeping and slapped her face *"get up bitch"* he shouted, but she was still motionless, *"why is the bitch like this"* he said to Mark looking at Cathy. *"She's still knocked out from the drug"* Mark said. John picked up the one litre plastic bottle of water on the table in the room and emptied it on Cathy's face *"get up bitch, it's time to pay for what you did to me,"* he furiously shouted again, when she didn't answer him, he slapped her on the face, Cathy sighed and passed out again, "at least you're not fucking dead now, you're not fucking going out easy" he said and looked at Mark, *"I just can't wait to get started, that bastard goes first"* pointing towards the room were Casey was locked in, *"then that bitch in the cage, but this bitch has to watch them scream before she goes"* he said fumingly and aggressively, *"but first, we show her the freezer"* he came out of the room and went to the big freezer in the corridor and opened it, there laid the dead body of Cathy's father, *"I want to see that bitch face when she sees this"* he said pointing to the dead body as he looked at Mark.

Superintendent Browne turned on his mobile phone after dressing up for work, it was going to 7am, he saw six missed call from inspector Julie, and then saw a message that says *"Cathy is gone missing, please call me"* he immediately rang her back, but the phone rang several times and went into voice mail, he left a message that he was on his way to the station. When he arrived at the station, he saw inspector Barry and Julie waiting for him, they had barely had any sleep during the night, they had been to John's apartment in the city, he was not there, they rang the mobile number they had for him, but it was not in service, they looked at one another, they have to do something, superintendent Browne said they needed to speak to Glenn, they believe Glenn might have information or heard information about the kidnap, there was an investigation about a post office robbery six months earlier that was still ongoing, and Glenn is a suspect in that robbery case notwithstanding that he has a good alibi of where he was when the robbery took place, the police believes he must have participated indirectly in the robbery, but the police have no concrete evidence to tie him to the robbery, only a tip off from a police informant that mentioned his name, so; they came to a conclusion that if he gives them a concrete information about how they can locate John, they'll cut him a deal to take him off the suspect list for the post office robbery, that was the suggestion given by superintendent Browne, and the two officer nodded in agreement to this. Twenty minutes after, the two officers were with Glen, *"why come to me, I have not talked or seen John for almost three years now"* Glenn said to inspector Julie and Barry as he sat on one sitter arm chair in his sitting room while the two officers stood opposite him, he appeared surprised to see them when he heard the doorbell and opened the door four minutes earlier, *"I only heard on the news two weeks ago that he was released from prison, you're wasting your time coming to me"* he said again. *"Well we are thinking that if you can help us to locate where he is hiding or any information about were Cathy is or taken, because we believe she has been kidnapped and is in danger, and if you can help us, we'll take you off the suspect list for the post office robbery,"* inspector Julie said. *"Well, you're not doing me a favour taking me off the list, because you're wasting your time putting me on the list in the first place, because I don't know anything about that robbery, which I have told you twice when you brought me in for questioning, and I don't have any information about John or Cathy as well, and it's another waste of your time and mine coming to speak to me about it"* says Glenn, *"I am sorry I can't help you"* he gesticulated with his hands and stood up to signal he's done talking to them, the two officers looked at each other, then back to Glenn, *"please if you hear anything about John, I believe you know how to reach us"* inspector Julie said as they left. As they drove off his property, Glenn was on the phone with Snake *"the fucking cops just left asking about John, the heat is on, I think we might need to suspend that job for now like I said"*

Superintendent Browne sitting in the office by his desk checked his wallet for the piece of paper with the mobile phone number Matthew gave him two months earlier when he last spoke to him in Midlands prison about John, but he couldn't find it, he wanted to check if it's the same number that they have on the case file for John that they have been calling and getting a message that the number is out of service, but he couldn't find the piece of paper, thirty minutes earlier, inspector Barry had rang him that they didn't get any concrete information from Glenn about John's were

- 145 -

about or Cathy's kidnap, he decided that he'll have to go and speak to Matthew again, he used his hand in gesticulation to invite inspector Barry and Julie into his office to tell them that he has to go and speak to a prisoner in Midlands prison that might help them with information about John's were about, the two officers left his office, he rang the prison to speak to chief O'Reilly to arrange a meeting to speak to Matthew, but before heading to the prison he needed to use the toilet, he was so pressed that he just quickly ran into one of the five cubicles in the toilet room and didn't turn on the switch to the florescent light in the toilet room, while using the toilet, he heard someone came in and turned on the florescent light, and overheard the person saying, *"he's on the way to Midlands prison to speak to a prisoner that can tell him where John is, you need to tell John to be careful, and I want my money unfailing before the end of today"* the person said and switched off the light again and left the toilet, he was shocked, because he recognised the voice of the person to be that of inspector Barry, he stood still, he couldn't flush the toilet, he peeped out of the cubicle to check if inspector Barry has definitely left the rest room, he discovered that he's gone, he flushed the toilet and headed straight to the prison thinking he now knows the answer to the puzzles he's been ruminating about, questions like how did the kidnappers knew that Cathy had a microchip on her thumb, he now knows that inspector Barry is the insider for this criminals, he wondered if inspector Julie is in on it as well, definitely not he thought again.

Mark stood at the front of the blackboard, trying to finish the solution to the mathematical equation Matthew gave to him to help him to solve as he doesn't understand the equation, but as usual, Mark is finding it difficult to solve, but just trying to arrive at any reasonable answer whether right or wrong he doesn't care, he just wants to get Matthew off his back, Matthew sat down and watched, he knew Mark was struggling, but he said nothing, he was the only prisoner in the class, because most other prisoners are not serious and determine as he is to finish a course that they started, Matthew's mission is to focus on completing the course successfully, Mr Roach came into the room *"hi Mark"* he said, *"please I need to get Matthew to help me out at the print shop with something very urgent if you don't mind"* he asked. *"Matthew"* Mark called as he looked at Matthew *"Mr Roach needs you, we can finish this on Tuesday"* he said, pointing to the equation on the board *"okay"* Matthew said and quickly parked his stuffs into the folder on the table. Fifteen minutes later Matthew sat on a chair talking to chief O'Reilly, Mr Roach and superintendent Browne, he handed a piece of paper with the mobile number John gave to him before he left the prison to superintendent Browne who compared it with another number on a piece of paper that he brought out of his *wallet*. *"It's a different number,"* he said, he got Matthew to ring the number from the land-line telephone in chief O'Reilly's office, the number rang several times and cut off, *"this number is active"* superintendent Browne said excitedly. *"Thank you Matthew,"* he said again, *"you're welcome sir,"* replied Matthew. Superintendent Browne stood up, *"chief, I have to quickly get back to work,"* he said to chief O'Reilly and Mr Roach and left the room. On his way back to the police station that is about one hour twenty minutes' drive from the prison, he rang a guy at the police department unit that can help him to put a trace on the mobile number Matthew had just given him, the guy told him that he'll call him back in thirty minutes to give him the location of the number *"please can you make it sooner because it's very urgent"* he said *"okay, I call you back in fifteen minutes then"* the guy replied. He decided not to divulge the new information to inspector Barry and Julie.

Cathy indistinctly opened her eyes as she tried to get up from the bed, but the rope used to tie her hands and legs to the bed hindered her from getting up, the room was dark, and she still felt lethargic from the impact of the sedative drug, she had the flashback of Snake hitting her with the butt of his handgun and being dragged into the van, she immediately felt an adrenalin rush knowing that she had been kidnapped *"help!!!, help!!!"* she shouted with a wailing sound, but she could only hear the echo of her utterance, the darkness of the room put her to reminiscent of when her father disappeared, two weeks before he went missing, she had sent a devoice letter to John in prison, and her father told her John called him from prison to reprimand him for supporting her to devoice him after getting the letter, she had told her father to get the prison to block John from calling him, and her father did just that, she remembered how her father went missing three days after that phone call from John, and also remembered how Lucy, her best friend, went missing two days after her father went missing, she tried to convince the police to believe that it was John that got them kidnapped, but after the police did their investigation, they said they couldn't get any evidence that John is linked to their disappearance, that it was even more difficult for them to charge John for their disappearance because of his good alibi of been locked away in prison while they went missing, Cathy was lucky to have missed meeting up with Lucy at the hair salon that day because they had an appointment to meet up the same day Lucy went missing, and the reason she didn't go for the appointment was because she got a call from the police to come down to the police station to get further updates on her missing father, as she came back to reality she was terrified by the dark room and thoughts going on in her head *"it's been over a year now that they've gone missing, what happened to them, how were they killed, they must definitely be dead"* she thought, *"and now I would be on the list of the missing people like them as well, John is definitely behind this"* she thought, she remembered the microchip that was implanted into her thumb, and a rush of adrenalin of how she would soon be found by the police, she picture inspector Barry and Julie and superintendent Browne on the way to rescue her, but she felt a sting and sharp pain on her left thumb, she turned her head towards her left hand towards her fingers, she felt something like a cloth or bandaged on her left thumb, why is her left thumb bandaged, has the microchip been removed, she thought, and just then, the door opened and the light from the bulb shone into her eyes, causing a serious ache to her eyes and made her to blink severally but she tried to look at the two bodies coming towards her. *"Please, please don't hurt me"* she frightfully begged, she blurrily saw Mark and John standing two foot away from the bed, John came closer to her *"you're awake bitch!!!"* he shouted, as he slapped her on the face and held her by the back of the head to race her head up and brought her face closer towards his face *"look at me bitch, it's payback time, but it's not going to be easy for you"* he dropped her head, she fell back onto the bed, *"get her up Mark!!!"* he shouted, as Mark came to untie her hands and legs from the bed, Cathy thought, this might be the opportunity to take on this monsters and escape, but John brought out a pistol from his pocket, Mark pulled her up from the bed and shove her towards John, she staggered as she tried to balance on her feet as she fell to the ground, Mark walked past them to the door, John held the pistol in his right hand from behind her to her side, poking her with the gun to get up from the floor and move, she managed to get up *"we go to that rat first"* they went into the room Casey was still sitting on the chair, John gave the pistol to Mark who stood by the door and shoved Cathy further into the room *"surprise,*

surprise" John said going over to Casey, and pulled his head up for him to see Cathy *"I brought you your slut, you see, can you see rat!!!"* punching him several times in the face *"I have been dreaming and waiting for this!!!"* John said in utter rage as he continued to punch him, Casey fell to the back on the chair as he wails in agony, Cathy started crying and begging John *"please, please, you are going to kill him"* she whimpered, but John continued to punch him, his right fist covered in blood that splatter on the floor and on his body, he stood up stamping on his head *"rat!!! rat!!! die!!!die!!!"* he shouted in rage, no sound came from Casey, Mark shouted from the door *"I think he's dead John!!!"* John kicked Casey's head, no sound from him, only the sound of Cathy's voice from squealing in the room, John grabbed Cathy by the arm *"now, you come with me bitch!!!, I'll show you your friend"* Mark stood aside for him to pass with Cathy, he went to the next room *"open the fucking door!!!"* he shouted to Mark, who immediately came and unlocked the door, John shoved Cathy into the room, Lucy sat on the single bed in the cage, she looked at Cathy who was in shock to see her, Cathy cried as she staggered to the cage to hold Lucy's hand who had started crying as well *"I think I have had enough fun for today"* John said to Mark smiling *"you are next tomorrow"* pointing to Lucy, *"and you are going to watch again bitch"* now pointing to Cathy that was now holding Lucy's hand and both of them sobbing, John pulled Cathy by the head *"I have one more thing to show you bitch!!!"* he shouted as he pulled her by the hand and shove her towards the door into the corridor were a big freezer was, Mark locked the door after himself, walking behind them with the pistol in his hand, John opened the freezer, pulled Cathy's head down to see what was inside the freezer, *"I told them to save this for you bitch"* Cathy sobbed convulsively, stretching her hand towards the frozen dead body of her father in the freezer. John pulled her by her hair again, she was now very irate thinking that she should be able to take John, but she saw the pistol in Mark's hand again, she thought to herself, that she's still got some couple of hours to try and safe herself from this monsters, she held her stomach as she vomited *"fucking bitch!!!"* John shouted again *"we throw her in the cage with that bitch"* he said to Mark, whom immediately opened the door again and brought out a bunch of keys from his pocket and unlocked the padlock to the cage while John shove Cathy into the cage *"am giving both of you a send-off, be ready for tomorrow"* he said as Mark handed the pistol back to him and locked the cage.

Superintendent Browne was on the phone with another police officer from the tracking department who gave him the address of where the mobile number he gave to him to track was currently located, he was still driving, on his way to the police station *"thank you sergeant, if the phone moves again please let me know immediately"* he drove straight to the police station, went to the office of his boss, chief superintendent Bergin, *"hi chief"* he said after knocking on the door and getting into the office, he told him the new development on John's case, and also told him that inspector Barry is the informant and insider for John, the chief told him that he needed proof that inspector Barry is the informant, they both agreed not to divulge the new development on the case to inspector Barry. When superintendent Browne was talking to the chief, inspector Barry was talking to inspector Julie in the open office, both of them sitting opposite each other with an office desk in between them, Barry had just came to Julie's desk *"what do you think would be our next move"* he asked, *"I don't know, maybe we need to stakeout John's apartment, we might be lucky, he might show up"* she replied, just then Barry's phone rang from his pocket, he brought it out, looked at the screen *"I need to quickly take this call"* he said as he stood up, quickly walked away talking on the phone, Glenn was on the other side of the phone *"your money is ready, if you want to come and collect it now"* he said, *"but I don't want to be seen at the joint or your house alone"* Barry replied, *"okay, you know what? I'll give it back to Snake, he's just going back to the farm yard, it's a safe and secluded place for you to collect your money, I'll text you his number now, then you can call him to get it from him"* says Glenn *"okay"* replied Barry and quickly left the building, Just then superintendent Browne came out of the chief's office, he went into the open office, saw inspector Julie at her desk, but didn't see Barry at his desk, he went to Julie, *"where is Barry?"* he asked, *"we need to go to somewhere now"* he said again. *"Okay, I'll go get him"* she said as she quickly stood up, briskly went outside the building and discovered that inspector Barry's car was gone, she rang his number, but it rang several times and went into voice mail, so; she left him a voice mail to get back to the office, that it's very urgent, she went back to superintendent Browne's office *"he's gone sir, his car is not there, but I left him a message on his phone to quickly get back that it's urgent"* she said, *"you know what, we have to go now, is sergeant Declan there?"* superintendent Browne asked *"yes, I think I saw him just now, I'll get him"* she said as she left his office. Ten minutes later superintendent Browne sat at the back of the car with inspector Declan driving and Julie sitting on the passenger's sit, *"I'll give you the direction of where we are going"* he said to inspector Declan.

"We will get out of this alive Lucy, I have a plan, we have to do something" Cathy said as Lucy cried, they both sat on the single bed in the cage, it's been about two hours that John and Mark left them *"but how Cathy, how"* she said and sniffles as she cried rubbing her nose, *"you know what"* Cathy said holding her wrists firmly to get her attention, *"I have a plan"* she said again, *"we need to fight and take our chances"* she said looking firmly into Lucy's eyes *"I don't want to die, and I know you don't want to die either"* Cathy said again, *"but how are we going to get out of here?, they have a gun, and even if they don't have a gun, how, how"* Lucy said and cried again. *"Look at me"* Cathy said as she shook her hand and then pulled her by the wrist to get her attention, *"will you at least listen to my plan!!!"* she said, Lucy stopped crying, sniffles, robbed her nose and reluctantly looked at her face to let her know that she has got her attention, ready to hear her plan.

Meanwhile, John and Mark threw Casey's body into the pit they've spent over an hour digging at the side of the main house on the farm yard, both of them took turns to use a shovel to scoop the sand earlier dug up to cover the dead body, filled up the pit and then level up the ground with the shovel, when they got back into the house. *"We need to give those bitches some food to keep them alive and ready for tomorrow"* Mark said *"yeah, but I think, we should just get it over with tonight,"* says John. *"Haven't you had enough for the day, I am fucking tired after burying that body,"* Mark said, just then they heard the sound of a car drove into the farm yard, it was getting to 6pm, John pushed the curtain to the window aside to look through the window. He saw Snake and Froggy come out the car, he opened the door as they got to the door, *"you fuckers missed the gig"* Mark said to both of them smiling *"what?"* Snake asked as they entered the house, *"Casey is gone, he was crying like a chicken"* says Mark *"we are about to start with that bitch Lucy, then I'll save Cathy for tomorrow"* John said, *"but you can't do that now, Barry is on his way to here to get his money"* Snake said, *"why here? I thought Glenn was supposed to give him is money at the pub"* John said irately, *"I know he works for us, but I don't want any cops coming around here"* says John again, *"we'll have to do the bitch tomorrow then, cause am tired, I'll just give them the food"* says Mark as he headed into the kitchen to get two sandwiches from the fridge and went down into the basement. Just then, another car drove into the farm yard, *"that should be Barry"* Snake said as he peeped through the window and went to open the door to meet him outside, John followed him.

They parked the car about eighty meters away from the entrance gate to the Farmyard, inspector Julie could see Barry's car with the binoculars she held to her eyes, and was even shocked to see Barry talking to Snake and John, *"superintendent Browne, John is here, and Barry is also here,"* she said flabbergasted and gave the binoculars to him, they crouch by the car that was hidden from John, Snake and Barry's view by the branches of shrubs that surrounded the farmyard, *"what is Barry doing there?"* inspector Julie asked astonished *"did you give him the address?"* she again asked superintendent Browne that was still glued to the binoculars, still surveying the farmyard, while Declan sat in the driver's seat of the car, trying to comprehend their discussion. *"Barry is in on this, he is the informant that told them about the microchip, and I think he's here to get his money"* superintendent Browne said as he handed back the binoculars to inspector Julie who was still in shock that inspector Barry is the informant, *"I'll call for back up, I think Cathy might be in there somewhere"* he said to inspector Julie again, and pulled his hand held transceiver from his pant, and radioed for back up.

The door opened, Mark came into the room with the plate of sandwiches. Lucy was sobbing over Cathy who laid flat on the floor in the cage, she looked up at Mark *"she's dead, she's not breathing, you can as well kill me too now"* Mark quickly put down the plate, brought out the key to the gate from his pocket and opened the cage, grabbed Cathy by the leg and pulled her out of the cage, Cathy thought in her head as Mark drop her legs on the floor and wanted to examine her chest to check if she was breathing *"this is the time"* she used all her energy to kick Mark in the balls, he squealed holding his balls as he crouched on the floor, Cathy quickly got to his back, rounded her hand around his neck falling with it to her back to be able to be in a position to use all her strength to suffocate him, Mark tried to pull her hands apart from his neck, but he couldn't, he tried to roll over and get up, but Cathy wrapped her legs around his thighs to pin him down, so he couldn't even move, he gasped for breath for some couple of seconds, it took just about forty seconds for him to pass out, Lucy just stood there completely petrified while all this happened, she was so horrified that she looked from Cathy pinning Mark to the ground to the pistol that fell out of Mark pocket and she just stood there fidgeting and couldn't pick the gun up to help Cathy, just then, upstairs, Froggy entered the kitchen, looked into the refrigerator, *"no fucking beer in here, there must be beer somewhere else in this house"* he muffled, he looked around the kitchen, *"hey Mark!!!"* he called, he saw the opened entrance to the basement on the floor, he climbed down the staircase, Cathy holding the pistol walked stealthily in the corridor with Lucy behind her, they were about to get to the staircase that will take them out of the basement when Froggy bumped into Cathy making her to fall to the floor and the gun accidentally went off when Froggy was falling down on her, Lucy watched both of them on the floor, terrified, and not knowing who the bullet hit, then Cathy sighed as she put the gun on the floor, pushed Froggy's dead body off her, stood up, picked up the pistol again, *"we have to get out of here"* she said to Lucy who was still in shock. Outside the house, five minutes earlier before the gun went off *"you need to stay away from your apartment for now, I'll say, stay here for now, this place is a good hideout"* inspector Barry said to John as Snake handed him the brown envelop that contained the money he came to collect, *"you make sure you keep Glenn informed"* John said *"as long as my envelopes keeps coming"* Barry said as he opened the envelop to check the money *"you don't need to worry about that"* Snake said, and just then, they heard pew!!! The sound of the gunshot. Five minutes earlier before the gunshot, superintendent Browne saw Snake gave inspector Barry the brown envelop, and saw John talking to him, he gave the binoculars to Julie to see what was happening, *"they seem to be having a meeting"* Julie said, then pew!!! They heard the sound of the gunshot, and saw Barry heading towards his car while Snake and John ran inside the house *"we have to go in now, Cathy may be in there somewhere and may be in serious danger"* superintendent Browne said to the two officers. When the gunshot sounded *"what is that"* Barry asked, John looked at Snake and then ran into the house, Snake brought out his gun, and followed him, *"Mark!!! what the fuck is going on"* John shouted angrily as he went into the kitchen to climb down the stair case to the basement, but Cathy was climbing up the staircase with Mark's pistol in her hand pointed to the exit ready to shoot, Lucy walked up the staircase slowly behind her, immediately she saw John, she fired the gun, but missed as John immediately turned back when he saw her with the gun, he climbed and ran back up to the kitchen, he ran past Snake who was at the top of the staircase and was about to climbed down, Cathy fired another shot which missed John again but the bullet hit Snake on the right shoulder making him to drop the gun he was holding, the gun dropped on the staircase down past Cathy and Lucy into the basement and Snake fell on the kitchen floor squealing in pain from the gun shot, Cathy ran past him, Lucy followed, by the time John got into the sitting room, he heard the sound of police siren outside the house so he turned and wanted to run to the back door to escape through the back garden of the house, but Cathy was now standing in his way with the gun, Lucy opened the front door, ran outside towards the police car coming closer to the house, John heard the siren getting closer, he wanted to make his move again to run pass Cathy, she tried to fire the gun at him, but the gun only clicked because it was out of bullet, she tried again, no bullet, the gun clicked as she tried, John smiled *"I am going to kill you bitch"* he said as he ran towards her swinging his right fist to hit her, Cathy saw it coming and moved her head aside to the right from the target to dodge the punch, and at the same time hardly kicked John in the balls, he wailed as he fell to the floor, Cathy used the butt of the gun to hit him in the face several times, making blood splatter from his face, John managed to grab her hands, but Cathy kicked him in the ribs as superintendent Browne came into the house through the front door, inspector Julie and Declan followed *"we are here now Cathy"* superintendent Browne said pointing his gun at John, while inspector Declan and Julie turned John on his face and handcuffed him *"you are under arrest John for kidnapping and murder"* inspector Declan said and read him his rights, while superintendent Browne went outside to meet Lucy who was standing beside Cathy by the ambulance that just arrived with two other police cars, *"I believe you are Lucy"* he said, *"yes"* she said whimpering as he held her closer to take her inside the ambulance, the other officers were already combing the farmyard and entered the house searching for other culprits, inspector Julie attended to Cathy who exhale deeply, and happy that it was all over now that John is back in custody for good, *"hello, Mr Foley, I have good news for you, I have Lucy right here beside me"* superintendent Browne said, he had just quickly made an important phone call, at the other end of the line was Ben, Lucy's father, *"I can tell you that she's alive"* he said and gave the phone to Lucy *"Dad"* she sobbed as she said that, *"Lucy, thank God, are you okay?"* he asked as he cried as well, they both cried. Snake was still crawling on the kitchen floor when the officers got to him, he was in deep pain and wailed as the police arrested him, the officers pointed their revolver towards the front as they climbed down into the basement, they saw Froggy's dead body laid on the floor in the basement right after the staircase, went past it, opening the door to the rooms before they finally got to Mark, not withstanding that he was unconscious, the officers discovered that he was still alive.

When Barry drove out of the farmyard after the gunshot, he didn't notice inspector Declan's car concealed by the shrubs, neither did he see the three police officers, he just wanted to get away from the farmyard as fast as he could, he drove straight back to the police station, but on his way, about five kilometres away from the farmyard, he saw two police cars and ambulance blowing siren driving fast towards the farmyard. Later after then, he saw superintendent Browne, inspector Julie and Declan came into the police station with John, but Snake and Mark were taken to the hospital under police security supervision, superintendent Browne went to Barry at his desk *"I was looking for you earlier on?"* he said to him *"sorry boss, my girlfriend was very sick, so I had to quickly go and take her to the hospital."* Barry replied *"so you were not at the farmyard earlier on today?"* *"No"* he reluctantly replied, but the expression on his face says otherwise that he was lying, superintendent Browne looked through his table, and opened the drawers as inspector Julie and Declan came to the table after locking John into one of the interrogation rooms, superintendent Browne saw the brown envelop that Barry collected from Snake at the farmyard earlier on, he took it out, opened it, and emptied the content on the table, piles of fifty Euro bills about one hundred bills fell on the table, *"can you explain this?"* he asked him as he looked directly at his face and back to inspector Julie and Declan and back to Barry that now looked startled by what was going on *"so you were at the farmyard today, and you took this from Snake"* superintendent Browne said to Barry, who continued to look startled and didn't say a word *"arrest this idiot"* superintendent

Browne said to inspector Declan and Julie as he packed the bills of fifty Euro back into the envelop and took it to the chiefs office as evidence.

Five days later, a prison officer pushing the trolley with prisoners food, stopped at one of the cell door at Clover Hill prison, the officer opened the cell door, took a plate marked with a red pen from one of the plates on the trolley, John got up from the single bed immediately the cell door opened, the officer handed him the covered plate *"you have thirty minutes, keep it quiet"* he whispered and locked back the cell door, John opened the covered plate, there was a small white nylon bag in it, he unwrapped it, took out the small black mobile phone, he looked at the screen, it was ninety three percent charged, he went to his bed, pulled the duvet cover over his head to conceal himself, and dialled a number, the phone rang twice and Glenn picked up the phone at the other end of the line *"what's the crack Glenn"* John said *"hello John, just really need to give you a very important information, the guy that got them to you is that guy at Midlands, the rat's name is Matthew"* Glenn said, *"yes I know that cunt"* John replied *"I am getting someone to take care of him"* says Glenn *"No no Glenn, I'll take care of that cunt myself, I need to look into his eyes when I take care of him"* John replied *"when is he out?"* Glenn asked, *"he's got about four more years left on his clock, I should be back in Midlands in the next two months, latest I'll say three months after my trial, then you'll be reading about that rat sent to hell on the news"* says John.

Chapter Eleven

Boxer Tony the Pilot

He stood aside with two other prisoners, watched Tony Kinsella teaching one other prisoner boxing techniques, as Matthew watched, he drifted into retrospection of how he met Tony, his new neighbour a month earlier the day after his former neighbour John the daddy devil was released from prison, after the first unlock that day in the morning that is used for prisoners to quickly get their breakfast, Matthew looked through the cell door peephole after coming back from collecting his breakfast, he held unto the small bowl of cornflakes and the small paper box that contained the two hundred and fifty millimetre milk as he peeped and saw someone lying on the single bed in the cell, on his way back into his cell, he gently closed his cell door, he wondered who his new neighbour was, he had looked at the card on the door that is used to show the name and sentence given to the prisoner in that particular cell, and saw that the name is Tony and the sentence says ten years the same sentence as himself. Another fifty minutes his cell door opened again, Matthew was ready waiting sitting on his bed holding his folder that contained stuffs he needed to use at the school for that morning, it was 9:15am and he had to get to the prison school, Tony was standing there at the front of his cell looking left and right at the other prisoners as they go back and forth on the corridor, some going into other prisoners cell, some going towards the prison officers room, some climbing the staircase to get to the exit gate on the second floor to wait for the prison officers that would come and take them to school, Matthew looked at Tony as he came out of his cell, Tony is about six foot five inches tall, he's in his late thirties, a big guy, he looks like a giant, like someone that plays rugby, and he was dressed up in a fancy blue jeans, white t shirt and white runners *"what's the crack, my name is Matthew"* he said as he looked at his face, *"my name is Tony"* he replied reluctantly, *"I need to get to the school, we'll see later"* says Matthew *"I am going to the school as well, but I need to see the governor, where do I see the governor"* Tony asked, *"it's on the second floor, the room by the exit gate from the landing, come I'll show you,"* he followed Matthew. When they got to the gate, there were about thirteen prisoners waiting to be taken to the school, *"that's the room to see the governor"* Matthew said pointing to a door to the last room on the right before the entrance and exit gate to the floor, there were about five other prisoners waiting in a queue to see the governor *"you queue on the line behind them"* Matthew said pointing to the prisoners *"when are they taking you guys to the school"* Tony asked, *"in about another four minutes, I don't think you can come with us, when you finish seeing the governor, just tell the officer on this landing or any officer you see to bring you to the school"* Matthew said *"thank you"* says Tony as he immediately walked to queue behind the other prisoners waiting to see the governor. About a week after then, they were sitting in Tony's cell playing chess, within that one week Matthew had come to know from Tony how he was arrested because of his dealings in drugs.

Tony used to be a boxer, he once represented the country at the Olympics which he won a bronze medal, but that was the farthest he went in boxing, he later finished his university degree course in Business Administration and went on to complete his masters in money management, after getting his masters, he started a security company and started supplying night clubs with bouncers and celebrities with bodyguards, in which he himself worked as a personal bodyguard for some celebrities, he was successful and made substantial amount of money, but he wanted more money, so he went and studied to be a pilot, when he finished the course, he was issued a licence to be a pilot, so he bought a small private jet from his savings from the security company and loan that he got from the bank, he had come across some drug dealers who are the owners of some of the night clubs he supplied bouncers to, so; they introduced him to drugs, he was invited to a meeting in Islamabad in Pakistan, were he met up with three other associate, one from Afghanistan, another European from Netherlands called Bakker and another Pakistani guy, the reason for their meeting was to agree on the price of per kilo of how much the drug would cost, which they agreed that a kilo would cost one thousand dollars in Afghanistan, then by the time it arrives in Pakistan it would cost three thousand dollars per kilo, then by the time it arrives in Netherlands it would cost twenty thousand dollars, and finally it would cost forty thousand dollars by the time it arrives in Ireland, Tony agreed with the permission from his associates in Ireland that he would pay the cost of what it is in Netherland, they arranged and concluded that they would start with hundred kilos, and also discussed how the drugs would be transported by land from Afghanistan were it is grown to Pakistan, then shipped by a yacht to Netherlands, then finally transported by air to Ireland, the four men guaranteed their own part of the mission for the deal, they finally discussed how the proceed from the sale of the drug would be transported back from Ireland to Netherlands, then to Pakistan and finally back to Afghanistan, the Afghanistan guy agreed to collect just twenty percent of the money for the first shipment upfront. Six weeks after the meeting, hundred kilos of heroine arrived in Netherlands by ship from Pakistan, *"hello Tony, the medical equipment is ready"* says Bakker, they use this code since Ireland imports loads of it medical equipment such as Orthopaedic appliances from Netherlands, the drugs was conceal in this equipment whenever it's to be transported to Ireland, Tony does the transportation of the drugs whenever he takes his clients that hired his private jet from Netherlands to Ireland, so he had a good alibi as a legit business man, he became successful and bought two more private jets and hired three more pilots, so; he stopped taking the risk of transporting the drugs and money himself just after four months of dealing in drugs, instead, he used the pilots that worked for him to take the risk of transporting the illegal stuffs without them knowing that the drugs was conceal in the medical equipment they were bringing into Ireland, this went on for several months, he made good money, several millions, he bought houses in Ireland, south Africa and Netherlands, he left his first wife that had two children for him, the woman who was there for him from high school through the years he was struggling to get his first degree and before he became rich for a younger beautiful lady that was about twelve years younger than him, he would take his new wife on a flight cruise and holiday almost every two weeks, splurging money on designer clothes, bags, shoes and jewelleries on her, while he abandoned his first wife and his two children, who are two teenage girls, the eldest daughter nineteen years and the second age seventeen, his new wife bore him his first male child, then just after the child was born, one of Tony's pilot got caught with one hundred kilos of cocaine that was about to leave

Netherlands for Ireland, the pilot cooperated with the police, he subtly implicated Tony as the organiser of the drugs that was found in the aircraft that he was about to fly off with that morning in Amsterdam. Tony was driving one of his flashy cars, a Range Rover Sport, when he got a call from his secretary from his office *"the police just came here looking for you John, they turned this place upside down searching for drugs"* says, his secretary, Elena *"how many of them?"* Tony asked *"about six police officers, they took your laptop and some files and documents, three of them are still here waiting for you, they called your phone several times, but they said you didn't pick up, what is happening Tony?"* Elena asked, *"I don't know, I'll call you later, I have to quickly make some calls"* Tony said and hung up, he rang his contact in Netherlands, *"Bakker, what's happening, did you deliver to my guy this morning?"* he asked. *"I was about to call you Tony, your guy picked up the goods this morning, but it's on the news now, just before your call, it says on the news that someone was busted at the airport this morning with hundred keys, since that was the amount of the product delivered to your guy this morning, then it's definitely your guy,"* Bakker replied, *"what the fuck!!!, but you guaranteed the safety of getting the products out of your territory, it's your error, so fix this!!!"* Tony said, *"No it's not my error, what my insider in the police told me is that the police in Ireland tipped the Interpol here in Netherlands that this pickup was happening this morning, so you need to investigate who the rat is at your own end there!!!"* Bakker said and hung up. Tony was in a deep thought as he parked his car by the side of the road, he looked at his phone, twenty one missed calls from a local number that he doesn't recognise, it must be from the police he thought, he thought who could have leaked the information about the deal to the police, his heart palpitating as he thought about Morris, his business associate in Ireland, one of his major distributor that was arrested three weeks earlier with twenty two kilos of Heroine, he is the only person that he thought that must have ratted him out, he thought to himself *"that bastard must have ratted me out to cut a deal with the police"* he thought *"cockroach!!!"* he screamed banging his fist on the staring of the car, *"I shouldn't have trusted him, what the fuck!!!"* he screamed again, holding the staring with his left and banging it with his right hand several times, his heart still palpitating, *"what am I going to do"* he said soliloquizing *"hundred fucking keys, that is twenty fucking years, fuck!!! I can't do that, I have to get out, go into hiding, fuck, fuck, fuck"* he said and bangs the staring again, just then the phone ringing again, he looked at the screen, it was an anonymous number calling him *"definitely, it's the police, fuck them, "* he said and cut off the phone, he called his wife *"Hello pretty, is the police there?"* he asked, *"No Tony, why should the police be here Tony?"* she frightfully asked *"they don't know the new house, there's a problem pretty, we have to move, or I go first then you and Alex can come and join me later"* he said, the name of the baby is Alex *"I am on my way home, I love you, we'll talk later"* he said and hung up, he had just moved to his new house three weeks earlier immediately after Morris arrest, it's a big mansion, and nobody knows the location except the builders that built it, he thought he still has the chance to go home, pack his stuff, money and disappear, he still has about four million euro cash in his personal safe at home. *"I'll go to South Africa, I'll be safe there,"* he thought as he drove to his house, what Tony didn't know was that the police had already discovered the address to his new house from one of the files they took from his office, and they were already waiting in the area, dressed up in mufti, three of them sat in an undercover white minivan with SPE Electricity inscribed on it to make it look like an electricity company van, with one officer monitoring the area and Tony's house from a computer installed in the van, the fourth officer was outside pretending to be working on an electricity box that was situated at the front of a house that was just two houses away from Tony's house, there was just one way in and out of the road to Tony's house which was a close, the time was going to about 1pm, they had been waiting for about twenty five minutes, Tony's house was a detached one storey building, the officer working outside was pretending to be focusing on solving an electrical fault from the box, creating no suspicion of police presence to any resident in the area, the officer on the computer saw Pretty, Tony's wife when she came outside ten minutes earlier when she was on the phone talking to Tony, the police guy on the computer saw Tony drove into the close, the secretary at his office told them that he drives a black range rover, he drove at seventy miles per hour on a road that he was legally supposed to be driving thirty miles per hour, he almost crashed into his house when he entered the compound, he came out of the car hurriedly, unlocked and opened the door to the house with his key and went and hugged pretty that was holding his three months old son, he kissed her on the four head, she was still dressed in her pyjamas, *"what is happening Tony"* she asked him with a squeaky voice *"why do you have to run Tony, why"* she sobbed *"listen Pretty, if I don't run, I am going to be spending a long time in prison because one of my pilot got busted this morning, and the cops are looking for me"* he said as he went upstairs and unlocked the personal safe in their bedroom *"we have about four million Euros in here, we can go and start another life somewhere else Pretty, like in South Africa"* he said looking into her eyes trying to convince her, just then they heard a loud knock on the front door to the house, *"Tony, Tony!!!"* the voice shouted *"it's the police!!! And you are surrounded, if you don't open the door, then we'll have to forcefully come in"* Tony looked at his wife who was now utterly petrified, stood there in shock hanging on to her baby *"am sorry"* he said as he kissed his wife on the four head again and also wanted to kiss his son, but just then he heard the door busted open by the police, three of them came into the sitting room downstairs, then separated themselves searching the whole house before one of them came into the master bedroom upstairs and saw Tony's wife sitting on the bed holding her baby fidgeting, he asked *"where is Tony?"* she was sobbing now and didn't say anything, one other officer came into the room, they both searched the room, and discovered Tony hiding under the bed, they pulled him out with his legs, but he punched them one after the other using his boxing skills, and overpowered them, he ran out of the room and down the staircase running as fast as he could, but when he got to the front exit door, another police man was waiting with a gun pointed at him, he stopped *"put your hands up and lie down on the floor!!!"* the police man shouted at him, he reluctantly obeyed the officer before one of the two officers that he overpowered earlier on came from behind him to handcuff him and read him his rights before taking him away to one of the police cars that was called as back up by the police officer on the computer in the van when Tony arrived at his house earlier on, the police discovered the four million euro cash in the safe in the house, but no other illegal stuffs were discovered, as Tony no more deals directly with the drug transportation, sale and supply, he uses other people to take the risk.

During interrogation, Tony continued to claim his obliviousness of the drugs discovered in the equipment intercepted by the police in Netherlands, which he continued to deny for five months until the day of his trial, when the prosecutor told his solicitor that he would make sure

Tony gets a minimum of twenty five years in prison if he's found guilty by the jury, the prosecutor also told his solicitor that a very important associate of Tony as agreed to come and stand as a witness in the law court to proof that Tony is the top three drug dealers in the country, and also Tony couldn't account for or explain how he legitimately came about the four million euro cash discovered in his house by the police, Tony was convinced with the witness coming to testify against him, which he knows that the witness is his former top business associate Morris that used to handle all his drugs distribution in the country and is now in prison awaiting sentence, Morris had already pleaded guilty, so; with all the evidence against Tony, including the cash found at his house he definitely knew that he would be found guilty by the jury if he goes to trial, so he decided to change his plea from not guilty to guilty before his trial began that day, so, at his sentencing two weeks after, he got the mandatory ten years sentence for drug possession, but three months into his sentence he saw it on the newspaper that Morris only got two years for getting caught with sixty two keys of cocaine, *"that is the guy that fucked me over to the cops"* he gave the newspaper to Matthew, as Matthew read the story *"I am going to fuck him up when I get out, I am here because of him"* Tony said again infuriatingly. *"Matthew, it's your shot now"* the prisoner doing the Sparring boxing training with Tony called him and handed him the boxing gloves, Matthew already had a blue fabric hand glove on, so he told the prisoner to help him to tie on the boxing gloves to his hand, the other prisoners watched as Tony talked him through the steps to be followed for the sparring training, *"Matthew you need to take a deep breath, in and out all the time, when you move, when you punch, when you defend, and you also need to stay at your level and always keep your eyes on your opponent"* says Tony as he checked the boxing gloves on his hands to see if it was properly tied on, the other three prisoners and two prison officers watched as they sparred, there were also eighteen other prisoners in the gym, some on the treadmill, some on the exercise bicycle and some doing the weight lift.

Three months later, Matthew was in the yard playing chess game with Tony, it was going to 1pm, it was a sunny day, about sixteen degrees Celsius, there were about forty other prisoners in the yard, most of them doing the three hundred and sixty degrees walk in the yard, Matthew and Tony were playing the game on two yoga mats that they brought to the yard with the chess board twenty minutes earlier on, seven other prisoners watched the game, *"checkmate, game over"* Matthew said as he got up laughing, dramatizing and gesticulating to be punching Tony, talking like a boxing sport commentator *"Matthew dodged the punch, Tony throw another right punch, Matthew dodged again, oh, oh Tony got caught on the chin, wow, Tony is on the floor, referee counting, is he going to get up!!!"* Matthew did all this gesticulating and dramatizing with his hand punching in the air to make it look like he was fighting Tony *"ooh, Tony can't get up, it's a knockout!!!"* the other prisoners laughed as Matthew was putting on this show off, Tony laughing, got up, came towards Matthew, and wanted to grab him, but Matthew ran away from him laughing, the other prisoners laughed as Tony ran after him, but Matthew continued to dodge him *"you're a fucking asshole Matthew"* says Tony as he laughed when he couldn't catch him, the three prison officers in the yard watched, gobsmacked that Matthew has also developed a close relationship with another mobster. They all knew Tony to be top drug baron and criminal, and they also heard about how Tony beat up five prison officers that tried to take him from his prison cell to isolation block for punishment because he spat on the face of another prison officer, that happened in Cloverhill prison after he came back from his sentencing in court, they had to get more officers, about ten of them to come and take him in the night to isolation, so, they were surprised to see how Tony as come to be very friendly with Matthew whom they believe is not a carrier criminal but only in prison because of his naivety, they were amazed, the same way they were astonished that Matthew became very good friend with another top mafia, John the daddy devil before he left the prison. There was a chess competition in the prison two weeks earlier, which sixteen prisoners participated in, including Matthew and Tony, the participants were put into two groups of eighth each, which Matthew was in group A and Tony with seven other prisoners in group B, Matthew won his first and second round of the competition and played another prisoner called Paul Hui, a Chinese guy, he's five feet six inches tall, Matthew believes he takes the shortness of his height from his Chinese father, he was a barber in the prison, he cuts other prisoners hair for a park of cigarette, he's half Irish and half Chinese, his mother is Irish, he was doing eight years for drug possession for sale and supply, he was arrested when he went to pick up three kilos of cocaine that a guy brought in from Spain, he didn't know that the police already caught the guy bringing in the drugs from Spain at Dublin airport, and after arresting the guy, he cooperated with the police to get them to Paul, the guy he was told to deliver the drugs to in Ireland, so the police was with him at the hotel where he earlier called Paul to come and collect the drugs, when Paul got to the hotel, he went into the lobby, it was about 10am in the morning that Thursday, the hotel was a four star hotel, there were about sixteen people in the lobby, which three people queued up to see the female receptionist, a family of four, a man with his wife and two children, a boy and a girl which look like teenagers sat down on a three seater couch, stood beside them was four luggage's, it looked like they've just seen the receptionist after coming into the hotel and waiting for a room to be allocated to them, they looked tired, the rest of the people sat in pairs, what Paul didn't know was that, there were two undercover anti-drug law enforcement officers sitting in the lobby, a man and a woman that pretended like a couple and a guest of the hotel, also there were two officers hiding in the room of the guy that Paul came to collect the drugs from, there were also three officers waiting in the car that was parked in the car park of a house that was directly opposite the hotel building, they saw Paul drove his black BMW into the hotel car park, *"hello, I am in the lobby"* says Paul *"you can come up to room 301"* the guy said, *"no, I don't want to come up, if you want to bring the package to the car park, you'll see a black BMW, you open the boot of the car and drop the package inside"* says Paul *"what about my money?"* the guy asked *"you'll see your money in a white nylon bag in the boot of the car, it's all in there, you can count it if you want"* Paul *replied "okay, I be down in two minutes"* the guy said and Paul disconnected the call. The two officers in the room with the guy said it's okay for him to do what Paul said, they called the two officers in the lobby and the three officers outside to update them on the new development, the guy did as Paul said, Paul saw him came down to the car park with a hand bag, saw him opened the boot of his car, dropped the hand bag into the boot, and saw him took the white nylon bag containing the money, and quickly walked back into the hotel past Paul that was now sitting on one of the single couch in the lobby, ten minutes later, after surveying the environment and checking that he was safe to live with his car, Paul was back in his car driving out of the hotel car park, but the three officers outside tried to use their car to block the BMW from leaving, but Paul drove round their car and sped off, the officers pursued him, there was a hold up on the street ahead, so Paul drove into another road, which the police followed him, but when he got to the end of the road he discovered that it's a close, there was a fence at the end of the road, he looked back, he saw the undercover police car closing in, Paul pulled up his car by the fence, ran out of his car, and jumped over the fence into a small field of about two hundred metres length and one hundred and twenty five metres wide, the officers jumped after him, one of the officers was a good runner, he caught up with Paul, jumped on him from behind and pinned him to the ground until two other officers joined him, he was arrested, at first, after his arrest, Paul denied knowing the guy that came into the country with the drugs, he claimed he was set up, but his finger print were all over the ten thousand Euros in the white nylon bag the guy picked up from his car, and the conversation he had with the guy since the guy contacted him after his arrest at the airport was recorded, the prosecutor actually told him during interrogation that he's going to get fifteen years if he goes to trial and found guilty, so when his solicitor advised him to plead guilty because of the overwhelming evidence against him, and told him he would get less than ten years sentence, he chose to plead guilty and got eight years. Matthew smiled at Paul as he pushed his pawn forward annoyingly and aggressively as a sign that he's going all out for attack, Paul just made a stupid move and lost his queen in exchanged for Matthew's pawn, *"Paul, have you seen enter the dragon?"* Matthew asked him, *"yes, it's by Bruce Lee"* replied Paul, *"you remind me of the scene of when Bruce Lee killed O'Harra, and Roper killed Bolo in that movie"* says Matthew *"You know when Han, the host of the tournament started telling all his boys to attack Bruce Lee and Roopa, he said attack, attack, now you are telling all your pawns to attack, attack"* Matthew said laughing, *"you are crazy Matthew!!"* Paul replied laughing, and the five guys that were watching the semi-final of the prison chess competition started laughing as well, the game took about just twenty minutes, because Paul is a fast player, even when he's stuck, he just think for about thirty seconds, that's the maximum time it takes him to think before moving his piece, Matthew won the game and Paul extended his hand in handshake which Matthew took, Paul is a very lovely guy, he plays the guitar at the Mass in the church and Matthew sang and they've become very good friends in the prison, there was a time Matthew's wife couldn't pay the house rent, and Matthew told Paul that he was looking for someone that can loan him money to give to his wife to pay for the house rent, Paul helped Matthew out by telling his mum to contact Delilah, Matthew's wife, to get her account number and loaned Matthew the money, and he paid Paul the money back with packs of cigarettes. The second semi-final was played between Tony and Frank, the cleaner on the first landing, Tony won the game and got into final to play Matthew, but Frank later confided in Matthew that Tony gave him five pack of cigarettes before their game to allow him to win, and said Tony told him that he would like to win the competition, so Frank allowed Tony to beat him after collecting the pack of cigarettes, Matthew has won the two previous competitions, and he has played chess with Tony several times and Matthew has won ninety percent of the game, the few times Tony won, he was always ecstatic, some of those times Matthew intentionally allowed him to win in other to put smiles on his face and to continue to have a good relationship with him, any time Tony lost to him, Matthew noticed that he was always totally devastated losing the game, Matthew also discovered that when Tony wins, he's always happy to train him the boxing skills and tactics, so when Frank confided in Matthew about allowing Tony to win, Matthew thought on that day of the final that he would allow Tony to win the competition, which he did, and Tony was very delighted and spirited, the winning price was fourteen pack of cigarettes and Matthew got two packs of cigarettes for being the runner up.

When Matthew got back from the yard to the landing, he was asked by one of the two officers on the landing to come into their office to sign for a letter, when he got back into his cell, he opened the letter, he discovered that the letter was from his solicitor telling him the date of his appeal case that would be coming up in two months, he could feel his heart palpitating as he read the letter, he sat down on his bed holding the letter and looked around his cell, he knelt down beside the bed resting his hand and upper body on the bed, he prayed in silence, his eyes watering and then tears trickling down his face as he prayed wholeheartedly to God to intervene in his matter when he goes for his appeal. The next morning, immediately after the second unlock, Matthew was on one of the three phones on the landing calling his wife's mobile phone, the phone rang several times and cut off, he was not surprised, she has been ignoring most of his calls for the past five months, and the last time she visited him was four months earlier in December, a week before the last Christmas, she came with his children, she had stopped wearing her wedding ring, when Matthew asked her why wasn't she wearing her wedding ring, she stood there at the other side of the table, just gazed at him for about one minute then tears trickled down her face, Matthew carried his four year old daughter and his six year old son, just sat there at the other side of the table from his wife, the visit only lasted for about ten minutes, not withstanding he was allowed one hour visit, his wife said she had to go, as Matthew walked away from the phone, he thought in his head that his wife as definitely abandoned him, he wrote her two letters every week for the past two year in which she has not replied to any of his letters for over one year now, once in a while when she picks Matthew's call, he would hear a male voice talking underground, and when Matthew asked who the person was, she would tell him that he doesn't know the person, that it's one of her colleagues at work, and sometimes she would say *"it's someone talking on the TV"* but Matthew knew that it was something else, he knew that she was having an affair. A week before his appeal, Matthew came back from school and discovered that a prisoner has been put in his cell, he saw the new prisoner lying down on a single mattress on the floor of his cell, taking almost the remaining vacant space in the cell, as Matthew stood at the door unsettled, some thought came to his mind *"how am I going to do my yoga? How am I going to study?, this is a single cell"* *"what's the crack"* the guy said as he stood up from the mattress, he is about five feet six inches tall and a small guy, he looked in his late twenties, he was wearing a jeans and a blue t shirt, *"my name is Collins"* he said as he extended his hand in handshake *"my name is Matthew"* he replied as he took the handshake *"I just need to quickly see someone"* Matthew said as he quickly went back to the landing to see one of the two officers that were now closing the cell doors after checking that the prisoners were back in their cell *"please officer, there is a guy in my cell, I believe it's a single cell"* Matthew said *"he's only going to be there for one night Matthew, we ran out of space, he's only here on transit going to another prison"* the officer replied as he moved to another cell, checked that the prisoner was inside and closed the door. Back in his cell, Matthew sat on the single bed and Collins sat on the only chair in the cell *"how long have you been here, what did you get ten years for?"* Collins asked curiously, *"well, I have been here for about three years now, I came from Cork prison"* Matthew replied *"what did you get ten years for, is it for robbery? drugs or what?"* Collins asked again, *"well, I was used by a malevolent individual that I thought was my friend to collect a package containing drugs"* Matthew replied. *"What do you mean you were used? You definitely knew you were collecting drugs, were you not told by this guy that you'll get paid some money after collecting the package?"* Collins infuriately asked. *"No, I never knew I was collecting a package containing drugs"* Matthew replied. *"Okay, how did you meet or know this guy that set you up?"* asked Collins again. *"Well it's a long story,"* Matthew said as he started telling him how he met Gordon the guy that used his naivety to get him to collect the package that got him ten years' imprisonment.

Chapter Twelve

Gordon The Malevolent

He drove his car towards a car park that is about ten minutes walk from Moore Street in Dublin, it was getting to about 10am, he had driven two hours from Waterford city that morning to get the maternity clothes and slippers that his heavily pregnant wife told him to get for her. After parking his car at the car park, he walked past several shops, people and stalls before arriving at the shop he was looking to buy the stuff from, there were two heavily pregnant women in the shop that were busy picking up stuff from the shelves, Matthew went to the lady at the till and gave her the list of stuff his wife told him to get. The lady went to the section of the shelves that had the items, picked the items from the shelve, went back to the till, five minutes later, Matthew was back on the street walking back to his car, just then he saw him, yes, that was when he came across Gordon, he was smiling as he removed his sunglasses as he looked at Matthew. He's about six feet tall and a slender guy, he was dressed in a black jeans, white t-shirt and white runners to match, he was also wearing a golden Rolex wrist watch. *"Matthew, what's up?"* he said, *"Gordon, my God, where did you come from?"* Matthew replied. *"My friend, it's been about eighteen years now that we finished school, right?"* Gordon said, *"yes, nineteen years precisely"* Matthew replied. *"You look great, this is a Rolex watch you're wearing?* Matthew said, pointing to the golden wrist watch on his left wrist as he took his handshake on the right hand, they both went to the same secondary school and was in the same class in their final year. *"Do you live in Dublin?"* Gordon asked, *"No, I came all the way from Waterford City, do you live in Dublin?"* Matthew asked. *"No, but I live not far away in Drogheda"* Gordon replied, *"well I have been to Waterford several times before, I was even there last week"* says Gordon, *"okay, I live right in the city, at the back of Tower hotel"* says Matthew *"yes, yes I know that hotel, it's by the road on the Quay, I have actually stayed in that hotel before, you see, I need to quickly get to a meeting, why don't you just give me your number, and we can talk later and arrange on how to meet up some other time"* Gordon said as he dipped his hand into his jeans pocket to get his phone, but it wasn't there, *"I think I left my phone in the car"* he said as he quickly walked back to a black Range rover parked at the other side of the road to get his phone, and got Matthew's *number "when are you going back to Waterford?"* he asked him after storing his number on his phone *"I start work at 4pm"* Matthew replied *"what do you work as?"* Gordon asked *"I work as a security officer, I mind construction sites"* replied Matthew smiling *"I can see you're doing fine with this your jeep"* says Matthew pointing to the black jeep, *"well I have my own business, that's one of the reasons why I got your number, so that we can do business together, I'll call you later today, okay"* Gordon said as he extended his hand in handshake again *"I am running late, I have to go"* he said and walked away. As Matthew drove back to Waterford city that day, he couldn't stop wandering what business Gordon is into that he drives such big Jeep, later that day around 6pm, his phone rang when he was doing the patrol check round the construction site, it was a new number that he doesn't have stored on his phone that appeared on the screen of his phone, he immediately picked the call because he was anxiously expecting a call from Gordon *"hello Matthew"* Gordon said *"hey!!! Gordon, I have been expecting your call"* he said *"well I am sorry that we couldn't really talk this morning, it was because of that business appointment that I told you I had to quickly get to"* says Gordon *"well how did it go?"* Matthew asked, *"it went well, thank you"* replied Gordon *"well I am really curious to discuss the business that you said you want to discuss with me, because this job I am currently doing is just to get survival money, to pay my bills, my wife doesn't currently work, I am the only one working"* says Matthew *"I understand, you see, that's the reason why I want to bring you into this business, and it's very easy"* says Gordon *"please, I really need a better job or get into a business that can get me out of my debts"* Matthew interrupted *"you see like I said, the business is very easy, and I have brought in some guys into it as well, and they are all doing well, I actually have someone in Waterford city that I do the business with as well, that is the reason why I come to Waterford at least every two weeks"* says Gordon *"okay"* says Matthew. *"I have a friend that works in a company that sells mobile phones and laptops, and he is able to post the mobile phones to the addresses given to him, I have a way to pay for the phones online, and my friend will just post it out to be delivered to the address given to him, but you see the delivery address has to be different addresses each time I want to place the order, and the name of the recipient won't be the name of the person collecting the package because we use different names as well."* "Why?" asked Matthew. *"Well that's the way my friend that sends out the package wants it, you don't need to worry about that, you can say that you are that name on the package, or tell the courier guy that comes to deliver the package that the person that owns the package is not around and you've been asked by the person to collect the package, mind you, this are latest mobile phones, and it would be coming in about twenty quantity maybe every week, it depends on how many addresses you can get for me, you don't need to be in the house at the address, you can just stand outside the house maybe couple of minutes before the courier driver arrives, he will call you while he's on his way to deliver the package maybe thirty minutes before his arrival to notify you that he's coming with your package, it's very easy, you can make at least five hundred Euros for collecting one package, or even more, I will give you the money when I come to Waterford to collect the package from you, normally I come on the same day after you've collected the package"* Gordon explained. *"whoop, it seems an easy business, I have loads of addresses I can give you, at my current job, I don't make up to four hundred a week most of the time, I only make that much when I do overtime, I am really interested, I can give you three addresses straightaway,"* says Matthew excitedly *"okay, you text me the addresses, and I will let you know when the phones would be coming, and I will also tell you the name on the package"* says Gordon.

Matthew was euphoric about getting started with the business after discussing with Gordon over the phone, but he thought about the reason why the guy that Gordon said sends the package sends it in different names and wants different addresses for the package to be sent to, the only reasonable reason to Matthew for that would be that there is a fraud going on in the company that the mobile phone is been sent from, this guy must be defrauding the company and he doesn't want to get caught, that would be the definite reason he sends it out in different names and to different addresses Matthew concluded. When he got home that night at around 9pm, he hugged and kissed his wife, went into his son's room and discovered that he was already asleep, his son was two year old, he looked at his face admiringly as he slept, he pulled the bed sheet cover that was beside him on the bed to cover him properly, his son moved his head with his eyes still closed, stuck his thumb into his mouth, sucked on it three times and back quiet sleeping, *"you look excited, what's the story, is it because of the baby coming?"* his wife asked him as he entered into their room, *"yes, yes, I can't wait for the baby to come, but I am also starting a new job that will make me an extra five hundred Euros a week"* Matthew amusingly replied *"and what type of job is that?"* Delilah asked in curiosity, *"well I ran into an old school mate in Dublin today, and he wants to bring me in on a business that I just need to collect a package containing mobile phones at an address here in Waterford, he will give me five hundred Euros when he comes to Waterford to collect the package"* Matthew said *"and why can't this your friend collect the package himself, and you have to collect it for him?"* Delilah asked curiously *"he doesn't live here in Waterford, he already has one person that does the same type of job for him here, think about us making extra five hundred Euro a week"* he said holding his wife hand, their second child was due within the next four weeks, and that would be more expenses *"do I know this your friend at all?"* Delilah asked *"you don't know him sweetheart, we were in secondary school together, about nineteen years ago"* he replied.

A week later Matthew was waiting in his car that was parked two houses away from the house address that the first package was to be delivered, he had got a call from the courier guy thirty five minutes earlier telling him the time he would deliver the package, and now it's five minutes to 10am that he said he would deliver the package, Matthew waited anxiously, when it was two minutes past 10am, he saw the courier van parked at the front of the house, he quickly got out of his car and went to meet the courier guy that was now at the back of the van bringing out a brown box with the name James Daniels *"hi, I believe you have something for me"* Matthew said, *"yeah, for James Daniels, if you just want to sign here"* the guy said as he handed Matthew the package, and also handed him a small hand device with a pen, and pointed to were Matthew should sign on the screen, *"thank you"* Matthew said when he finished signing for the package, the guy got into the van and left as Matthew took the package to his car, five minutes later he was on the phone to Gordon *"I have the package"* Matthew said *"okay, I am almost in Waterford city, if you just want to meet me up at the front of McDonalds on Cork road in fifteen minutes, I'll collect the package and give you your money"* Gordon said. *"Okay, I'll be waiting for you at the front of McDonalds then"* says Matthew. Eight minutes later, Matthew was parked at McDonalds car park waiting for Gordon, it wasn't a busy morning at McDonalds, so; there were just seven other cars at the car park, just another six minutes after his arrival, Gordon also drove into the car park, after collecting the package from him *"here is your money, and you can also have this phone, it cost about two hundred and fifty Euros, so that is you getting seven fifty for this package alone"* says Gordon, *"thank you, my wife actually need a new phone, she'll be very happy when I give her this"* Matthew said as he walked with Gordon back to his Jeep. Matthew looked at the phone when he got back to his car, it was a fancy phone, it had a pink cover, the type of colour his wife likes, he felt ecstatic as he drove home, he pictured the expression on his wife's face when he gives her the phone, he had already counted the ten fifty Euro notes given to him by Gordon immediately he got back inside his car, he was very delighted that he had this extra cash because he's being worried about how he would keep up with the expenses of having another child, but with this new business of collecting package, at least he can make extra five hundred a week, he has not gotten half of the stuffs his wife told him they'll need for the new baby, since it's going to be a girl, they would have to buy completely new stuffs. When he gave the phone to his wife, she was over the moon, she kissed him passionately *"I love this, I love you"* she said as she sat down on the three sitter couch in there sitting room and immediately trying to get the sim card from her old phone into the new phone in other to start using the phone immediately *"sweetheart, is this phone unlock"* she asked him, *"yes, it's unlock, just put your Sim card into the phone, and you're ready to go, do you want me to help you"* he asked, *"no, no, I'll do it, you just get some rest before you go to work"* she said, Matthew would be starting work at 4pm at Ferrybank, *"Gordon also gave me five hundred Euros for collecting the package"* he said as he brought out the money from his pocket. *"Wow"* she said putting her hands to cover her mouth to gesticulate her excitement, *"you can keep it as part of the money for the stuffs for the baby"* he said as he gave her the money. *"Thank you"* she said and stood up to kiss him on his lips. Within the four weeks to the birth of the baby, Matthew collected a package each week and he got five hundred Euro and a mobile phone whenever he handed the package to Gordon, so he and his wife bought all the stuffs for the new baby, and they also bought a new TV as well, because the old analogue TV in the sitting room had been having problem with the picture breaking up off and on for over a year and they just had to managed watching programmes on it. Matthew was at work two weeks before the baby was due, he got a call from his wife *"Sweetheart you'll have to come now and take me to the hospital, it's like the baby is coming now"* she screamed. *"Am on my way sweetheart"* Matthew immediately replied as he quickly closed the construction site gate, and immediately rang his boss to tell him that he had to leave work to get his wife to the hospital, his boss said it was okay for him to go, that he should just make sure that the gate was properly locked, his boss understood because he knows Matthew is a very diligent reliable worker, but when Matthew got his wife to the hospital that night after the nurse examined her they were told that the baby wasn't ready to come out, this happened on two other occasions that he had to live his work to rush down to his flat to get his wife to the hospital, and then been told that the baby was not due yet, thinking about his wife going into labour without his physical presence at home with her to quickly get her to the hospital made him unsettled at work, so what he did was that, he got two weeks of his holiday off work to stay with his wife until the baby came, and the baby came a week earlier than the date the hospital originally gave that she would arrive, the day the baby finally arrived, that morning around 4am, his wife started complaining about the baby coming, that the water to her ovary as broken, Matthew could see that her pyjamas was wet and the bed was wet as well, luckily, his mother in law was around to look after their son, she arrived from England three days earlier, Matthew immediately got his wife to the hospital, the drive from his apartment to the hospital took him fifteen minutes, after thirty five minutes of their arrival at the hospital, Delilah gave birth to their baby girl, when the baby was about to be delivered, there were four midwifes in the room with a doctor and Matthew, his wife was screaming, this made Matthew perturbed, Delilah was told by the midwifery's to push, she screamed as she pushed, this she did for about twenty minutes *"I can see the head coming, please just continue to push"* one of the midwifes said to Delilah, Matthew looked at his wife and saw something like a head with loads of black curly hair slowly coming out of her virginal *"please push, you have to push"* one of the midwifes said again, *"haaa, haaa, haaa"* Delilah screamed as she pushed, by this time the baby came out, Matthew saw the baby and immediately started crying, tears trickled from his eyes, immediately the baby came out of Delilah, she stopped screaming, she just relaxed on the bed, she looked completely fatigued, one of the midwifes immediately took the baby, wrapped her with a white blanket, and gave it to Matthew, he held the baby carefully as tears continued to trickle from his eyes, the four midwifes came to hug and patted him on his shoulder. *"It's okay, the baby is out, ooh he's so excited, am sure it's tears of joy"* one of the midwifes said trying to calm Matthew down while the doctor examined his wife's vaginal for any complications like tear, the baby looked like an angel, she cried when she first came out, but immediately stopped crying when she was given to Matthew, the midwifes laughed at Matthew *"you are crying as if you gave birth to the baby"* one of them said as she laughed, it took Matthew another three minutes after holding the baby to compose himself to go and comfort his wife, by then the doctor was clearing all the excretes from her body, the doctor said she'll have to sew her vaginal up because of tear, his wife had a difficult time before the baby came out not withstanding that she was giving an injection on her back bone called epidural to make the delivery to be easier and successful, Matthew was admiring her daughter when one of the midwife came and collected her from him *"I need to go and weigh her and also to do some medical checks"* she said, the doctor sewed his wife virginal up, Matthew looked at her as she was in pain and really pitied her, he missed the birth of his first child, his son, two and half years earlier, he was in Dublin that day when his wife called him that she has called the ambulance to get her to the hospital, he immediately drove down to Waterford hospital, but by the time he arrived his wife gave birth ten minutes earlier, so he missed the birth of his son by just ten minutes, but for the birth of his daughter that he didn't miss, the whole scenario has got him completely overwhelmed with emotions.

A week after his daughter's birth, they all went to the church for her naming ceremony, they named her Deborah, but they call her Debbie, they invited some friends and church members about twenty of them back to their flat for a small party, it was a lovely day, Matthew has been attached to the baby since her birth, it was now been two weeks that he took some time off work, he had called his boss to tell him that he needed another two weeks to assist his wife with the children, so he had another week to go before going back to work, but he had been collecting a package weekly for Gordon, and with the payment from collecting the package, he was able to pay for the house rent and also provide for his wife and children. A day after he finally got back to work, his boss came to him at the Ferrybank site that he was minding, he gave him a check of one thousand euro, he told Matthew that it was refund from the tax revenue office for the overtax on his wages for the past one year, Matthew was very delighted, he thanked his boss, the next day he lodged the check into his bank account, he had plans to save up money to buy his wife a second hand car to help her move around with his two kids, not withstanding that his wife doesn't know how to drive, he had plans to teach her how to drive every weekend before going to work. The fifth week after the birth of his daughter, Gordon called Matthew as usual, *"hi Matthew, the package would be delivered this Friday, I will send you the name and address"* *"okay, thank you"* Matthew replied. That Friday, he was waiting at the front of a house that was three houses away from the house he was expecting the package to be delivered to, he couldn't park on the same street of the house with the address because there was no parking space available, so he parked his car at the car park on the Quay, and walked for about six minutes to the front of the house he was standing at, he had got a call from the courier guy about twenty minutes earlier on that he was almost there at the house to deliver the package. Immediately Matthew saw the courier van, he quickly approached the courier guy as he went to bring the box from the back of the van, *"Hi, please I am expecting a delivery for flat number thirty"* says Matthew, *"are you Stewart Davis"* the guy asked as he wanted to hand the package to Matthew *"no, I am his brother, he's not at home, and he just told me to collect the package for him"* Matthew replied, *"okay, just sign here"* he said as he gave him the package and also gave him the electronic device for him to sign on the glass to proof that the package was delivered and collected, Matthew put the package on the ground, and signed the electronic device, *"thank you"* the guy said as he closed the door to the back of the van and got into the driver sit, Matthew noticed another guy sat at the front on the passenger sit of the van before the delivery guy drove off. Matthew picked the package to go to his car, Gordon had called him earlier about three times to asked him if he had collected the package and had told him to meet him up at Tesco Poleberry in the same Waterford city, so he had plans to call him immediately he gets to his car with the package to tell him that he was on the way, just then as he was walking to the car park with the package, he was surrounded by four undercover police men, and two cars pulled up beside him, they immediately took the package from him, and told him he was under arrest for drug trafficking for sale and supply. Matthew was shocked, he immediately told the officers that he was only collecting mobile phones and not drugs, and that the guy that sent him to collect the package is waiting for him at Poleberry by Tesco, that the officer should follow him to Poleberry, that they would be able to arrest Gordon the owner of the package, but the police said no, and took him to the police station, locked him in a cell for about one hour and then one of the officers came to bring him to the interrogation room were two other officers were waiting for him, Matthew said he continued to plead to the officers to allow him to help them to apprehend the real culprit that used him to collect the drugs, he said he cried as he told them that he was oblivious of the drugs inside the package, but a female officer started sneering at him as he cried, the female officer started singing a song by Timberland that featured One Republic *"it's too late to apologised, it's too late, it's too late to cry, it's too late"* the two other male officers in the interrogation room laughed as their female counterpart sang, then they put him back in the cell, after which a guy in his early twenties was brought into the cell, the guy was very drunk, he was causing the police, banging the cell door with his feet and hand for over fifteen minutes, and spat into the squatting toilet pan on the floor before sitting down beside Matthew on the only single mattress on the floor *"what did you do? Why are you here"* he asked Matthew that was clinging to the Holy Bible that his wife brought him two hours earlier after the police had gone to his apartment to ransack the whole place to search for drugs or any illegal stuffs, but found nothing there that was incriminating to use as evidence to back their case, that was the reason why the police tried so many times after bringing him out of the cell before getting him to the interrogation room to admit that he knew about the drugs that came in the package, they'll tell him *"Matthew, we really want to help you, but you are not helping yourself if you continue to deny that you didn't know that drugs was coming in the package, if you go into the interrogation room now, you just say you knew about the drugs, and then we'll be able to help you"* Matthew would reply *"okay officer"* when he gets to the interrogation room before the recorder start playing, the three officers would tell themselves smiling *"he's going to do it now"* but when the recorder starts playing, Matthew would say *"I never ever knew about the drugs in the package, I was only told I was collecting a package containing mobile phones, and if you had cooperated with me when you arrested me with the package and immediately followed me to Poleberry, you would have apprehended the real culprit that used me to collect the drugs."* The expression of devastation on the face of the officers in the room when he said this was very obvious, that was the reason why they have arranged with this undercover policeman to act like a drunkard to be locked in with him in the same cell to get a confession out of him *"why are you here?"* he asked Matthew again *"I was used to collect a package containing drugs, and the police refused to apprehend the real culprit that sent me to collect the package"* Matthew replied *"so you didn't know about the drugs? you should know that the drugs were coming in the package"* the guy said *"no I didn't, if I knew why would I want the police to get the real guy that sent me, I didn't know about the drugs"* Matthew replied again. Has he explained how he got into his ordeal to Collins, his new cell mate in utter retrospection, he was almost in tears, *"had it been the police cooperated with me has I was ready to get them to apprehend the guy that sent me to collect the package, they would have arrested the real culprit"* says Matthew, *"there was another guy that Gordon used to collect the same type of package in Cork city two weeks after I was arrested, the guy was brought to Cork prison, if they had arrested Gordon when he was waiting for me at Polebery, he wouldn't be out there using naive people like myself to collect his drugs supplies"* Matthew said again, *"well it is hard to believe that you didn't know about the drugs in the package, anyone can say that"* Collins replied, *"well I don't blame anyone that doesn't believe my obliviousness of the drug in the package, but the reprehensibility of the police refusing to cooperate with me to apprehend the orchestrator of the drug importation, which is Gordon, is highly irrefutable, because they would definitely have found out that I was unaware of the drugs in the package if he had been arrested, I definitely won't have been charged for the drugs, they would have charged me for something else, may be for my stupidity for collecting packages at different addresses for Gordon, but not for drugs"* Matthew replied, *"honestly, you just have to do your whack, because it's very hard for anyone to believe that crap of a story that you've just told me, not withstanding that the few minutes that I have known you Matthew, honestly, I kind of believe you, because it's possible, because if you were ready to give up the main guy that sent you to collect the package and the police refused to immediately arrest the guy, then there is a fault on their side, maybe one of the cops knows this Gordon guy, and wanted to protect him, because most police officers would immediately want to get this guy arrested and locked up, well that's life, you got ten years for been very stupid and greedy as well, I don't want to blame you for your own mistake of collecting the package, but now you know"* says Collins, *"well I am going for my appeal next week, and my defence wants to do their best to get the judges to understand that I wasn't aware of the drugs in the package"* says Matthew, *"well I wish you best of luck, I won't be here, I am going back to Cork prison tomorrow, and hopefully by next week my wife would have gotten someone to pose my bail money and I'll be out"* Collins replied *"what are you in for"* Matthew asked *"well I was caught driving without insurance and suspended drivers licence, I'll be out on bail next week anyway"* Collins replied again.

The next day when Matthew came back from the print shop, Collins was gone, it was on a Thursday going to 12pm, all the cells were opened because it was time for lunch and prisoners were queuing up to get their lunch, Tony the boxer came by to his cell door, talking quietly *"you know what Matthew"* he said *"what?"* Matthew asked, *"did Dave told you that he was going for his appeal today?"* Tony asked *"no, he didn't, no wonder I didn't see him at the print shop this morning, he's in D block, is he back? Or did you see him?"* asked Matthew *"I didn't see him, but it was on the news about ten minutes ago that he got extra two years for appealing his sentence, now he has to do another two years for wasting the court's time"* Tony said as he looked at Matthew that was all the expression of shock *"you see, that's why I told you that you are taking a big risk appealing your conviction, if you don't drop the appeal, you might get more years Matthew, the court won't believe you, the court always support the police, they are on the same team, you need to think about that, and Matthew, who was that guy in your cell this morning?"* Tony asked *"ooh!!! His name is Collins, he was just here for yesterday night, he's going back to Cork prison today, I think he might be gone already"* says Matthew *"the idiot spoke to me this morning, I think after you left for school, he was asking me if I believe that you didn't know about the drugs in the package you collected, I told him I don't know, but I said I believe you, I don't know why he should be asking me about that, I don't know or ever met that idiot before this morning, some people are just too nosey getting into other people's business, I'll just need to quickly grab my lunch"* Tony said and left, Matthew was still in shock while he left, he just sat on his bed, he could hear the officers closing the cell doors to signal that most of the prisoners as gotten their lunch and the guys from the kitchen were about to finish serving the lunch and leave the landing, but Matthew immediately lost his appetite after hearing that Dave got more years because most of the prisoners that knows about his appeal tells him that he would get more years, ninety nine percent as told him explicitly that he would get more years, most especially when it comes to drugs, some prison officers has advised him to get his solicitor to withdraw the appeal if he loves himself, since he came to prison, he has witnessed about eight prisoners that went for their appeal, about five of them got more years, the rest of them were lucky that they didn't get more, there sentence was just told to remain, one of those three prisoners that got their sentence reinstated was very happy that he didn't get more years, he celebrated.

The next day, Matthew saw David at the print shop *"you are next Matthew, you are definitely getting more years if you go for your appeal, if you love yourself get your lawyer to withdraw your appeal, I am regretting now that I didn't do that, if there is a time clock that can take me just back to last week, I would get my solicitor to withdraw my appeal, now my wife told me after the appeal that she's tired of waiting for me, that she can't wait anymore, that it's finished between me and her, can you imagine that, after getting another two years, the bitch came to me right there at the court after the judgement to tell me that it's over between me and her, I am just sorry about my children, the bitch should go, I have been told that she's sleeping with one of my friends anyway, and I have only been in prison for three years, with the two years added now, I am now doing ten years, that is another about five years to go for me, Matthew!!!"* Dave said as he touched him on the right shoulder *"if you don't withdraw your appeal, you will get more years, I went there and I saw that the judges were not happy with me appealing my sentence, that is just my advice to you, of cause, you do what you want to do, I just don't want you to get more years"* Dave said to him *"thank you Dave"* Matthew replied, there were four other prisoners that were there and Mr Roach looked at Matthew, maintained eye contact as he stood by the photocopy machine, printing some documents, he nodded his head to Matthew in support of what Dave as just said *"I told him Matthew that he might get more years, and see what happened"* says Mr Roach as he took the photocopied documents from the machine and walked out of the room. The next four days to his appeal, Matthew felt completely apprehensive, he called the Potters to tell them to continue to pray for him, he asked them if they heard from his wife, they said they didn't hear from her, they said they tried to contact her, but she didn't pick up their call, and they sent her a text message, but she didn't reply as well, they encouraged and advised him to concentrate on praying that they believe he's going to be alright at the appeal, *"we'll see you there brother Matthew"* Joseph Potter replied, "thank you sir" says Matthew. A day before his appeal, it was on a Wednesday morning around 10am, at the print shop *"are you still going for your appeal?"* Dave asked *"yes, I am going, I am not doing ten years for a crime I didn't commit"* Matthew replied, *"well, I believe you committed the crime, and so the judges there at the court of appeal, and I believe you are going to get more years"* Dave said emphatically as he looked from Matthew to Mr Roach *"he's going to get more years, I will tell him that I told him when he comes back tomorrow"* Dave said again laughing to Mr Roach, Matthew thought about Dave's case and his, they are two different events, not withstanding that Dave is in for drugs as well, Dave has a previous conviction for drug possession before he got caught again with drugs, he was given a three years suspended sentence on his first drug sentence and given the chance to turn a new leaf, but he refused to change, he pretended to have changed for two years after the verdict, but the third year the police discovered that he was back in the game, so they put him under surveillance, they sent an undercover police to do business with the guy that Dave does business with, not withstanding that Dave doesn't touch the drugs, he drove his associate to deliver the drugs, the undercover police man took several deliveries from Dave associate, when the car arrives at the undercover cop's location for the delivery, Dave always sits in the car while his partner delivered the drugs, when the police had enough evidence to arrest both of them, on that day, Dave arrived with his partner in crime as usual, they didn't know that some undercover policemen were waiting, immediately Dave's associate went in to deliver the drugs, there were three police officers waiting to arrest him in the apartment, and there were three other undercover policemen sitting in a car outside the house, but Dave surveying the area to see if there was anything suspicious going on, he's always doing that, surveying any location of delivery, he learnt this from his mistake when he got caught the first time, he was able to noticed the three men sitting in a car parked on the other side of the road on the street through the side mirror on the passenger's side, and he thought he knew one of them as a cop, by this time his partner was already arrested in the apartment that he went to deliver drugs, Dave could see one of the undercover cop talking on the phone, so his instinct immediately told him something was definitely wrong, so he pulled the car out on the road and started driving away, but the cops followed him, so he increased the accelerator, driving about hundred miles per hour in an area that he was supposed to drive fifty miles per hour, but the cops caught up with him in a traffic hold up and arrested him, they searched the car, and discovered two kilos of cocaine that was bound to be supplied to other suppliers, during interrogation, Dave denied and said he wasn't aware of the drugs in the car, he said he didn't know that his partner was dealing in drugs, his partner also testified that Dave wasn't aware of the drugs in the car, but Dave's fingerprint was discovered on the plastic bag that was used to cover the drugs in the boot of the car, so the prosecutor charged him and he was found guilty by the jury and he got eight years, so; when Matthew compares his own case with loads of other prisoners that got more years when they went for their appeal, he sees that they were hundred percent culpable in the crime and deserved to be found guilty, but himself, he hundred percent believes that he didn't get a fair trial and judgement, not withstanding that as the hours to his appeal drew closer, the more he became anxious and restless, and couldn't wait for it to be over, something told him the judges at the appeal court would see the truth, and do the right thing by setting him free. He couldn't go to sleep that night he was overwhelmed with the thoughts of what would happen at the court the next day.

The next morning, one of the prison officers opened his cell door at 6:am to tell him to get ready for court, he would take a shower and dress up, he already got his suit ironed and his black shoe cleaned the previous day.

Chapter Thirteen

The Unexpected Judgement

John the daddy devil stood in his cell with another prisoner that just came into his cell at Cloverhill prison, he had been told earlier on by one of the prison officers that he would be transferred to Midlands prison that he should get his stuffs ready, as the prisoner helped him to park his stuff, "I can't wait to cut out the balls of that rat that got me back in this fucking hole, I had my perfect plan laid out and that cunt blew it all up, now I have to deal with all this shit all over again, when I see that rat, I am going to cut him into one thousand pieces" John ranted as he arranged his stuff into the nylon bags given to him by the same officer that came earlier on to tell him about his immediate transfer, he was sentenced to life imprisonment at the Cloverhill Circuit Court two weeks earlier for the murder of Casey, in which Mark and Snake got life as well for the murder of Cathy's dad and also for the kidnapping of Lucy and Cathy, the time was going to 11am, one of the two male prison officers standing outside John's cell came into the cell to tell him it was time to leave, he carried some of his stuffs packed in four small nylon bags and the other prisoner helped him to carry the remaining nylon bag to the exit gate on the landing. Meanwhile earlier on that day Matthew sat in one of the holding cells by the reception at Midland prison with four other prisoners, he was dressed in a black suit with a blue checkers shirt and a black shoe to match, the other prisoners were all dressed in jeans and t shirt, they looked at Matthew, one of them said, *"you look like a solicitor Matthew, you are crazy if you think you dressing like this will prevent the judges giving you more years"* the three other prisoners laughed as he said that, Matthew smiled back at them, he didn't say anything, he was in fasting and prayer, he held unto his holy bible, *"what is this?"* another prisoner asked him as he pointed to the bible *"it's my bible"* Matthew replied, *"you are crazy Matthew!!!"* they all laughed again, *"are you going to give that to the judge to proof that you are innocent or what?"* they all laughed again, Matthew continued to smile, *"this keeps me company that I am not alone"* replied Matthew *"well, I bet you won't be alone when you get three extra years"* another guy said and they all busted into laughter again, Matthew shook his head in disappointment as they all laughed, he thought as he looked at them *"they are all going for their sentence or appeal, they are supposed to be sober or at least anxious about what would be the outcome of their appeal"* Matthew thought *"but it seems these guys are enjoying themselves, they don't care about getting more years or been locked up."* They all rolled up a tobacco and smoked, not withstanding that Matthew doesn't smoke cigarettes, he has gotten use to coping with the atmosphere of the incessant smoke coming from their tobacco as they drag from the cigarette and puff out the smoke, he doesn't have any other choice than to endure inhaling the smoke, that is prison for him, no were to run, no were to hide, this guys that he was surrounded by, don't care if they spend the rest of their life in prison, they've been in and out of prison several times, they have come to be institutionalize to the prison system of been locked up, that is what they call it, they believe they are been smart by been in prison, and that is the reason for the high rate of recidivism, this irresponsible cohorts believe that by staying in prison they won't have to be out there to pay for bills like electricity bill, gas bill and several other expenses like payment for going to the gym and also, they get free three square meals in prison, they even have television to watch for free and most of them even have access to console games like play station, which they play for several hours till late in the night most times because they know that they can get up from bed at any time they want to, they are not forced to take advantage of loads of the facilities that the prison authority has put in place to better their life when they finish their sentence, such facilities like school, workshops were they can learn a profession such as carpentry or welding or woodwork or several other trade, they believe that been outside the walls of the prison is like hell to them, they have become so institutionalized that when they finish one prison sentence they immediately go and commit another crime in other to be sent back to prison, prison is their home, they sing a song about home sweet home whenever they are on their way back to prison, there was a time Matthew was having a discussion with Mr Roach, chief O'Reilly and Dave at the print shop, they were discussing about how most prisoners in the prison are re-offenders, which Matthew said that he believes some of the major reason for recidivism is because of the conduciveness of the prison environment for the prisoners, he said that if he were in charge of the prison authority, he would make life in prison uncomfortable for re-offenders, he said that a first time prisoner or offender is entitle to stuffs like TV, single cell and every other amenities currently available to them in the prison, but he said that re-offenders should be deprive of such amenities like TV, consoles games and play stations, they should only have access to educational facilities like school and workshop to get them to learn a profession that can help them to change from their criminal activities, and they should also make it mandatory that re-offenders work in the prison, he said he is absolutely certain that if the prison system is run in that way, it would really help to reduce recidivism, Mr Roach said he doesn't believe that would reduce re-offenders, but chief O'Reilly laughed, *"Matthew what do you then think would happen to the job of a prison officers if we don't have prisoners coming back"* he laughed as he said that *"Matthew, you prisoners are our client, we are here to look after you, it's the human right of every prisoner that we take good care of you as long as you don't break our rules, we'll keep you happy, we'll look after you"* he said again in a smirk way, but he noticed the dismayed expression on Matthew's face. *"Matthew am only joking, it's crazy the way most prisoners come back here, if there is one person that I am absolutely certain that won't be back here, it's you Matthew"* he said explicitly as he pointed to Matthew, *"thank you sir"* says Matthew. *"What about me chief?"* asked Dave *"you Dave, you'll definitely be back here, I know you Dave"* says chief O'Reilly laughing as Dave looked utterly disappointed from what he just said *"yeah sure, Dave will be back, and Matthew won't be coming back, you're correct chief"* Mr Roach chipped in, *"ooh thank you sirs"* Matthew said again as Dave looked in embarrassment and walked off.

The door to the holding cell opened and two prison officers came in to tell the prisoners that it was time to live for court *"Matthew you are going into the truck first"* one of the officers said and brought him out of the cell as the other prison officer closed the cell door after him, *"give me your hand"* the officer that brought him out of the cell said as he brought out the handcuffs and handcuffed him *"is it too tight"* he asked him as he put on the handcuff on his wrist, Matthew checked that he was still able to hold his bible properly *"no sir, it's okay"* he replied. He brought him to the prison truck, opened one of the six cubicles for him to sit inside, and then locked the door to the cubicle, Matthew managed to sit in the small cubicle, it was so tight that he just managed to sit almost like in a crouching position, he heard as the officers brought in the other prisoners one at a time to the truck, opened the cubicle, set them in and locked the doors, it was getting to about 8am, the journey to the appeal court should be about two hours, he thought, it was a bright day, it was the month of June, he heard the engine of the truck started, revving up and the radio came on, the news about the weather forecast was on, he heard that there would be showers of rain later in the day, he thought to himself *"it would be shower of blessings for him"* but something immediately came to his mind *"what if you get more years like you have been told by several prisoners and officers!!!, well I just have to believe that I won't be getting more years, I need to hold my faith!!!"* he said to himself, *"prayer without faith is a waste of time, stop being negative!!!"* He heard that voice told him louder in his thought, he thought about his wife, he hasn't been able to speak to her for almost four days, he was only able to speak to her the day after he got the letter for his appeal to notify her the date, but the way she spoke back to him, he has set his expectation that she won't be coming to the court and he won't be seeing her there, but he was looking forward to see his pastors, Ruth and Joseph Potter there, the two angels in his life, he was utterly apprehensive, shivering from cold because of his anxiety, he was in a deep thought throughout the journey, he thought about his children, tears trickled from his eyes as he thought about them, he missed them so much, he had missed his daughter's birthday three weeks earlier, she celebrated her fifth year birthday, Matthew made her a pink teddy bear and duvet cover at the beginning of June from the prison school tailoring class and also made her a lovely birthday card with her picture printed on the card, he made the card from the print shop, he sent everything to her in the post, he was very delighted when he rang his wife on her daughter's birthday and was able to speak to his daughter who said she loved the teddy bear and the card, he could remember his wife telling him that afternoon that his daughter has not let go of the pink teddy bear since she gave it to her in the morning of that day, tears continued to trickle from his eyes has he thought about his children, he prayed to God that if it's just because of one thing, one good reason for God to make the three judges to have mercy upon him at his appeal, they should do it because of his children, he's a good father that loves his children, a voice told him immediately *"you are very stupid if you think the judges would show you mercy for collecting a package full of drugs, you should have thought about your children when you were collecting the package"* his heart started palpitating again *"I rebuke you Satan, I rebuke you in Jesus mighty name"* he prayed silently clinching to his holy bible to try and be positive *"the almighty God will use the three judges to show me mercy in Jesus mighty name, I promised you God, I make a covenant with you that if you deliver me today, I will never ever do such a thing again in my life, please God, please give me this final chance"* he cried as he prayed wholehearted, *"you have to have faith, you just have to believe that God will set you free"* he said trying to reassure himself that he would be alright, he was still in his realm of prayers when he discovered the truck had stopped, he thought they have arrived at the court, so he stooped and looked through the small window at the top of his head in the cubicle, but they were just stopped at a traffic light that was about six hundred meters from the court house, it was a busy morning in the city of Dublin, it was going to 10am, there were loads of cars and people busy walking hurriedly to their respective place of work and destination.

Seven minutes later they arrived at the back of the court house, the prison truck door opened, and his cubicle door opened, one of the prison officers took him through the entrance door to the reception, there were two court officers at the desk, one female officer that looked in her early thirties, she had a red hair, about six feet tall and the other court officer a male, he looked like he's in his late forties, they were both tall and big, *"I want to book this prisoner in"* the prison officer that brought him from the prison truck said to the two court officers at the desk, *"what's his name?"* the female court officer asked *"Matthew Williams"* the prison officer replied, the other male court officer checked the list on the wall on his left hand side, he saw the name and put a tick beside it with the pen he was holding, he told the prison officer to bring Matthew, they followed him to the court holding cell, when they got to the cell door, the court officer opened the cell door, there were six other prisoners in the cell, the prison officer removed the handcuffs from Matthew's wrist and told him to go into the cell. The cell was small, about six feet long and four feet wide, four of the prisoners were smoking, the cigarettes smoke in the room made the room looked misty, there was a toilet by the entrance of the cell, there were two flat bricks one each on each side of the room, about one feet from the floor, three prisoners sat on each side of the cell on the flat brick meant as the seat in the cell, Matthew joined the prisoners on the right side of the cell, they created a space for him to sit on the flat brick, *"what's the crack"* the guy that sat right beside him asked him *"Still Alive"* Matthew replied, *"barely"* the guy replied laughing, *"what prison did you come from"* the guy asked *"I came from Midlands"* Matthew replied, *"that's a good prison, I was there twelve years ago, I am in Mount Joy prison, and what sentence are you appealing?"* the guy asked again *"I got ten years for collecting a package containing drugs"* Matthew replied *"and what is the quantity of the drugs, I mean, is the price above ten thousand euro"* the guy asked again *"well the police put the value of the drugs at about forty thousand euro"* Matthew replied *"and did you pleaded guilty?"* the guy asked *"no, I pleaded not guilty because I didn't know that there was drugs in the package"* Matthew replied, the guy started laughing, *"you're crazy, you knew you were collecting drugs, and you should have pleaded guilty and got a lighter sentence like six years"* the guy replied *infuriatingly* *"and you think the judges will believe that you didn't know about the drugs after the jury found you guilty, you must be completely deluded to think that will happen, you might even get more years"* the guy said again. *"I pleaded guilty for getting caught with almost half of what you got caught with and got the same ten years that you got, I pleaded guilty, that should have been a mitigating factor for the judge not to give me the mandatory ten years, my solicitor told me that I would get maximum seven years, but the judge said because I had previous convictions for drugs, that's the reason why she gave me the mandatory ten years, she's crazy, I know this judges here will reduce my sentence, but you my friend, you'll be lucky if you don't get more years"* he said *"but I can't plead guilty to a crime that I didn't commit"* says Matthew again *"whatever"* the guy said and asked for a cigarette from the guy sitting on his left hand side. Just then, the cell door opened, the two court officers that Matthew saw at the reception brought in some small paper bags of McDonald containing burgers, chips and coke and handed one each to each prisoner, Matthew asked the guy that he had been talking to if he wants his *"you don't want it?"* the guy asked, astonished, *"yes am alright"* Matthew replied, he didn't want to tell him that he was fasting and praying, he knew he would make jest of him, the guy took the burger, and asked the other prisoners if anyone wants the chips, another prisoner took the chips, and another prisoner took the coke. Just then the cell door opened again, the male court officer stood at the door *"Brian O'Keefee!!!"* he called a name from a paper that he was holding *"yes, that's me"* one of the prisoners jumped up as he answered him, *"come on, let's go"* says the office.

Thirty-five minutes later, the cell door opened again, the female officer that opened the door removed the handcuffs on Brian's hand and stood aside for him to get back into the cell, she called another name from the folder that she was holding and took another prisoner away. *"Those bastards gave me an extra twelve months, fuck them"* Brian said angrily, *"for fuck sake!!!"* another prisoner said, *"now I have to do eleven years"* says Brian again, he's in his early forties, but looked like he's in his sixties, he's about six feet tall, for the past twenty three years he has spent almost ninety percent of his life in prison, he's been going to prison since he was fifteen years old for dealing in drugs, he started been sent to juvenile detention centres, and by the time he was eighteen years old, he got his first sentence of two years for dealing in drugs, came out, but his freedom only lasted for three months because he got busted with four kilos of cocaine and was lucky to get eight years, the prosecutor was very unhappy with the sentence, so he appealed the sentence asking that Brian should get more years, but at the appeal court the judges upheld the eight years sentence based on the fact that Brian pleaded guilty and cooperated with the police to apprehend another culprit, after serving six years, Brian was released early for good behaviour, but again his freedom only lasted for about six months before he got busted again with three kilos of cocaine and was sentence to ten years two years ago, not withstanding that he pleaded guilty, what he doesn't understand is that on his two first charges since he became an adult, the judges in those cases gave him a chance to repent and change, but he continued with his illicit drug business that was the reason why the judges at the appeal court gave him another twelve months for wasting the court's time. *"Matthew Williams!!!"* the officer called as the cell door opened again, *"that's me officer"* says Matthew as he got up holding his bible, before then, three other prisoners had gone for their appeal and all of them came back with the story that their sentence was upheld, one of the prisoners was very happy that he didn't get more years, he was given the mandatory ten years for dealing in drugs, not withstanding that he pleaded guilty, Matthew continued to pray silently in his mind as he witnessed each prisoner coming back with their sentence been upheld or gotten more years, and none coming back with good news that their sentence was reduced, but in Matthew's case, he's fighting for his conviction to be overturned, well, he told himself that his own case is different, this guys did the crime and he believes that it was a poetic justice for them to get the sentence they got, *"I am culpable for collecting packages in other peoples name that I don't know, which I lied to the courier delivery guys that I know them, but I am not culpable for the drug charges as I didn't know that I was been used to collect drugs"* he said this to himself to encourage himself that he was doing the right thing to appeal his conviction and sentence. Immediately the officer closed the cell door after Matthew, he handcuffed him and brought him through the reception, climbed up a staircase then opened a door that led them into the court room and told him to sit on a small wooden bench that is used for defendants to sit on, there were about sixty other people in the room, at the front row was seated four senior counsels and three barristers with several files seated on a desk, Matthew saw Daren O'Kelly, the senior counsel representing him, and right behind them seated on a wooden bench were seven solicitors looking at files getting ready with documents to assist the senior counsels and barristers with their case, but Matthew didn't see Luke Hoare his solicitor that represented him at his trial, and also didn't see the barrister that represented him during his trial, but he saw another solicitor handing documents to Daren O'Kelly, and seated on the other benches behind the solicitors are the families and friends of defendants that has come to appeal their sentence or conviction was Ruth and Joseph Potter with their daughter Pamela, they smiled at him as their eyes came into contact, he couldn't smile back because he was overwhelmed with anxiety, his apprehension was so obvious that he was shivering like someone that has got serious cold, but he still managed to hold the bible that he was carrying, he kept praying silently saying psalm 23 quietly to himself, he knew it off hand, *"The LORD is my shepherd; I shall not want. He makes me lie down green pastures. He leads me beside still waters.[a] He restores my soul. He leads me in paths of righteousness for his name's sake. Even though I walk through the valley of the shadow of death,[c] I will fear no evil, for you are with me; your rod and your staff, they comfort me. You prepare a table before me in the presence of my enemies; you anoint my head with oil; my cup overflows. Surely[d] goodness and mercy[e] shall follow me all the days of my life, and I shall dwell[f] in the house of the LORD forever"* he murmured all this sobbing, he looked down at his bible most of the time and could not hear the deliberation between his senior counsel and the three judges, the tears from his eyes trickled unto his bible, he fidgeted throughout the hearing, just before the judges passed their judgement, he slightly raised his head towards Ruth and Joseph Potter, they nodded their head to reassure him that he would be alright, he looked towards the back of the courtroom, then he saw his wife standing at the back of the benches, Delilah was dressed in a pink long sleeve shirt and blue jeans, she nodded her head to him to greet him and to let him know that she was standing there, her presence didn't surprise him because he was more overwhelmed with what would be the outcome of the decision of the judges, but he was gobsmacked to see Collins, the guy that was his last cell mate two weeks earlier, their eyes met, he was also standing at the back of the court room, about six meters away from his wife, he smiled at Matthew, but Matthew was still fidgeting and startled to see that Collins was talking to two of the prison officers, but what Matthew didn't know was that, one of the three judges that was presiding over his case sent Collins to Matthew and some other prisoners in prison as an undercover court employee to get the fact about Matthew's involvement in the crime that he was put in prison for, in other to use the investigation as part of the outcome for the decision he would arrive at that day, because he found it hard to believe that Matthew was oblivious of the drug in the package, just then, the senior counsel representing him smiled at him immediately after the judgement was passed, but Matthew didn't smile back, he just looked at him and bow his head in courtesy to great him because he didn't know what has just happened, the solicitor that he saw giving Darren O'Kelly documents earlier on came to him to great him *"congratulations"* he said to him, Matthew looked at him in astonishment and confused, he looked towards the judges seat and discovered that they had left the court room *"didn't you hear the judgement passed?"* the solicitor asked Matthew *"what, I didn't hear the judgement, I don't know"* he replied in befuddlement, curious to know what happened, now seriously fidgeting and finding it more difficult to hold his bible as his heart continued to palpitate, the bible fell on the floor, *"you have been released on time served"* the solicitor said, *"I have been released?"* asked Matthew *"yes, you have been released, congratulations, wipe your face, it's time for you to stop crying, it is over"* the solicitor said again as he patted him on the shoulder and gave him a tissue to clean the tears streaming from his eyes. *"Thank you sir"* Matthew replied as he took the tissue and the solicitor left, Matthew looked towards his pastors, Ruth and Joseph Potter who looked jubilant, smiling and talking to one of the prison officers, their daughter Pamela waved to him jubilantly as well, he managed to smile back, he looked at his wife who looked crestfallen as she still stood at the back of the court room, she looked confused, Joseph Potter came closer to him, *"congratulations brother Matthew, we did it, but they said you still have to go back to the prison to get your release processed, God did it for us brother Matthew, you can call me whenever they release you from prison"* he excitedly murmured to him. *"Thank you sir"* Matthew replied. Joseph Potter then walked over to Ruth Potter and Pamela who were now talking to Delilah at the exit door of the court room, just then the prison officers came to take him back to the holding cell *"what did you get"* one of the prisoners asked immediately he entered back into the holding cell *"what happened"* another prisoner asked *"am sure they gave him more years"* another one said laughing, Matthew sat on the flat brick bench still flabbergasted that he was about to be release from prison, he thought about his wife and children, his wife had told him two years earlier that she moved house from the house they used to live together before he went to prison and reluctantly gave him the new address when he asked for it. *"What happened"* Brian, the last prisoner to speak to him since he came into the cell asked, *"am sure you got more months or years"* he too said. *"I am going to the prison to get my release processed,"* Matthew quietly said to him *"it's a joke, you're lying"* another prisoner said, *"yes, I got time served, I think I am just going to the prison to sign some documents of my release,"* Matthew said again, *"wow, then you should be happy man, I got fucking extra twelve months"* Brian said. It was going to about 3pm, the cell door slightly opened, and the two court officers peeped into the cell, *"Matthew, you go first"* the female court officer said to tell them that it was time to go back to the prison, they didn't handcuff Matthew, they handed him over to two prison officers at the reception after signing the sheet of paper on the wall to proof that they have collected him from the court house, one of them told Matthew to follow him to the prison truck, they didn't handcuff him, it was the same prison truck that he came with in the morning, the officer opened the same cubicle that he sat in on the way to the court, he told him to go inside, as he sat down without being in handcuffs he felt the sign of his potential freedom, on the way back, he thought about his wife, he pictured her confused after the judgement of his release, is she going to take him back, has she moved on with the man she was having an affair with, well, if she doesn't take him back at least she would allow him to see his children, he thought, he was more restless as he was before the judgement, the only difference is that he has stopped crying, he thought about all the discussion between him and Tony the boxer, he had told Matthew about them doing business together when they get out of prison, Tony had told him that he has substantial amount of money saved up in a bank in South Africa that they can invest in drug business, Matthew thought about their discussion in retrospection *"you are a smart guy Matthew, we can do business together and make loads of money, then we can retire, I have all my connections and contact, but I need a smart guy that would be my right hand man, and I believe you are the right man for the job Matthew"* says Tony. *"I am down Tony, look at me, I have lost my wife and with all my hard work out there before I started collecting the packages that got me into this trouble, I used to work as a labourer on a building site from 8am to 2pm, and then go and start a security job on another construction site from 4pm to 10pm, doing sometimes eighty hours a week, and at the end of the week when I get my pay checks from both jobs, I barely made six hundred euro a week after tax, that was why I was happy to make extra five hundred a week collecting the package for that asshole that I believe was making thousands euro weekly using naive people like myself to collect his drugs"* says Matthew *"well, I will be hundred percent honest with you Matthew, I guarantee you that within six months of doing business together, you can make at least one million euro"* says Tony, *"wow!!!, that's a lot of money"* Matthew chipped in excitedly *"well, we are both doing ten years, and you started your sentence seven months before me, so you'll definitely be out before me, you just wait for me, I'll give you my dad's number in the UK, and you just contact him to find out when I am out"* Tony said as he wrote his dad's mobile and landline number and gave the piece of paper to Matthew. *"Thank you Tony for believing in me, I will never disappoint you,"* replied Matthew. *"I know that you'll never disappoint me Matthew, I trust you,"* says Tony smiling, the conversation between the other prisoners in the prison truck brought him back to reality, *"yes, we are back home"* one prisoner shouted, *"home sweet home"* another prisoner said, *"I am hungry, what was for lunch today?"* another prisoner asked *"today is Wednesday, I think it's Stroganoff beef and rice"* another prisoner answered *"yum yummy"* the first prisoner that asked about the food said.

In another prison truck, John Dunne the daddy devil sat in one of the cubicles, the expression on his face was the epitome of anger and vengeance, he was in deep thought, planning how he's going to torture Matthew to death when he gets back to Midlands prison, he had loads of his associates which are not just prisoners, but also two prison officers that are on the payroll of Glenn, it was one of the two prison officers that leaked the information that Matthew was the prisoner that gave superintendent Browne the information that led to his arrest, John was so overwhelmed with the thoughts of how he would kill Matthew that when the news of Matthew's release came on the radio; *"A man in his early forties that was doing ten years sentence at Midlands prison has been released today by the court of appeal on time served after serving three and half years of his sentence."* John didn't hear the news, he was still engulfed in his own world of planning what he believes would be Matthew's doomsday when the prison truck he was been transferred in arrived at Midlands prison. A Male prison officer pushed a trolley with prisoners foods towards one of the two holding cells by the prison reception, he unlocked the cell door, he handed a plate of food to each of the four prisoners in the cell, Matthew removed the cover from the plate, it was going to 5pm, but he was not feeling hungry, he was still overwhelmed with his new plight of getting released into the outside walls of the prison that he has been locked up in for over three years, he thought about how he would immediately call Joseph Potter when his release is finalized by the prison authority, he hoped they finished all the paper work that same day so that he can leave the prison that day, he just wanted to get out of the prison, he has really suffered prison confinement because of his claustrophobic nature but as managed to survive for the past three years, when he first came to prison, he thought he wouldn't last a year, he found it difficult to breath properly because his heart was always palpitating from thinking about his separation from his wife and children, but with time, with the prayers and fasting, and later started doing some physical and mental meditation from doing Yoga and going to the prison gym, he got to know how to manage stress and started to have hope that there is light at the end of the tunnel if he just hang on, keep focus and just wait for his appeal, and he has managed to pull it off, he looked at the plate of food that he had in his hand, the food looks yummy, he started eating the food, just then the same male prison officer that brought the trolley with foods unlocked the cell door again, and brought in another prisoner, the face of the prisoner looks familiar to Matthew, he is a bald headed guy, a tall guy of about six feet, three inches, he was dressed in a t shirt, black jeans and runners, he gazed at Matthew as he sat down directly opposite him on the brick bench, as Matthew continued to ruminate on where he came across this prisoner *"what's the crack? Where did you come from?"* one of the prisoner asked the new guy that was just brought into the cell *"I just came from court, I got sentenced today"* the new guy replied reluctantly *"what did you get?"* another prisoner asked the new guy. *"I got two years"* he replied *"for what, what did you do?"* they asked him. *"For fraud, I think I know you"* the guy said excitedly as he suddenly remembered where he knew Matthew *"remember seven years ago in Waterford city, myself and two other guys sold you a laptop"* the guy said smiling, Matthew immediately had a flashback of when he first met the guy, followed by the retrospection of how he got scammed by the guy and his accomplice, it was on a sunny lovely afternoon during summer, Matthew was walking with his wife and son that was sitting in the pram pushed by Matthew, it was a busy afternoon, loads of people came out to enjoy the lovely weather shopping or window shopping at the city centre *"do you want to buy this expensive lap top for a giveaway price?"* one of the three guys that stood by a grey mini jeep asked him opening the lap top that was in a black lap top bag, it was a brand new Dell lap top *"this is the receipt from Curry's shop, the cost price is two thousand eight hundred, but we want to sell it for the half price, it belongs to me, I need money urgently for something very important"* one of the three guys said to Matthew and his wife as he showed them the receipt *"sorry we are not interested, sweetheart lets go"* his wife said to him as he gently pulled him by the hand to get them away from them *"wait wait Sweetheart, this lap top is very cheap, it's an opportunity for me to own a lap top"* Matthew replied and he further negotiated the price of the lap top down to two hundred and fifty euro, which was agreed by the guy holding the lap top while his two other accomplice watch from the mini jeep, Matthew had already checked that the lap top was working, it was a brand new lap top with all accessories included and looked intact *"but I don't have the money here, if you can wait for me to quickly go home and get the money, it will only take me about twenty minutes"* says Matthew *"do you want us to take you in our car?"* the guy holding the lap top asked *"yeah, that would be perfect because my car is parked about ten minutes' walk away, let's go"* Matthew replied, but his wife tried to stop him again *"Sweetheart, just wait for me at the front of Argos, I'll should be back in thirty minutes"* he said and entered the mini jeep, when they got to the house of the blocks of apartment that Matthew reside in, he ran into his apartment to bring the money, by the time he came out, the guy gave him a black lap top bag after collecting the money *"I need to quickly drop this into my apartment and I can follow you guys back to the city centre"* says Matthew *"okay"* the guy sitting at the driver's seat replied, Matthew quickly ran back inside the house, he had plans to quickly connect the power cable to the lap top to quickly check that the cable is working, but when he unzipped the black bag immediately he got inside his apartment he discovered that there were eight boxes of one litter milk perfectly packed in the black bag to make the bag look as if it contained the lap top, the weight of the bag containing the boxes of milk was also the same weight with the black bag containing the lap top, what Matthew didn't know was that when he came outside with the money and counting the money to the guys after they've showed him the lap top again, the guys switched the bag that contained the lap top to the bag that contained the boxes of milk, when Matthew discovered that he had been scammed, he quickly ran out of his flat, down to the car park were the guys were parked earlier on before he came to his flat, he discovered that they were gone, he ran out of the compound to the road and saw the guys mini jeep far gone down the road, he ran after them holding the black bag containing the boxes of milk but he saw them disappeared as they turned right into a major road. He walked down to the city centre completely devastated losing the money because he initially saved up the money for his son's one year birthday coming up the following week, when he got back to the city centre as he walked towards his wife that was waiting for him with his son at the front of Argos store, he opened the black bag about ten meters away from his wife for her to see the boxes of milk *"they scammed me, they gave me this instead of the laptop"* he said to her looking utterly miserable, his wife started laughing. *"I warned you, did you give them the money?"* she asked. *"I gave them the money and they drove off before I came back outside"* he replied, his wife started laughing again, she couldn't stop laughing *"you don't listen, I warned you"* she said again. Matthew back to reality *"this guy scammed me of two hundred and fifty euro seven years ago"* says Matthew to the other prisoners in the cell pointing to the new prisoner that just came into the holding cell, the guy started laughing, *"what did you do with the boxes of milk?"* the guy asked Matthew laughing *"I threw it away, what do you think I did with it, drink the milk?"* Matthew asked as the other prisoners laughed, just then the cell door opened again and one of the officers stood at the door *"Matthew come with me"* he said, and locked the cell back after he came out of the cell *"you are going to park your stuffs, your release has been authorized by the governor"* the officer said *"thank you officer"* says Matthew excitedly *"you are one lucky man Matthew"* says the officer, as they got to the first landing on B Block, Mr Roach was waiting at the front of the officers room, *"congratulations Matthew, you did it, I have just come to say goodbye, you are a very good man Matthew, I wish you best of luck out there."* He held Matthew's hand, pulled him towards himself and hugged him *"I needed to give you that hug, I am very happy for you Matthew"* he said smiling, three other officers smiled as he spoke to Matthew *"thank you Mr Roach, you are the best, kindest officer I ever come across, thank you for everything"* replied Matthew. He was almost in tears *"I'll let you go now"* Mr Roach said and walked off, Matthew walked towards his cell, it was going to half past 6pm, most of the prisoners had gone to the yard, some locked in their cell playing board games or playing games on the play station or just lying down watching the telly, but there were three prisoners walking towards Matthew to go to the exit gate on the landing, one of them came to him, *"you've been released Matthew, you deserve it men, you are a good man, how long did you pray for Matthew?"* the prisoner asked, but Matthew looked at him and smiled *"please pray for me Matthew, I am going for my appeal next week"* the prisoner said, took Matthew's hand and placed it on his own forehead for Matthew to pray for him, but Matthew smiled *"you need to pray yourself, read psalm 23 and Isaiah 45, I have been praying for over three years since my incarceration"* Matthew replied, the officer that brought him to the landing from the reception that was talking to the two officers on duty on the landing about thirty metres away waved to him to signal to him to hurry up, *"I have to quickly go and park my stuffs"* says Matthew, as he got to his cell, he saw that the door to Tony's cell was opened, but he quickly went inside his cell and started packing his stuff into the six big nylon bags that the officer on the landing gave to him earlier on when he was talking to Mr Roach, eighty percent of his stuffs were his Open University books, just then Tony came into his cell, *"hey Matthew, you did it men, everyone heard it on the news"* says Tony. *"Thank you"* Matthew replied as he continued to park his stuffs *"are you leaving now"* he asked *"yes I have been released now, the officer is waiting for me by the gate"* he replied, *"well you have my number Matthew, you call my father, you get in touch, you know our discussion and mission"* says Tony *"yeah Tony, I can't miss that opportunity, I really appreciate that"* replied Matthew as he continued to park his stuff, just then the officer came with a trolley for him to put his stuffs on, Tony extended his hand to him to give him an handshake to say goodbye, fifteen minutes later, Matthew was talking on the phone to daddy Potter to come and get him, he was very excited, the three prison officers at the final gate told him to leave the trolley by the gate after unloading his stuffs into the car that is coming to pick him, then they locked the final exit gate of the prison after he stepped out of the prison precinct, Matthew stood there rested his back on the last fence to the prison outside the last exit gate to the prison, he looked at the car park meant for the prison staffs and visitors to the prison, he also saw the bus stop by the major road that is about ninety metres away from where he was standing, he was given his wrist watch, his money, three hundred and twenty euro saved up in his prison account and also given a free bus ticket that can get him home, he was given all this earlier on before he was told to sign his release papers at the final gate, he looked at his wrist watch as he waited for Joseph Potter, he was coming from Waterford City to pick him up in Portlaoise, which is about one hour ten minutes' drive, Matthew rang him earlier on at about 7pm, and it was going to about 8pm, so he had to wait for another fifteen minutes.

Meanwhile, John the daddy devil sat in one of the holding cell by the reception at Midlands prison, he has been sitting there for about three hours since he arrived from Cloverhill prison, he was sitting at the other cell that was directly opposite the cell Matthew was kept in earlier on, he got his dinner immediately after Matthew was given his dinner by the same prison officer that gave Matthew his, but he didn't know that Matthew was sitting in the other holding cell across from him, the same officer that gave both of them their dinner earlier on unlocked the cell door with another female officer, *"John, your cell is ready"* the male officer said, *"it's about fucking time it's ready"* John said infuriatingly, the officers took him to B landing, he was very excited when the officer told him that they were taking him to a cell on B landing, he believed that it would make it easier for him to get to Matthew, it was going to 8pm, all the other prisoners in the prison had been locked in their cells ten minutes earlier, when he got to B Block, the two officers handed him over to two other male officers on duty on the first landing on B block, *"Hi John, you are back"* one of the officers said smiling, *"yes I am fucking back for life"* John replied as the other officer asked him to come into the office, handed him a clean bedspread, pillow case and other utensils that is issued to prisoners that has just arrived at the prison, *"I'll get you to your cell"* the other officer said when he noticed that his colleague had finished giving John the accessories *"we'll take care of you John"* the officer said as he walked with John to his cell *"you better fucking do"* John replied, when they got to cell number 28, the officer unlocked the door, John noticed that it's Matthew's cell, he thought the officer made a mistake, but he was curious to quickly see Matthew before he tells the officer, but when he peeped through the door, he saw that the cell was empty, his heart started palpitating *"so Matthew has been moved from this cell, were is his new cell?"* John curiously asked, *"ooh, so, you don't know?"* the officer said, *"know what? Is he dead or what?"* John asked furiously, *"Matthew is a free man, he was released from court today when he went for his appeal"* the officer said as he told John to get into the cell so that he could lock the door, *"what the fuck do you mean?, the fucking bastard was doing ten years"* John said again intensely, he thought the officer was joking with him, and he felt a rush of adrenalin, something telling him to drag the officer into the cell, torture him to tell him the truth, *"John, you need to step back, I need to lock the door"* the officer said as he tried to close the cell door, just then, suddenly apoplectic with rage, John lost his head and jumped on the officer and tried to pull the officer by the shirt into the cell, but the other officer saw what was happening, he ran to the scene, and both officers managed to push John into the cell and banged the cell door to lock it, the first officer's shirt was turn, the other officer peeped through the peep hole, he could see John smashing the TV and other stuffs in the cell, *"what was that?!!!"* the second officer that came to rescue the first officer asked, *"the fucking lunatic asked about Matthew, and I told him Matthew has been released and he lost his head"* he replied. The two officers radioed for help, they needed to get John to solitary, that is the protocol.

Meanwhile Matthew stood by the fence outside the prison walls, another prisoner called Alex stood beside him, he's in his late twenties, he's a slender guy, about six feet tall, he was dressed in a black jeans and a long sleeve shirt, he wore a white runners to match, he too was just released from Midlands prison after serving six months out of a one year sentence for driving without insurance, he had asked Matthew immediately he came out of the prison who he was waiting for and where he is going and Matthew had told him, and since he was going to Tramore which is a village that is twelve miles away from Waterford city, he asked if he can get a ride to Waterford city, and Matthew said yes because he knows Joseph Porter won't mind dropping him off at the bus station in Waterford City for him to get on the bus that would finally take him to Tramore village, *"I can't wait to see my daughter"* says Alex, *"how old is your daughter?"* Matthew asked, *"she's two years old"* he replied *"how about you Matthew, you have two children right?"* he asked *"yes, I have a five year old daughter and my son is seven years old"* Matthew replied *"are they coming with the person that is coming to pick you?"* he asked *"no, they are with their mum"* replied Matthew *"how long were you locked up for?"* Alex asked *"three years and seven months"* replied Matthew *"wow, that's long, but at least you are out and can see them tonight, you must be very excited?"* Alex asked *"well, I am not seeing them tonight anyway, I am going to spend some days with my pastor, because I don't really know if my wife waited for me, I think she's moved on with another man"* Matthew replied *"that's crazy!!!, you are a good man Matthew, why couldn't she wait for you for four years?"* Alex said angrily *"well she thought I would be gone for ten years, I got ten years you see"* says Matthew *"that's no fucking excuse Matthew, she should have thought about the children, there are crazy unrepentant carrier criminals in there doing longer sentence or life and you see their wife comes to visit them every week encouraging them to be strong because they are waiting for them"* says Alex again, just then the Potters drove towards the gate in an eight sitter car and parked right in front of them, they smiled at Matthew *"thank you sir, and thank you ma"* Matthew said as he smiled back at them, Joseph Potter came down, he was dressed in the same black trouser, grey suit, white shirt and black shoe that he wore earlier in the day at the appeal court, he went and opened the booth to the car for Matthew to put his stuffs in, *"please sir, this my friend is going to Tramore, but he needs a lift to Waterford bus station"* Joseph potter interrupted *"yes we can get him to the bus station in Waterford city."* *"Thank you sir, his name is Alex, this is pastor Ruth and Joseph Potter"* Matthew introduced them to Alex *"thank you"* Alex replied, thirty five minutes later they were in Carlow, *"we are just going to pull over here at this restaurant, they have lovely steak here, I believe you guys are hungry"* says Joseph Potter as he drove into the car park to the restaurant. There were about fifteen other people in the restaurant, it was going to 9pm, the food was really nice, Matthew enjoyed the steak with mashed potato, it was the best meal he has had in over three years, *"this is lovely, thank you sir"* says Matthew, *"thank you"* says Alex as well, *"are you a Christian?"* Joseph Potter asked Alex *"yes, I am a catholic"* Alex replied *"okay, well we have a lovely church in Waterford city, I am wondering if you'll like to worship with us this Sunday?"* Joseph Potter asked, *"I would have loved to come but am not allowed to drive , I am suspended from driving for three years, I went and drove while under suspension last year, that was why I went to prison."* Alex replied, *"well I can come and pick you and drop you back after service"* says Joseph Potter *"okay, but I will check with my wife tomorrow if I can come, then I'll let you know"* replied Alex *"okay, here is my card with my mobile number"* Joseph potter said as he gave him his personal card that he just pulled out of his suit. They finally got to Waterford city around past 10pm, Alex quickly grab his bag from the boot of the car, *"thank you again"* says Alex as he quickly ran towards the last bus that was about to live for Tramore.

Six prison officers, all dressed in riots gear, had protective helmet, held a shield and baton all stood at the front of John's cell, it was going to half 9pm, just over one hour earlier, John had assaulted one of the prison officers, John stood in his cell, he had just removed all his clothes, so he was naked *"common, you fucking bastards, come and get me,"* John shouted, one of the officers held the key in the keyhole ready to unlock the cell as he signalled to the other officers that were ready to move in immediately he opens the door to the cell, immediately he unlocked and opened the door, the five officers jumped into the cell one after the other pouncing on John, within thirty seconds he was pinned down to the floor with his arms locked behind his back and brought out of the cell by four officers each holding each arm and legs, John struggled to break free but he couldn't, the grip on his arms and legs were so tight that he ran out of energy *"you fucking bastards"* he screamed and tried to spit on the officers, but the fifth officer held unto his bald head as he was taken to solitary confinement.

Chapter Fourteen

Unexpected Reunion

"Here is the phone I got you, I believe you need one" Ruth Potter said has she handed Matthew a mobile phone, and a piece of paper with his new mobile number written on it *"that is your number, and there is a twenty euro credit on it, so it's ready to go"* she said *smiling "thank you, I don't know how much to thank you and daddy Potter, you are angels sent to my life from God, I feel like touching you guys to check if you are really human beings because I believe both of you are angels"* Matthew said, Ruth and Joseph Potter laughed as they looked at each other *"angels?"* says Joseph Potter as they arrived at their house in FerryBank in Waterford, it was going to half past 10pm, the house is about nine kilometres distance from Waterford city, about sixteen minutes' drive from the city centre, it is a big house, six bedroom, four toilets, two sitting rooms, a big kitchen and a big garden. *"I want to hug you brother Matthew, it's been long that I hugged you"* Joseph Potter said smiling as he got out of the car *"thank you sir"* says Matthew, and Ruth Potter hugged him as well, *"hello brother Matthew, good to see you, thank you Jesus"* Pamela said as she came out of the house excitedly to greet him, *"thank you sister Pamela, free at last"* Matthew said smiling. That was the first time Matthew has been to the house because they moved from the house Matthew knew before he went to prison, Joseph and Ruth Potter gave him the tour of house after bringing his stuffs to one of the six bedrooms in the house, in Matthew's room, there is a small door, about four feet high and two feet wide that leads to another smaller room that has got two single beds, you'll have to bend your head through the door to go into the room because of the height, that night after Matthew finished taking a shower in the en-suite shower toilet in his room, he laid down on the double bed that had been neatly made with a clean bedspread and duvet

cover, there were four pillows on the bed, as he laid there on the bed he thought about his wife and children, he tried to call his wife earlier in the car since he was given his new mobile phone, her phone rang several times, but she didn't pick up her phone, Matthew guessed she might have gone to work after arriving back to Clonmel from the court, he knew she works the evening shift from 4pm to 12pm that week, he looked at the clock on the wall in the room, it says past 11pm, he wondered if his wife saw the text message he had sent her to let her know that he's out and that's his new number, he wondered if she would call him back, he thought if she doesn't want to take him back, she still needs to allow him to see his children, he missed them so much.

Meanwhile, earlier on that same day, in the afternoon after Delilah left the court of appeal, she immediately called her boyfriend *"they are releasing him on time served, what are we going to do"* she sadly asked "are you serious or joking?" her boyfriend asked at the other end of the line, "what do you mean am joking, does someone joke with such serious thing, he's been released, they could have released him from the court, but they had to take him back to the prison to make it official, and I think by tomorrow or unfailingly within the next forty eight hours, he'll be out" Delilah explained again, *"this is serious!!!"* her boyfriend replied, *"so what are we going to do"* Delilah asked again *"I don't know, I am confused, I think you should just tell him about us, just tell him, you said he already knows"* he said, *"well I don't know how to tell him, I think he knows that I am seeing somebody else, but he doesn't know that you have moved in with me"* says Delilah, *"you know what, we'll discuss this when you get back home"* he said, *"okay then, I am just getting in the car to start driving back"* she said *"I love you"* he said *"bye"* she replied and disconnected the call. After speaking to her boyfriend, Delilah rang her mum in the United Kingdom, *"Matthew is getting released from prison"* she said. *"What!!!"* she shouted, *"I went to the court today for his appeal, and he's been released for time served"* she said *"thank God!!! that's good news"* her mum said excitedly, *"but what am I going to do about Garvin?"* Delilah asked *"you stop seeing him, have you told him that your husband has been released from prison?"* her mum asked *"yes, I did, but he wants me to tell Matthew about our relationship, he said I should tell him that I have moved on with him"* replied Delilah, *"he's crazy, well before I advise you, do you still love Matthew?"* her mum asked *"yes I do still love him, but how do I get reed of Garvin? he's moved in with me"* she said, *"moved in with you? Since when?"* her mum asked, *"since last year November, about nine months ago"* she replied, *"but you didn't tell me all this while, I thought you go to him and he comes to you, I didn't know that your relationship as gotten to the state of him moving in with you, you see my daughter, Matthew is a very good man, he made a mistake, and he's now been released, he's the father of your children, the only advise I can give you is to get Garvin out of your life and start all over again with Matthew"* replied her mum, *"okay, I will call you when I get home"* replied Delilah. She was so overwhelmed with the dilemma of the new development of Matthew's release from prison that when she got back to Clonmel, she rang her work place that she was sick that she couldn't come to work.

Garvin was sitting in his car, parked at the car park of Tesco supermarket in Clonmel, he just bought a bottle of whiskey after hearing on the phone from Delilah that Matthew was going to be release, he is in his late thirties, he's a big guy, about six feet tall, he was as well overwhelmed with the new development as Delilah, he thought about what he's going to do, he has to convince Delilah to tell Matthew about their relationship, about both of them in love and that she has moved on, he remembered Delilah telling him just a month earlier when he proposed to her that she wants to spend the rest of her life with him when he proposed to her to marry him and gave her an engagement ring to which Delilah accepted, they've been dating now for over a year, he knew Matthew at Bolton before he went to prison, he used to do the same shift with Delilah in the same department, while Matthew worked another shift in another department, in fact he has been interested in dating Delilah before Matthew went to prison, but she rejected all the love advances that he made towards her then because she was very happy in her marriage and he noticed that she was in love with Matthew, he met Matthew on either the way to his department when he was on the night shift when Matthew had just finished the morning shift or when he was on his way to clock out when Matthew was coming in to do the night shift, they both always had an handshake, talk a bit about the weather and job, smiled and they wished themselves good luck before going on their separate ways, but when Matthew went to prison, Garvin managed to convince Delilah about his love for her by helping her out with getting a minder that would mind the kids when Delilah was at work, and also helped her with the payment of some house bills and child minder, there was a time Delilah's car was repossessed because of late payment for the finance of the car and the car was taken from Delilah to the Dublin office of the finance company, Garvin had to go and make the payment of fifteen hundred euro before the car was released two weeks after it was ceased from Delilah. He had to go and get a loan from the credit union to be able to make the payment, he remembered that day, when he brought the car back to Delilah at the house, she kissed him passionately because she was very delighted and took him into her room where they made love, and that led to the beginning of their intimate relationship, he later went with Delilah and her children to England to meet Delilah's mum, her mum supported their relationship because she wanted Delilah to move on with her life since she believed Matthew would be locked away for ten years, Delilah also introduced him to her younger brother that lives in London, he too supported their relationship and gave them his blessings, Garvin was there that day before they left for England when Matthew rang Delilah from prison, when she told Matthew that she was going away for five days on holiday that Matthew won't be able to speak to her for five days, when Matthew asked her where she was travelling to, she said it's none of his business that she was just telling him that she was going away because he would not be able to reach her cell phone and she hung up the phone, and Garvin had been there several times when Matthew called from prison and Delilah would not pick up his call, and sometimes when she picked up his call and Garvin was talking on the phone to another person or talking to Matthew's children, when Matthew asked who is the male voice in the house? Garvin heard her telling him that it was the TV, that she was watching a programme, and sometimes she would just hang up, but there was a time Garvin heard her shouting on the phone to Matthew that she's having an affair, that she has moved on that Matthew should stop calling her, that he should call another person, Garvin was very happy because he thought she has given Matthew the message that she's moved on with him, and also Garvin has witnessed that she has not replied to all the letters that Matthew had been sending her from prison for the past over one year that they began their relationship. He had himself received the letters from the postman and had read the content which was mostly Matthew pleading to her not to forget about him, and that he'll soon be out and their Ordeal would soon be over, and the rest of the content would be him telling her to remember their marriage vows to love each other for better, for worse, and

Garvin would destroy the letter and throw it in the bin, Garvin just changed job two months earlier working in another company in Cashel village that is just twenty minutes' drive from Clonmel, he works in a higher position as a team leader and earns better money than the one from his previous job at Bolton, he was enjoying the new job and his life with Delilah, and was also looking forward to them getting married soon before getting the news of Matthew unexpected early release, he's become unsettled by the information but he still believes Delilah loves him and won't want to lose him, he just needs to convince and encourage her to stand her grounds and tell Matthew that she has moved on he thought.

When Delilah got home after arriving from Dublin that day, she discovered that Garvin car was not on the drive way, immediately she got into the house, she told the child minder that was minding her children that there was a new development that she won't be needing her service anymore, she said she would pay whatever she owes her into her bank account. When the childminder left, she brought her children into the sitting room, *"you will be seeing your daddy very soon,"* she said, the children were just seven and five year old so they didn't really understood what she said, they thought she meant they would be going to visit their dad in prison, just then Garvin came in, normally they would hug, but when Garvin wanted to hug her, she subtly ignored him by telling him to follow her to their room, "we have to talk" she said and walked up the staircase to their room, he looked at her children who were busy watching a cartoon programme on the TV, he then followed her, he closed the door, *"they are releasing Matthew, I think by tomorrow and I don't know what to do, I have been really unsettled since I was told in the court today, what are we going to do?"* she asked, Garvin sat there on the bed with his head rested on his hands, he was slightly tipsy from the half bottle of whiskey, *"you should tell him about us, not withstanding that he knows already, I am surprised you are asking me this question"* Garvin replied as she looked into her face passionately, *"you know I love you dearly, and we are engaged, and you said you'll like to spend the rest of your life with me, or as that changed because Matthew is getting out?"* asked Garvin again standing up to place his hands on her shoulder as he continued to look into her eyes, *"but it's not that easy, I am still married to him you know, and I have his children, you need to understand that"* she replied as she moved away from him and rested her back on the wall crying, *"I think you still love him, I want to know, please tell me"* Garvin moved closer to her by the wall, *"I thought you said you don't love him anymore, that you want to spend the rest of your life with me"* he said emphatically overwhelmed with emotions. *"You don't understand because you are not the one in my plight"* she replied furiously, moving away from him again, *"tell me the truth that you still love him, I need to know, please!!!"* Gavin asked again *"okay, okay, I still love him, but I love you more, but my children needs their father, that is why it's so difficult for me, do you think I want this?, no!!!, I don't want this"* she said crying again, he pulled her closer and kissed her on the forehead and wanted to kiss her in the mouth, she tried to resist, but he continued to kiss and caress her, she relaxed and kissed him back, he carried her to the bed removing her jeans pants, she tried to push him away, but he dipped his hand into her virginal, she relaxed and held his head as they both kissed passionately and had a rough sex that lasted for about three minutes, she pushed him away from herself immediately after reaching orgasm, got up from the bed abruptly, *"you know what!!!, we need to take a break for now,"* she said this assertively as she looked him directly in the eyes as he still laid on the bed, *"what do you mean babe?"* he asked her curiously pretending that he didn't understand what she just said. *"You need to pack your things and leave for now!!!"* she said affirmatively maintaining eye contact, and then went into the bathroom, locked the door, turned on the shower, sat under the shower with her shirt still on, and started crying, Garvin knocked on the door several times, but she ignored him.

Matthew slightly opened his eyes, he thought he was dreaming, he remembered that he was released from prison the previous day, his heart started palpitating, is it true that he's out and free at last? he thought, yes, I am free, he wanted to jump out of the bed, but he felt very comfortable lying on the double bed, the sunlight beam through the window, he felt very relaxed again after reassuring himself that he wasn't dreaming, that he's now a free man for real, he wanted to go back to sleep, but managed to look around the room, he saw his phone with the charger on the table, he remembered that he hasn't spoken to his wife and children, he jumped out of bed and went for his phone to quickly check if his wife had called him, but he discovered that she hasn't called or replied to his test message, he checked the time on his phone, it was going to 9am, he remembered he was still up till 2am, and must have drifted to sleep after then, he tried calling his wife again, but her phone went straight into voicemail, the previous day when he rang her phone it rang several times but she didn't pick up, he thought why all of a sudden her phone is going straight into voicemail, did she switch off her phone so that he won't be able to get through to her, he thought, well, maybe he would have to call her mum, and he did, *"good morning, this is Matthew speaking"* he said, *"ooh, hello Matthew, congratulations, Delilah told me that you were going to be released, I am really happy"* she said. *"Thank you"* Matthew replied *"I have been trying to call Delilah since yesterday but she refused to take my calls or call me back"* says Matthew *"you don't need to worry Matthew, she'll call you, where are you now?"* she asked *"I am in Waterford with my pastor"* he replied *"they came to pick me up from prison yesterday after my release"* he said again *"you don't worry, Delilah will call you, I will call her and tell her to call you"* she replied, *"okay, thank you,"* says Matthew.

Meanwhile, Delilah was with Garvin that same morning, he had parked all his belongings overnight after she managed to convince him to let them separate temporarily for her to sought herself out with Matthew, she said she would know how to frustrate Matthew to live her and they would come back together, she promised him to give her three months, that they would definitely come back together, so; that morning, Garvin left with all his stuffs, and Delilah made sure that she got read of any evidence or anything that can show or prove that Garvin stayed in the house with her, she told her children that they shouldn't say anything about uncle Garvin, yes, that's what her children calls Garvin, she lectured them that morning when she was parked outside their school gate before taking them to their respective classes *"daddy would be coming back to the house, and when you see your daddy, please don't ever say anything about uncle Garvin, okay?"* she said, *"okay mummy, we won't say anything about uncle Garvin"* they replied *"promise?"* she asked them again *"promise mummy, we won't say anything about uncle Gavin"* the children replied, she then went to the phone shop to get another sim card in other to change her mobile number because she wanted to cut all communications with Garvin and his family after Garvin left, she planned to work things out with Matthew, she assured herself that it's a new start, a new beginning with Matthew and her children, but she was sceptical if Matthew would want to still be with her after hearing that she was having an affair while he was locked up in prison, she thought, if she had to beg Matthew, she would beg him, she knows hundred percent that Matthew truly loves her, and she believes he would forgive her, she had seen his missed calls and text message the previous day, but she decided not to respond because she was still with Garvin and wanted to get reed of him first before starting any conversation with Matthew after his release from prison.

"Have you been able to talk to your wife and children yet?" Ruth Porter asked Matthew as they sat at the dining table eating that morning, *"no I have not been able to talk to her, I called her several times yesterday but the phone rang several times but she didn't pick up, and I sent her a text message since yesterday but she hasn't reply my message, and this morning I called her phone I couldn't get through, I got a message that the number is not in service, I called her mum, and her mum said she would call me, that I shouldn't worry, I just want to see my children, I missed them so much"* says Matthew *"don't worry brother Matthew, the most important thing is that you are out and free, we need to continue to thank God for that"* she said smiling, as she looked at him, she remembered what Delilah told her and her husband six months earlier when they rang her after visiting Matthew in prison when he complained to them that Delilah didn't come to visit him and hasn't been replying to his letters and has refused to take his calls several times, *"please mummy Porter, I am done with this, I have moved on with my life, I can't pretend anymore"* that was what Delilah said to them when they told her to take the children to go and visit Matthew in prison *"so you've moved on?"* Joseph Potter asked, *"yes, please don't call me about Matthew anymore, I don't want to get involve anymore, I am done"* she said again, *"well, I think and believe your husband really misses you and the children, please if you can take the children to visit him it will really help him, I know it's not easy for you, but we are praying for you guys, if there's anything we can do to help, even if you want us to come down and take you to visit him or help you with some money, please let us know"* says Ruth Porter , *"I'll see what I can do"* says Delilah and the call dropped, by then she had stopped attending the church about five months earlier before that discussion, and after that discussion, she stopped picking Joseph and Ruth Potter's calls, when they couldn't get through to her over the phone, they paid her an unexpected visit, they noticed a second car parked behind Delilah's car on the driveway, when they rang the doorbell, it took over fifteen minutes before Delilah reluctantly opened the door, and with the way she was acting suspiciously,

they knew that there was another man in the house somewhere, they saw the kids, they love children, they stayed there for about thirty minutes playing with the children, when they wanted to leave, they gave Delilah five hundred euro *"ooh thank you sir, I will try and go and see him next week with the children, I am going because he needs to see his children, like I told you before, I am done with the marriage"* she told them before they left, but Ruth and Joseph Potter has never mentioned this to Matthew after several visit to him in prison and also after his release.

Joseph and Ruth Potter owns a charity shop were people bring and donate unwanted stuffs like clothes, furniture, books, toys, shoes, DVD's and loads of other home accessories to their charity shop, the proceeds from the sale of those stuffs is used to support the needy that comes to their church in Waterford city. Later on that day, around 2pm, Matthew was at the charity shop helping out with arranging stuffs like DVD's and books on the shelves, but Ruth Porter noticed that he was restless trying Delilah's phone every five minutes, *"maybe you should just leave her alone for now, I know you are missing your children, I and my husband can arrange to go and see your wife tomorrow to speak to her on how you can see her and your children, I know she knows you're out"* says Ruth Potter, *"well, what I don't understand is why her phone that was ringing yesterday, has been saying not in service since this morning whenever I call her phone"* he replied *"well, relax brother Matthew, I promise you that me and daddy will go and see her, and you will see your children"* she said to assure him again. A lady from the church that knew Matthew came running into the charity shop, her name is Joy, she visited Matthew in prison with her husband and three children several times, she's in her late thirties, *"my brother, how are you, it was Pamela that told me that you've been released from prison, thank you Jesus"* she said as she hugged him, *"thank you my sister"* Matthew replied managing to smile back at her *"you look great, how is Delilah, did you know that she was having an affair, have you seen her at all?"* she asked whispering, *"I know, but I have not even seen her and my children"* he replied *"Pamela said you've been out since yesterday and Delilah has not come to see you with your children?"* asked Joy *"well I have not seen her, and I have been trying to call her phone, but I couldn't get through to her"* Matthew replied, *"that is not good, well you are out, that's the most important thing, I would have really love to cook you a very nice meal, but I am working late today, I am actually on my first break and already late, but I was so excited that I just had to quickly drive down to see you, and here you are for real"* she said smiling and touching him on the shoulder to check that it was him for real *"I will see you in church tonight, I know you are definitely coming for bible study with mummy and daddy Porter"* she said, *"yes I am definitely coming"* he replied as she left the shop.

Around 6:30pm, Matthew arrived at the church with Ruth and Joseph Potter, the church was now at another location from the one the service used to be held before Matthew went to prison, this current church has a bigger auditorium, the service used to be held in hotel halls rented by the Potters, but they've now managed to lease this magnificent space in a building with apartments of offices, the bible study starts at 7pm and finishes at 8:30pm, the members of the church that knew Matthew came to hug him as they arrived, what they normally do for the service is; they start with praise and worship for about fifteen minutes by singing about four to five Christian songs, and then pray for about another ten minutes before Joseph Potter now goes on the pulpit to preach from the bible. There were about forty members in the auditorium that evening singing and dancing during the praise and worship when Delilah and Matthew's children came into the church, Matthew was standing by the sits which was about five metres from the entrance door, Delilah holding his children walked to him and handed them to him, Matthew immediately bent down and picked both of them up, they both hugged him giggling, Delilah just stood there beside them as everyone in the church watched them, smiling as they continue to sing the praise and worship song "thank you Lord for everything, thank you Lord for everything, thank you thank you Lord, thank you Lord for everything" they all sang, Delilah was dressed in a shirt and skirt and wore a brown sandal. That night at the end of the sermon, Joseph Potter *said "we have our brother Matthew here, praise the Lord!!!"* everyone responded by saying *"hallelujah!!!"* he invited Matthew out to come and say some few words to the church and handed him the microphone, *"I want to thank the church, every one of you that prayed for me, God answered your prayers, that's the reason why I was set free, and I also want to thank Mummy and Daddy Potter for their unconditional love and support throughout my ordeal, they are angels sent from the Almighty God to me and my family, I made a covenant with God that if I am set free when I go for my appeal that I would sing a special song to you my brothers and sisters"* says Matthew, he sang a song *"When you believe"* by Whitney Houston and Mariah Carey *"there can be miracles, when you believe"* when he finished singing the song he handed the microphone back to Joseph Potter as everyone in the church gave a tumultuous applause. After the service, everyone came to congratulate him, his wife and his children, Joseph and Ruth Potter took Matthew, his wife and children out to a nice restaurant, they celebrated Matthew's freedom, his wife and children ended up spending the night with him at the Potters house, that night his wife told him that she changed her phone number, and gave him her new number, she begged him that a lot has happened since he was away locked up in prison, but told him to allow them have a new start in their relationship, that night he made love to his wife for the first time since over three years that he has been a celibate. His wife left the next day, on Friday morning with his children after breakfast, but they came back the next day, Saturday morning to spend the weekend with him at the Potters house, they all went to church together the next morning, Matthew and Delilah got Baptized after the service, about over hundred members of the church were in attendance who watched them baptized by Joseph Potter, as they stood inside a big metal tank used for the baptism by the church that was already half filled up with a lukewarm water, Joseph Potter dipped their head in the water one after the other to symbol that old things has passed away in the water, and raised their head up as a sign of a new beginning for them, the members prayed and sang some praise and worship songs as the baptism was done, Matthew and Delilah held unto each other's hand after the baptism, some members got emotional with watered eyes but managed to smile as streams of tears of joy trickled from their eyes, that Sunday, Matthew parked his stuffs from the Potter's house and followed Delilah and his children home back to Clonmel, it was his first time in the house because his wife moved to the house over a year earlier when he started her affair with Garvin, it is a three bedroom house with three toilets, that night as he laid on the bed looking at the list of telephone numbers on a piece of paper that he held in his hand, he was more interested in a particular number, the number that Jason, the guy that collected the same type of package that he collected gave him at Midlands prison before Jason was released on bail five months earlier, as he continued to look at the number, the thought of how he can get Gordon the guy that used his naivety to collect the drugs arrested by the police so that he's innocence of the crime that sent him to prison can be proven and his conviction can then be overturn occupied his mind, he grabbed his phone from the small bedside table, he looked at the time on the screen of his phone, it says 10:22pm, he looked at his wife that laid down beside him on the bed, she was fast asleep, he got up from the bed and climbed down the staircase into the sitting room and rang the mobile number *"Hello"* a voice came from the other end of the line *"it's me Matthew, I believe I am talking to Jason"* asked Matthew, *"hey Matthew, when did you get out? I heard about your release"* he said *"I got out five days ago, you live in Cork right?"* asked Matthew. *"Yes, actually in Mallow, about fifteen minutes away from Cork city"* Jason replied *"okay, I am coming to see someone in Cork so I just saw your number in my diary, and I said I'll give you a call to say hello or maybe see you on my way back from Cork city"* says Matthew *"yeah man, it will be my pleasure, I'll text you my address"* says Jason. After the call, when Matthew got back on the bed, as he lay there, he ruminated on what he needed to do to convince Jason to unintentionally get him to Gordon.

Meanwhile at Midlands prison, John the daddy devil was in solitary confinement because of his attack on prison officers, but he still managed to use his connection in the prison to gain access to a mobile phone after spending four days in isolation. *"Hi Glenn, that rat has been released before I got here"* says John *"what!!!, I thought you said he has six years to go? Well I'll have to take care of him then, do you have any information about his new location?"* Glenn asked, *"I can get that, but no fucking way you getting rid of that rat without me watching, I have to kill that rat myself, I need to fucking get out of here, you'll have to arrange something for me"* says John, *"how the fucking hell am I going to get you out of there John?"* Glenn screamed, *"I have a plan that can get me out of here to the hospital within a month Glenn, then I can bolt from there, I'll tell you what you need to do for me"* says John.

Acknowledgements

Some of the contents in this novel is inspired by true events but most of the write ups has been fictionalized to make the story fascinating and to create more suspense from the beginning of the book till the end.

This book took me over a decade to write, there were daily challenges and huddles that occurred in my personal life that immensely wanted to dissuade or discourage me from completing the book, but I managed to soldier on with the help of some people that encouraged and boosted my morale daily in writing and completing the book, so; first of all, I want to thank my daughter Debbie Akinola for her continuous support and positive criticism that got me going in the times that I almost gave up, and I also want to thank Debbie for helping out in the drawing out the artistry design for the cover page of the book; I also want to thank my son Olamide Akinola for his daily inquisitiveness to know how far I have gone in writing the book and for the aftermath daily kudos I get from him whenever I told him how far I have gone in writing the book which always encouraged me to go further in finishing the book.

I also want to use this opportunity to thank the two most important, lovely Angels God sent to my life during my ordeal, to whom I am immensely indebted to, Thomas Potter who has been called Home to Heaven, and his wife Linda Potter, for their unconditional love and exceeding support for me and my family.

I want to thank Teddy Hughes, who has been called Home to Heaven, Elizabeth Paul who has been called Home to Heaven, Josh and Annett Oviri, Chris and Grace Kanwei, to name just a few, all these wonderful people sacrificed their time to visit me several times to encourage me during my ordeal when most people that I considered close friends and family found it easy and unconcerned to abandon me.